"The Changing Same"

"The Changing Same"

BLACK WOMEN'S LITERATURE, CRITICISM, AND THEORY

Deborah E. McDowell

INDIANA UNIVERSITY PRESS

Bloomington and Indianapolis

The paper used in this publication meets the minimum requirements of American National Standard for Information Sciences—Permanence of Paper for Printed Library Materials, ANSI Z39.48-1984.

Manufactured in the United States of America

Library of Congress Cataloging-in-Publication Data

McDowell, Deborah E., date
    "The changing same" : black women's literature, criticism, and theory / Deborah E. McDowell.
        p.   cm.
    Includes bibliographical references and index.
    ISBN 0-253-33629-5 (alk. paper). — ISBN 0-253-20926-9 (pbk. : alk. paper)
    1. American fiction—Afro-American authors—History and criticism.
    2. American fiction—Women authors—History and criticism.
    3. Women and literature—United States—History. 4. Afro-American women—Intellectual life. 5. Afro-American women in literature.
    6. Afro-Americans in literature. I. Title.
PS374.N4M37   1995
813.009'896073—dc20   94-10663

1 2 3 4 5 00 99 98 97 96 95

In Memory of My Parents

Jimmye Ziegler McDowell
and
Wiley McDowell

CONTENTS

ACKNOWLEDGMENTS

I am grateful to the friends and colleagues who have richly assisted the completion of this book. I thank William L. Andrews, Susan Fraiman, Janice Knight, Arnold Rampersad, Cheryl Wall, and Richard Yarborough for comments and suggestions on drafts of various chapters. I thank Cheryl Wall, especially, for demonstrations of patience. I have lost count of the phone calls I've made to her in the middle of the day, at the dinner hour, and at what is most people's bedtime. And to my question, "Cheryl, do you have a minute to hear this paragraph?" her answer is always, "Yes." I also thank Nellie McKay for urging me on to the finish line and for understanding if not encouraging my bouts with paralysis. Doris Smith Witt, Mason Stokes, Matthew Brown, and Michael Furlough have all assisted my research while stimulating my imagination and pushing me to see beyond my complacencies.

While the intellectual support has been indispensable, I also thank many others for spiritual and moral support: my cousin, Cora Ivory; my oldest, dearest friend, Gwen Rigby Williams; Marilyn Richardson; Jeanne Maddox Toungara; Toni Morrison; Janet Beizer; Orson Watson; Farzaneh Milani; and Teju and Moojie Olaniyan. I am especially grateful to Moojie, Farzaneh, and Jeanne for their great cooking. There is nothing like akara, tadik, and groundnut stew or sauce gumbo to nourish the body and the soul when the mind just has to take a holiday.

I can never adequately thank the staff of the University of Virginia library. Their responses to my calls for help are always speedy and cheerful. Thanks especially to Doug Hurd for being ever-patient about my delinquent inter-library loan returns.

Various parts of this work were supported by grants from the Mary Ingraham Bunting Institute of Radcliffe College and the National Research Council of the Ford Foundation.

Thanks to Emma Dunham Kelley, Frances E. W. Harper, Alice Walker,

Jessie Fauset, Nella Larsen, Toni Morrison, Sherley Anne Williams and all the other "black women writers" here and gone for the wealth of their wisdom and the examples of their lives.

Only "Precious" knows the troubles I've seen and has guided me over the rocky shoals to safety.

PREFACE

Speaking To *You about the "Changing Same"*

> But I write here, speaking to you,
>   where discoveries end, opposed within myself.
>   —Jay Wright, "Beginning Again"

This book has been a long time coming and has had at least two conceptions and one stillbirth. I began it proper in 1984,[1] though I actually started before that—in 1978—when I commenced my dissertation over the vigorous objections of not a few who found fiction by African American women not altogether fitting subject matter for intellectual pursuit. While I have held on to the subject,[2] nothing of the dissertation remains, for between its completion and the product you now hold in your hand, literary studies underwent a wrenching upheaval, or, as we are now wont to say, à la Thomas Kuhn, a "paradigm shift" from the "Age of Criticism" to the "Age of Theory." This, of course, is a popular and reductive reckoning, but let's grant it explanatory validity for the moment. While "Criticism" had stakes in close analysis and interpretation, "Theory" had stakes (and imperatives) in grand frameworks—semiotics, structuralism, poststructuralism, psychoanalysis—and methodological systems, even as it cast systems-building in a suspicious light.[3]

Though unbeknownst to me and others trained outside the academic epicenters, by 1978, the year I began this work, "Theory" had already rendered the claims and causes of the dissertation obsolete. As you might well imagine, this discovery sent me (and others who had blithely invested in projects much the same) into convulsions and, quiet as it was kept, occasional paroxysms of rage.

People responded variously to the quake. Some ignored it and kept right on doing what they were doing before it hit. Others experienced conversions, much like Saul's on the road to Damascus.[4] Still others set about crawling from underneath the rubble to see what they could salvage while trying to rebuild. I place myself in this latter camp.

I offer these details of history in a straightforward (and some would say shameless and unseemly) act of what Nancy Miller calls "autographics" or "personal criticism." It is writing that "opens an inquiry on the cost of writing . . . and its effects."[5]

The costs of "doing" literary studies in the 1980s—the historical frame of the following essays—were often high: retooling as the "parts" of the critical machinery were changing by the day and while the professionalization of literary studies seemed to accelerate to the point of near collapse. (Call it the Industrialization of Academe, with its own versions of speedups and work stoppages.) The stakes were nothing less than the rights and privileges of academic life.

These details of personal and discursive history are pertinent to the shape, concerns, and methods of these selections, which are all engaged with matters of literary CHANGE, in capital letters, all engaged with the shifting aesthetic, critical, cultural conventions and values that influence, and at times determine, writing *by* and *about* black women.

But first, more of the history of this project's formation. Formerly titled *"The Changing Same": Generational Connections and Black Women Novelists,* the study's original emphases lay in literary history conceived as patterns of generational influence. It sprang from my concerns about the direction in which knowledge about these writers was headed. I wanted to show that contemporary novelists, who were the focus of such intense discussion—popular and critical—had not emerged *in vacuo,* but were preceded by an earlier generation of women writers, albeit those with limited popular appeal. I would select from the number of diverse novels by black women spanning roughly 130 years, tracing the effects of writers and texts on other writers and texts. I planned simply to isolate the continuities and discontinuities, the transformations and retentions between and among the writers of this tradition, ignoring other lines of influence that might be traceable in their work. As I put it in an early description of the project, "the novels by black women up to and through the Harlem Renaissance are all unified by their common concern with the question of black women's struggle for self-realization, wholeness, and autonomy in a racist and sexist society fundamentally antagonistic to individualism and the ideal of autonomy for women and blacks. The Harlem Renaissance writers' concern with the possibilities for black women's autonomy is revoiced in the contemporary writers, along with a range of themes that aggregate under this general concern: the tension between social dictates and personal integrity; the possibilities for and constraints on black female creativity, both from within and without; the question of female bonding; and of female heroism, to name but a few."

I scratched this approach early in 1984, because further study revealed to me its conceptual limitations. But more importantly, I shifted my approach because, by then, fiction by black American women had become, in the words of Hortense Spillers, "a vivid new fact of national life," generating a broad-based, archeological effort that unearthed "lost" and neglected titles and made them available through such auspices as the Beacon Black Women Writers Series and the Schomburg Library of Nineteenth-Century Black Women's Literature.[6] This project of excavation, combined with the growing popular appeal of black women novelists, had a corresponding effect on scholarship focused on their work.

Barbara Smith had laid the ground much earlier of what she called "black feminist criticism," a reading strategy attentive to the intersections of gender, race, and class in the writings of black women. Now, of course, that mystical, holy trinity has become a household phrase, a three in one, a mantra to be uttered to mark (and mock) oppositional credentials and a form of "paper" resistance. While Smith's 1979 call for nonhostile interpretations of black women's writing has been prodigiously answered, it is useful to remember that, a scant fifteen years ago, scholars in search of criticism on black women writers faced a daunting vacuum that abandoned them to their solitary carrels with only their own thoughts to bounce against each other. Since that time, however, several collections—not all devoted exclusively to literary criticism—and several book-length studies have been published in steady succession. Add to these anthologies placing selections of black women's literature in thematic frameworks, countless essays on the subject in literary journals, and more conferences than either time or money would permit any single person to attend, and we have, arguably, a small industry.

Constituting an epochal moment in U.S. publishing and intellectual life, writing by and about African American women in the 1970s and 1980s was proliferating at such a pace, was such a moving, protean object, that it would not hold still long enough to be "universalized," to be confined within a single explanatory system or grand discursive unity. The texts of the "tradition" weren't even firmly in place. For example, while scholars of African American literature had long operated on the assumption that Frances E. W. Harper's *Iola Leroy* inaugurated black women's tradition in the novel, the discovery of Harriet Wilson's *Our Nig* (1859) pushed back that beginning several decades. In the midst of such energy, this book took on a life of its own, its choices and concerns beckoned and dictated by the increasingly visible and sometimes controversial role black women's fiction was playing in the world.

Discussions about "Black Women Writers" (falsely understood as a unity with plural names) raged throughout the country from university lecture halls and academic symposia to television talk shows, public radio, and "The MacNeil-Lehrer Newshour." I joined in those conversations at the academic end of the discursive spectrum, and the essays gathered here are the fruits of that activity and exchange. Each is a response to a specific assignment or topic or to a critical issue demanding immediate address and intervention.

Because these essays were written over a period of years, the temptation is strong to erase from them all traces of their times. I have largely resisted that urge, except to provide transitions between chapters and remove repetition of expository material. I have resisted the urge, for it would constitute an effort to write over history. While my thinking on the subject of black women writers has evolved, I have allowed these chapters to stand, for the most part, as they were originally published. I do so for several reasons. I want to suggest something of a round table, moving from place to place, the mode of dialogue and discussion that surrounded the study of black women writers in the 1980s. These essays are not only in dialogue with each other, but they also record parts of a continuing dialogue among a variety of critics and critical perspectives.

Taken together, they chronicle something of my own intellectual development, although I present them out of chronological sequence to avoid any teleological coding, to avoid any implication that this development constitutes a progressive unfolding toward some analytical completeness or conceptual resting place.

The structure of the book—designed to evoke a series of conversations—works aggressively against any such teleology. Interpolated commentary in italics is scattered throughout, reopening discussion of particular issues. Some interpolations respond directly to questions and criticism raised by others; others are second thoughts of my own that allow me to adjust some of my own positions, based on my ongoing negotiations with developments in African American, feminist, and literary studies more generally. Needless to say, these developments are, themselves, anything but final.

While events and assignments of the 1980s occasioned their writing, the focus of these pieces is much more broadly historical in stress, encompassing the general history of fiction by African American women and the history of its interpretation. My efforts are far from comprehensive, and whatever generalizations I dare to tender are inevitably compromised by my own arbitrary selections of texts and contexts through which to pursue the critical issues I address. I have chosen texts from what I consider to be the central or defining moments in the fictional tradition of black women: what Frances Harper coined the "Woman's Era" of the 1890s; the Harlem Renaissance of the 1920s and 1930s; and the 1970s and 1980s, a period during which a small but significant group of black American women secured a toehold in U.S. publishing for the first time in history.[7]

Just as I do not attempt a chronological or comprehensive sweep of the writers here, I do not attempt to endow to these writers a false homogeneity. Nor do I attempt to endow a false unity to these essays, despite the obvious correspondences and recurrent ties that bind them loosely to each other. They are all conceived, to some extent, with materialist matters of reading and reception in mind and, reciprocally with the conditions under which literature is produced, published and reviewed. The essays in part 4 take up these questions in fuller detail, pursuing a now commonplace observation: the various subject positions that readers assume during the act of reading are intricately related to variables of sex, race, sexual preference, and class. These influence, if not determine, readers, readings, and "misreadings."

As several chapters will conclude, the work of the writers considered here has been subjected historically to criticisms that revealed as much (if not more) about shifting aesthetic, critical, and cultural conventions and values as about merits or properties intrinsic to the writers' work. Nowhere is this more transparent than in the central controversy about black women writers sustained throughout the 1980s. It stemmed from the charge that the work of contemporary black women writers was determined and programmatic in its attacks on black men, some of whom fired back with a round of attacks of their own in op-ed pieces and partisan reviews featured in the popular press.

In both "Boundaries: Or Distant Relations and Close Kin" and "Reading Family Matters," I attempted to unravel the central issues and expose the stakes in the rapid-fire attacks on the fiction of contemporary black women. I wanted to extract from the cacophony, rancor, and just plain confusion of the controversy some underlying unity of concerns. I quickly discovered that these attacks and the reading prerogatives blurred beneath them relied on an enfeebled black nationalism, long past saving, which, like other nationalist rhetorics, was bound up in masculinist anxieties and gendered ideologies of dominance and control. Metaphors of "family," "kinship," and "community" structured these attacks that bordered on calls for censorship and attempted to demand that black women writers meet a representational ideal in the name of creating racial unity and wholeness. That ideal held familiar injunctions for women that seemed to echo those that the German National Socialists (Nazis) held for "their" women—*kinder, kirche, kuche* (children, church, and kitchen). In this respect, it ironically obeyed the same commandments as the Reverend Donald Wildmon's American Family Association. Because the writings of contemporary black women indeed seemed to hold little sacred about pietistic views of family, they were read and loudly proclaimed to be threats to a unified black community, healthy and whole.

While I wanted to ferret out the underlying unity—contained in rhetoric of family—in the broadside attacks on contemporary black women writers, I sought as well to articulate alternative reading strategies with implications that might extend beyond the specifics of this controversy. The shifting aesthetic standards, cultural values, and ideological assumptions that drove this 1980s controversy to its fever pitch are likewise at the base of the different, but no less gender-based, critical reception of Jessie Fauset and Nella Larsen in the 1920s and 1930s, whose work I consider in part 3.

In assessing these authors' place in the canon of Harlem Renaissance writers, a long-standing and intractable challenge must be confronted: the "black middle class" as conceptual problematic. Both as a social group and as a category of analysis, the black middle class has been frequently invoked as a self-evident, transhistorical, and conceptual given. Students of African American culture have tended to work with loose, narrow, and vague definitions of the term, many derived from the type E. Franklin Frazier portrayed pejoratively in his still-influential study, *Black Bourgeoisie*. According to Frazier, the black bourgeoisie wanted to "forget the Negro's past" and conform to the "behavior and values of the white community in the most minute details." Comprised largely of intellectuals, this class, Frazier continued, "never dared think beyond a narrow, opportunistic philosophy that provided a rationalization for their own advantages."[8]

Although Frazier's representation of the black middle class was based on and situated in a fairly limited purview—the black middle class of Washington, D.C., of a particular moment—it has entered the store of "common" knowledge and contributed to entrenched critical positions. Ironically, as Wilson J. Moses is astute to note, the bourgeois class of "educated black Americans in turn-of-the-century Washington made possible the existence of an E. Franklin Frazier."[9]

Moses is one of the few critics to examine the hostility of the critical establishment to what it terms the "genteel," Victorian values of the black bourgeoisie. He traces this hostility to what he calls "the proletarian/bohemian tradition in criticism," which "has been granted a sort of moral and political superiority over any other framework of analysis in black literary and intellectual history." While I would question the name Moses gives this dominant paradigm, as well as what appears to be an apology for the middle class, I agree with him that the reflexive relegation of the middle class to a category of disrepute needs to be rethought, for "the legitimate roots of black American culture are not confined to "plantation folklore, the blues style, and proletarian iconoclasm" or any of their equivalents.

According to this critical tendency to demonize and expend anything or anyone associated with black middle class existence, Fauset and Larsen have always been easy targets. While Nella Larsen has taken her share of criticism by those who think prescriptively and pejoratively about the black middle class, it has in no way compared in severity to what Fauset has received. While Fauset and Larsen should not be regarded as forming an aesthetic pair or articulating a program of consensus on the subject of the black middle class, reading the two together usefully complicates the class question and often reveals both writers in a more nuanced light.

While each of these chapters explores to some degree patterns and ruptures in the history and interpretive history of fiction by African American women, they engage simultaneously matters of critical methodology. The framing chapters—one and nine, written at either end of the 1980s—confront more explicitly and in fuller detail the sometimes vexing problem of methodology that was so feverishly contested throughout the decade. The paradigm shift to which I alluded at the beginning of this preface—popularly melodramatized as the Age of Criticism meets the Age of Theory—sent tempers flying and temperatures climbing as "Theory" seemed to put everything outside itself on notice and on trial, and "Criticism" went skulking into the chambers of disgrace.

As varieties of poststructuralism, all unified and constructed as a synonym for "Theory," came to be incorporated into African American literary study, some students in the field voiced their suspicions that poststructuralism was incompatible with the traditionally "humanistic" imperatives of scholarship on African American literature.

Taking "a" position about these developments is not as easy as it seems, and in "New Directions for Black Feminist Criticism" and "Transferences: Black Feminist Discourse: The 'Practice' of 'Theory,'" I approach the matter from a position away from the most explosive points of reference, one that avoids the implied and oversimplified imperatives of "for" and "against." For such imperatives rest on false notions of separate and discrete (and certainly unequal) methodological entities, marking separate and discrete moments in time. But I accept *this* moment's critical axiom that self "identity" always gives way to "difference," thus making difficult any easy and clear-cut identifications and alliances. And thus, it will be readily apparent that this study does not fit neatly within either conceptual or disciplinary boundaries, but rather selects aspects from a variety of discourses in order to formulate its questions and reading strategies.

As Kenneth Burke puts it, "a critic's perspective implicitly [and explicitly, I would add] selects a set of questions that [she] considers to be key questions." We usually think of *answers* as the primary pointers of direction in a critic's work. The point about differences in critical methodologies, and how we reconcile the disparities and contradictions that might exist among them, lies "not in answers, but in *questions*." But lest I appear to be advocating some naive position of "anything goes," let me rush to add that the questions we ask are never neutral, and thus their implications can never be wholly disregarded. Even questions have political and institutional consequences that are very real.

While the questions posed in the following essays reflect a variety of critical perspectives, some are more influential on my thinking than others. Without accepting all that has been written under its banner, this study draws heavily on the grounding strategies of black feminist criticism, particularly its investments in how categories of race, gender, class, and sexuality figure into literary analysis and critical inquiry. It draws as well on feminist reading strategies, more generally, particularly as they seek to expose ideologies of male dominance, question traditionally masculinist standards of evaluating literature, and critique the sex/gender arrangements that exclude women from symbolic activity.

These concerns stretch outward to reach (and at times contest) general developments in literary study—varieties of poststructuralism, new historicism, and cultural studies. Taken together, these essays chart an ever-widening circle of intellectual influence, exchange, and reciprocity, reinforcing Kenneth Burke's assertion that a critic's "methodology should be formed, at every turn, by reference to the 'collective revelation' of accumulated critical lore" (p. 68).

The lore reflected here, accumulated throughout the 1980s and beyond, bears the imprint of a variety of critical moments and their shifting vocabularies and points of stress. While we can see the shapes and ridges of critical and literary change written on their surfaces, on closer look we see that a certain cycle of terms and modes of inquiry has remained the same. But even when we think we see the same, we look again and know with certainty that the ways things stay the same are always changing.

If there be nothing new, but that which is
Hath been before, how are our brains beguiled,
Which, laboring for invention, bear amiss
The second burden of a former child!
                              —*William Shakespeare*

All change and progress from within comes
about from the recognition and use of difference
between [and among] ourselves.
                              —*Audre Lorde*

Repetition is the ground of both the new
and the same.
                              —*Kum Kum Sangari*

Now the fragments have been put together again
by another self.
                              —*Frantz Fanon*

PART I

Thinking about Methods

1

New Directions for Black
Feminist Criticism

"What is commonly called literary history," writes Louise Bernikow, "is actually a record of choices. Which writers have survived their times and which have not depends on who noticed them and chose to record their notice."[1] Women writers have long fallen victim to literary history's arbitrary selections, their writings "patronized, slighted, and misunderstood by a cultural establishment operating according to male norms out of male perceptions."[2] Both literary history's "sins of omission" and literary criticism's inaccurate and partisan judgments of women writers have come under attack since the early 1970s by feminist critics.[3] To date, no one has formulated a precise or complete definition of feminist criticism, but since its inception, its theorists and practitioners have agreed that it is a "corrective unmasking the omissions and distortions of the past—the errors of a literary critical tradition that arise from and reflect a culture created, perpetuated, and dominated by men."[4]

Early theorists and practitioners of feminist literary criticism were largely white females who, wittingly or not, perpetrated against black women writers the same exclusive practices they so vehemently decried in white male scholars. Seeing the experiences of white women, particularly white middle-class women, as normative, these scholars proceeded blindly to exclude the work of black women writers from literary anthologies and critical studies. Among the most flagrant examples of this chauvinism is

Patricia Meyer Spacks's *The Female Imagination*. In a weak defense of her book's exclusive focus on women in the Anglo-American literary tradition, Spacks quotes Phyllis Chesler (a white female psychologist): "I have no theory to offer of Third World female psychology in America. . . . As a white woman, I'm reluctant and unable to construct theories about experiences I haven't had."[5] But, as Alice Walker observes, "Spacks never lived in nineteenth-century Yorkshire, so why theorize about the Brontës?"[6]

Not only have black women writers been largely "disenfranchised" from critical works on the "female tradition," they have also been frequently excised from those on the Afro-American literary tradition by black male scholars. Robert Stepto's *From behind the Veil: A Study of Afro-American Narrative* is a case in point. The study purports to be a "history . . . of the historical consciousness of an Afro-American art form—namely, the Afro-American written narrative."[7] Yet, black women writers are conspicuously absent from the roster of writers on whom Stepto focuses. Although he does include a token two-page discussion of Zora Neale Hurston's *Their Eyes Were Watching God,* describing it as a "seminal narrative in Afro-American letters,"[8] the novel merited no chapter of its own, nor was it accorded the thorough analysis reserved for Frederick Douglass's 1845 *Narrative,* Booker T. Washington's *Up from Slavery,* W. E. B. Du Bois's *The Souls of Black Folk,* James Weldon Johnson's *The Autobiography of an Ex-Colored Man,* Richard Wright's *Black Boy,* and Ralph Ellison's *Invisible Man.*

Even when black women writers are given critical consideration, their writings are generally misunderstood and summarily dismissed, especially those whose work was published before the "protest" era of the 1940s. While praising black fiction in this latter period, David Littlejohn denigrates the work of Fauset and Larsen. He maintains that "the Newer writers are obviously writing as men, for men," and are avoiding the "very close and steamy" writing that is the result of "any subculture's taking itself too seriously, defining the world and its values exclusively in the terms of its own restrictive norms and concerns."[9] An example of what Mary Ellman terms "phallic criticism,"[10] Littlejohn's assessment is based on masculine-centered values and definitions, which have dominated the criticism on black women writers and done much to guarantee that most would be, in Alice Walker's words, "casually pilloried and consigned to a sneering oblivion."[11]

Recognition that various critical communities have not favored black women writers and have, in many cases, actively suppressed their work, has given rise to black feminist criticism, the terms of which Barbara Smith sets forth in her essay "Toward a Black Feminist Criticism." The salient postulates of this critical position are, at this point, only skeletally defined; however, it proceeds to challenge a fundamental assumption: that the experiences of white women, white men, and black men are normative, and black women's experiences are deviant. That signal challenge has taken a joint form: resurrecting forgotten black women writers and revising misinformed critical opinions of their work. Justifiably enraged by the critical establishment's neglect and mishandling of black women writers, many critics have found common cause in Barbara Smith's call for "nonhostile and perceptive analyses of works written by persona outside the 'mainstream' of white/male cultural rule."[12]

Although it is an urgent and timely enterprise, no substantial body of black feminist criticism—either in theory or practice—exists, a fact that might be explained partially by our limited access to and control of publishing media.[13] Barbara Smith offers another explanation for the paucity of black feminist criticism: the lack of a "developed body of black feminist political theory whose assumptions could be used in the study of black women's art" (p. 159).

Despite the strained circumstances under which black feminist critics labor, the committed few have broken necessary ground. For the remainder of this chapter I would like to focus on selected writings of black feminist critics, discussing their strengths and weaknesses and suggesting new directions toward which the criticism might move and pitfalls it might avoid.

Unfortunately, black feminist scholarship has been decidedly more practical than theoretical, and the theories developed thus far have often lacked sophistication and precise details and have been marred by slogans, rhetoric, and idealism. These limitations are not without reason. As Dorin Schumacher observes, "the feminist critic has few philosophical shelters, pillars, or guideposts," and thus "feminist criticism is fraught with intellectual and professional risks, offering more opportunity for creativity, yet greater possibility of errors."[14]

As the earliest theoretical statement on black feminist criticism, the importance of Barbara Smith's "Toward a Black Feminist Criticism" as a groundbreaking piece of scholarship cannot be denied. It suffers, however, from a lack of definitional precision and supportive detail. Smith justified the need for a black feminist aesthetic that would embody the "realization that the politics of sex as well as the politics of race and class are crucially interlocking factors in the works of Black women writers." She insisted that such an approach was an "absolute necessity," for without it, "we will not ever know what these writers mean" (p. 159).

Smith argued for the existence of a black female literary tradition that cohered "thematically, stylistically, aesthetically, and conceptually." Black women writers' "common approaches to the act of creating literature," she continued, was a "direct result of the specific political, social and economic experience they have been obliged to share" (p. 164). She offered, as an example, the incorporation of rootworking, herbal medicine, conjure, and midwifery in the stories of Zora Neale Hurston, Margaret Walker, Toni Morrison, and Alice Walker. While these folk elements certainly do appear in the work of these writers, they also appear in the works of certain black male writers, a fact that Smith omits. If black women writers use these elements differently from black male writers, such a distinction must be made before one can effectively articulate the basis of a black feminist aesthetic.

Smith maintained further that Zora Neale Hurston, Margaret Walker, Toni Morrison, and Alice Walker use a "specifically black female language to express their own and their characters' thoughts" (p. 164), but failed to describe or to provide examples of this unique language. Of course we have come recently to acknowledge that "many of our habits of language usage are sex-derived, sex-associated, and/or sex-distinctive," that "the ways in which men and women internalize and manipulate language" are undeniably sex-related.[15] But this realization in itself simply paves the way for rather than closes investigation, investigation that must engage some difficult critical questions.

For example, is there a monolithic black female language? Do black female high school dropouts, welfare mothers, college graduates, and Ph.D.s share a common language? Are there regional variations on this common language? Further, some black male critics have tried to describe the uniquely "black linguistic elegance"[16] that characterizes black poetry in general. Are there noticeable differences between the languages of black females and black males? These and other questions must be addressed with precision if current feminist terminology is to function beyond mere critical jargon.

Turning from her discussion of the commonalities between black women writers, Smith describes the nature of her critical enterprise. "Black feminist criticism would by definition be highly innovative," she maintains. "Applied to a particular work [it] can overturn previous assumptions about [the work] and expose for the first time its actual dimensions" (p. 164). Smith then proceeds to apply such an innovative reading to Toni Morrison's *Sula*. She begins by classifying it as a lesbian novel, which she sees in "the emotions expressed . . . the definition of female character and in the way that the politics of heterosexuality are portrayed" (p. 170). Smith vacillates between arguing forthrightly for the validity of her interpretation and recanting or overqualifying it in a way that undercuts her own credibility.

According to Smith, "If in a woman writer's work a sentence refuses to do what it is supposed to do, if there are strong images of women and if there is a refusal to be linear, the result is innately lesbian literature" (p. 164). She adds, "because of Morrison's consistently critical stance toward the heterosexual institutions of male/female relationships, marriage, and the family" (p. 165), *Sula* works as lesbian novel. This definition of lesbianism is vague and imprecise; it is, oddly, a desexualized sensibility that subsumes far more black women writers, particularly contemporary ones, than not into the canon of lesbian writers. For example, Jessie Fauset, Nella Larsen, and Zora Neale Hurston all criticize major socializing institutions, as do Gwendolyn Brooks, Alice Walker, and Toni Cade Bambara. Further, if we apply Smith's definition of lesbianism, there are probably a few black male writers who qualify as well. All of this is to say that Smith has simultaneously oversimplified and obscured the issue of lesbianism and stripped it of any explanatory power. Obviously aware of the delicacy of her position, she interjects that "the very meaning of lesbianism is being expanded in literature" (p. 170). Unfortunately, that qualification does not strengthen her argument. One of the major tasks ahead of black feminist critics who write from a lesbian perspective, then, is to define lesbianism and lesbian literature precisely. Until they can offer a definition that is not vacuous, their attempts to distinguish black lesbian writers from those who are not will be hindered.[17]

Even as I call for firmer definitions of lesbianism and lesbian literature, I question whether or not a lesbian aesthetic is finally a reductive approach to the study of black women's literature that possibly ignores other, equally important aspects of the literature. For example, reading *Sula* solely from a lesbian perspective overlooks the novel's density and complexity, its skillful blend of folklore, omens, and dreams, its metaphorical and symbolic richness. Although I do not quarrel with Smith's appeal for fresher, more innovative approaches to black women's literature, I suspect that "innovative" analysis is pressed to the service of an individual political persuasion. While personal and political presuppositions enter inevitably into one's critical judgments, we should

> be wary of reading literature as though it were polemic. . . . If when using literary materials to make what is essentially a political point, we find ourselves virtually rewriting a text, ignoring certain aspects of plot or characterization, or over-simplifying the action to fit our "political" thesis, then we are neither practicing an honest criticism nor saying anything

useful about the nature of art (or about the art of political persuasion, for that matter).[18]

Alerting feminist critics to the dangers of political ideology yoked with aesthetic judgment is not to deny that feminist criticism is a valid and necessary cultural and political enterprise. Indeed, it is both possible and useful to translate ideological positions into aesthetic ones, but if the criticism is to be responsible, the two must be balanced.

Because feminist criticism is a cultural and political enterprise, the majority of those who practice it believe that their efforts can effect social change. Smith argues emphatically for socially relevant criticism in her conclusion that "Black feminist criticism would owe its existence to a Black feminist movement while at the same time contributing ideas that women in the movement could use" (p. 164). This is an exciting idea in itself, but we should ask: What ideas, specifically, would black feminist criticism contribute to the movement? Further, even though the proposition of a fruitful relationship between political activism and the academy is an interesting (and necessary) one, I doubt its feasibility. I am not sure that either in theory or in practice black feminist criticism will be able to alter significantly circumstances that have led to the oppression of black women. Moreover, as Lillian Robinson pointedly remarks, there is no assurance that feminist aesthetics "will be productive of a vision of art or of social relations that is of the slightest use to the masses of women, or even one that acknowledges the existence and struggle of such women."[19] I agree with Robinson that "ideological criticism must take place in the context of a political movement that can put it to work. The revolution is simply not going to be made by literary journals."[20] I should say that I am not arguing a defeatist position with respect to the social and political uses to which feminist criticism can be put. Just as it is both possible and useful to translate ideological positions into aesthetic ones, it must likewise be possible and useful to translate aesthetic positions into the machinery for social change.

Despite the shortcomings of Smith's article, she raises critical issues on which black feminist critics can build. There are many tasks ahead of these critics, not the least of which is a clearer formulation of the principles and parameters of black feminist criticism. I use the term in this paper simply to refer to black female critics who analyze the works of black female writers from a feminist perspective. But the term can also apply to any criticism written by a black woman regardless of her subject or perspective—a book written by a male from a feminist or political perspective, a book written by a black woman or about black women authors in general, or any writings by women.[21]

In addition to defining the methodology, black feminist critics need to determine the extent to which their criticism intersects with that of white feminist critics. Barbara Smith and others have rightfully challenged white women scholars to become more accountable to black and Third World women writers, but will that require white women to use a different set of critical tools when studying black women writers? Are white women's theories predicated on culturally specific values and assumptions? Andrea Benton Rushing has attempted to answer these questions in her series of articles on images of black women in literature. She maintains, for example, that critical categories of women, based on analyses of white women characters, are Euro-American in derivation and hence inappropriate to a consideration of black women characters.[22] Such distinctions are necessary and, if held uniformly, can materially alter the shape of black feminist scholarship.

Regardless of which theoretical framework black feminist critics choose, they must have an informed handle on black literature and black culture in general. Such a grounding can give this scholarship more texture and completeness and perhaps prevent some of the problems that have had a vitiating effect on the criticism so far. This footing in black history and culture serves as a basis for the study of the literature. Such "contextualism" is often frowned upon, if not dismissed entirely, by critics who insist on exclusively textual and linguistic analysis. Its limitations notwithstanding, I firmly believe that a contextual approach to black women's literature exposes the conditions under which literature is produced, published, and reviewed. This approach is not only useful but necessary to black feminist critics.

To those working with black women writers prior to 1940, the contextual approach is especially fruitful. In researching Jessie Fauset, Nella Larsen, and Zora Neale Hurston, for example, it is useful to determine what were the prevalent attitudes about black women during the time that they wrote. There is much information in the black "little" magazines published during the Harlem Renaissance. An examination of *The Messenger*, for instance, reveals that the dominant social attitudes about black women were strikingly consistent with traditional middle-class expectations of women. *The Messenger* ran a monthly symposium for some time titled "Negro Womanhood's Greatest Needs." While a few female contributors stressed the importance of women's equality with men, socially, professionally, and economically, the majority emphasized that a woman's place was in the home. It was her duty "to cling to the home [since] great men and women evolve from the environment of the hearthstone."[23]

One of the most startling entries came from a woman who wrote:

> the New Negro Woman, with her head erect and spirit undaunted is resolutely marching forward, ever conscious of her historic and noble mission of doing her bit toward the liberation of her people in particular and the human race in general. Upon her shoulders rests the best task to create and keep alive, in the breast of black men, a holy and consuming passion to break with the slave traditions of the past; to spurn and overcome the fatal, insidious inferiority complex of the present, which . . . bobs up ever and anon, to arrest the progress of the New Negro Manhood Movement; and to fight with increasing vigor, with dauntless courage, unrelenting zeal and intelligent vision for the attainment of the stature of a full man, a free race and a new world.[24]

Not only does the contributor charge black women with a formidable task, but she also sees her solely in relation to black men.

This information enhances our understanding of what Fauset, Larsen, and Hurston confronted in attempting to offer alternative images of black women. Moreover, it helps to clarify certain textual problems and ambiguities of their work. Though Fauset and Hurston, for example, explored feminist concerns, they did so ambivalently, Fauset especially so. Her novels are alternately forthright and cagey, radical and traditional, on issues that confront women. Her first, *There Is Confusion* (1924), is flawed by an unanticipated and abrupt reversal in characterization that brings the central female character more in line with a feminine norm. Similarly, in her last novel, *Seraph on the Suwanee* (1948), Zora Neale Hurston depicts a female character who shows promise for growth and change, for a departure from the conventional expectations of womanhood, but who, in the end, apotheosizes marriage, motherhood, and domestic servitude.

These two examples alone clearly capture the tension between social pressure and artistic integrity which is felt, to some extent, by all women writers. As Tillie Olsen points out, the fear of reprisal from publishing and critical arenas is a looming obstacle to the woman writer's coming into her own authentic voice. "Fear—the need to please, to be safe—in the literary realm too. Founded fear. Power is still in the hands of men. Power of validation, publication, approval, reputation. . . ."[25]

While insisting on the validity, usefulness, and necessity of contextual approaches to black women's literature, the black feminist critic must not ignore the importance of rigorous textual analysis. I am aware of many feminist critics' stubborn resistance to the critical methodologies handed down by white men. Although the resistance is certainly politically consistent and logical, I agree with Annette Kolodny that feminist criticism would be "shortsighted if it summarily rejected all the inherited tools of critical analysis simply because they are male and western." We should, rather, salvage what we find useful in past methodologies, reject what we do not, and, where necessary, move toward "inventing new methods of analysis."[26] Particularly suggestive is Lillian Robinson's assertion that "a radical kind of textual criticism . . . could usefully study the way the texture of sentences, choice of metaphors, patterns of exposition and narrative relate to [feminist] ideology."[27]

This rigorous textual analysis involves, as Barbara Smith recommends, isolating as many thematic, stylistic, and linguistic commonalities among black women writers as possible. Among contemporary black female novelists, the thematic parallels are legion. In Alice Walker and Toni Morrison, for example, the theme of the thwarted female artist figures prominently.[28] Pauline Breedlove in Morrison's *The Bluest Eye,* for example, is obsessed with ordering things.

> Jars on shelves at canning, peach pits on the step. Sticks, stones, leaves. . . .
> Whatever portable plurality she found, she organized into neat lines,
> according to their size, shape or gradations of color. . . . She missed
> without knowing what she missed—paints and crayons.[29]

Similarly, Eva Peace in *Sula* is forever ordering the pleats in her dress. And Sula's strange and destructive behavior is explained as "the consequence of an idle imagination."

> Had she paints, clay, or knew the discipline of the dance, or strings; had
> she anything to engage her tremendous curiosity and her gift for metaphor,
> she might have exchanged the restlessness and preoccupation with whim
> for an activity that provided her with all she yearned for. And like any
> artist with no form, she became dangerous.[30]

Likewise, Meridian's mother in Alice Walker's novel, *Meridian,* makes artificial flowers and prayer pillows too small for kneeling.

The use of "clothing as iconography"[31] is central to writings by black women. For example, in one of Jessie Fauset's early short stories, "The Sleeper Wakes" (1920), Amy, the protagonist, is associated with pink clothing (suggesting innocence and immaturity) while she is blinded by fairy-tale notions of love and marriage. However, after she declares her independence from her racist and sexist husband, Amy no longer wears pink. The imagery of clothing is abundant in Zora Neale Hurston's *Their*

Eyes Were Watching God (1937). Janie's apron, her silks and satins, her head scarves, and finally her overalls all symbolize various stages of her journey from captivity to liberation. Finally, in Alice Walker's *Meridian,* Meridian's railroad cap and dungarees are emblems of her rejection of conventional images and expectations of womanhood.

A final theme that recurs in the novels of black women writers is the motif of the journey. Though one can also find this same motif in the works of black male writers, they do not use it in the same way as do black female writers.[32] For example, the journey of the black male character in works by black men takes him underground. It is a "descent into the underworld,"[33] and is primarily political and social in its implications. Ralph Ellison's *Invisible Man,* Imamu Amiri Baraka's *The System of Dante's Hell,* and Richard Wright's "The Man Who Lived Underground" exemplify this quest. The black female's journey, on the other hand, though at times touching the political and social, is basically a personal and psychological journey, the state of becoming "part of an evolutionary spiral, moving from victimization to consciousness."[34] The heroines in Zora Neale Hurston's *Their Eyes Were Watching God,* in Alice Walker's *Meridian,* and in Toni Cade Bambara's *The Salt Eaters* exemplify this theme.

Even though isolating such thematic and imagistic commonalities should continue to be one of the black feminist critic's most urgent tasks, she should beware of generalizing on the basis of too few examples. If one argues authoritatively for the existence of a black female "consciousness" or "vision" or "literary tradition," one must be sure that the parallels found recur with enough consistency to support these generalizations. Further, black feminist critics should not become obsessed with searching for common themes and images in black women's works. As I pointed out earlier, investigating the question of "female" language is critical and may well be among the most challenging jobs awaiting the black feminist critic. The growing body of research on gender specific uses of language might aid these critics. In fact, wherever possible, feminist critics should draw on the scholarship of feminists in other disciplines.

An equally challenging and necessary task ahead of the black feminist critic is a thoroughgoing examination of the works of black male writers. In her introduction to *Midnight Birds,* Mary Helen Washington argues for the importance of giving black women writers their due first. She writes:

> Black women are searching for a specific language, specific symbols,
> specific images with which to record their lives, and even though they can
> claim a rightful place in the Afro-American tradition and the feminist

tradition of women writers, it is also clear that, for purposes of liberation, black women writers will first insist on their own name, their own space.[35]

I believe likewise that the immediate concern of black feminist critics must be to develop a fuller understanding of black women writers who have not received the critical attention black male writers have. Yet, I cannot advocate indefinitely such a separatist position, for the countless thematic, stylistic and imagistic parallels between black male and female writers must be examined. Black feminist critics should explore these parallels in an effort to determine the ways in which these commonalities are manifested differently in black women's writing and the ways in which they coincide with writings by black men.

Of course, there are feminist critics who are already examining black male writers, but much of the scholarship has been limited to discussions of negative images of black women found in the work of these authors.[36] Although this scholarship served an important function in pioneering black feminist critics, it has virtually run its course. Feminist critics run the risk of plunging their work into cliché and triviality if they continue merely to focus on how black men treat black women in literature. Hortense Spillers offers a more sophisticated approach to this issue in her discussion of the power of language and myth in constructing a "politics of intimacy" in James Baldwin's *If Beale Street Could Talk*. Arguing that the present diction of that "politics" is "demonstrably outmoded," Spillers urges critics to formulate "new notations for our time" and offers her own as a working model.[37]

Black feminist criticism is a knotty issue, and while I have attempted to describe it, to call for clearer definitions of its methodology, to offer warnings of its limitations, I await the day when black feminist criticism will expand to embrace other modes of critical inquiry. In other words, I am philosophically opposed to what Annis Pratt calls "methodolatry." Wole Soyinka has offered one of the most cogent defenses against critical absolutism. He explains:

> The danger which a literary ideology poses is the act of consecration—and of course excommunication. Thanks to the tendency of the modern consumer-mind to facilitate digestion by putting in strict categories what are essentially fluid operations of the creative mind upon social and natural phenomena, the formulation of a literary ideology tends to congeal sooner or later into instant capsules, which, administered also to the writer, may end by asphyxiating the creative process.[38]

Whether or not black feminist criticism will or should remain a separatist enterprise is a debatable point. Black feminist critics ought to move from this issue to consider the specific language of black women's literature, to describe the ways black women writers employ literary devices in a distinct way, and to compare the way black women writers create their own mythic structures. If they focus on these and other pertinent issues, black feminist critics will have laid the cornerstone for a sound, thorough articulation of the black feminist aesthetic.

1980

Decades make convenient, if not always tidy, units for taking stock of movement and for anticipating change. In rethinking this essay roughly ten years since its initial publication, I prefer to undertake the former; that is, to assess rather than predict. That way I avoid the challenge as well as the presumptive grandiosity of charting directions. But more importantly, I avoid the danger of having those directions rigidify into the kind of doxology to which I alluded and cautioned against near the end of the original essay. Such critical orthodoxy, I suggest, brooks no departure from itself and, in its scrupulous plotting, often forecloses the unexpected delights of detour, or the pleasures to be found in just plain getting lost.

But in declining to map future directions in order to take a retrospective glance, I am aware that I engage in a different form of plotting, one with all the trappings of narrative; more so, because it is a nonlinear narrative of my own intellectual sojourn within a specific critical terrain. In tracing the distance in my own thinking about black feminist criticism between 1980 and 1991, I trace a distance that parallels and intersects in places and crisscrosses at others, with broader questions and developments in literary and cultural studies. I trace a distance that has brought me in touch with a breadth and variety of critical positions either unavailable or untapped when I began to write this piece in 1979. But finally, and perhaps most importantly, I trace a distance that reaches beyond the bounds of "literary" texts proper to confront the slippery, controversial, and ultimately irresoluble matters of racial identity, subjectivity, and the political realities of institutional life. Acknowledging the problematics and politics of "speaking for" the "other" has become a reflexive gesture of this critical era, an acknowledgment that is, on the one hand, a salutary recognition of "difference," but, on the other, a handy justification for sticking with "our own" kind and kin. This tension between "insider" and "outsider" groups lay at the heart of Barbara Smith's attempt to found and define a "black feminist criticism." In her landmark essay, "Toward a Black Feminist Criticism" (1977), widely and rightly considered the origin and benchmark of the discourse, Smith confronted the weight of an established critical tradition and challenged the consistently negative judgments it meted out to black women writers, when it deigned to judge them at all. She sought a corrective in arrogating to black women critics the exclusive or proprietary authority over the writings of black women. She argued for a connection between the "politics of Black women's lives, the content of their writings, and their situation as artists." Only a black woman, in her estimation, could appreciate the "profound subtleties of this particular body of literature."

Smith's effort to define the boundaries of black feminist criticism restrictively was necessary to this emergent discourse. As Jane Gallop has observed, "the fencing off of a field of literature always involves glorifying and strengthening the territory in a defensive relation to the outside, keeping out the foreign element."[39] Uneasy with Smith's restrictive parameters, I went too far in the other extreme by attempting to formulate a definition so inclusive in its scope that it nearly gutted black feminist thinking of any distinctiveness and explanatory power as a critical category.

Whereas Smith had sought to make biology the sole criterion of a black feminist critical sensibility, I maintained that biology was inessential. The principles of black feminism could be found in the work of whites and blacks, men and women alike, across a broad spectrum of often mutually antagonistic positions. My critics were quick to point out the naivete of such a full embrace. Hazel Carby was astute to notice that "black feminist theory is emptied of its feminist content if the perspective of the critic doesn't matter." In a more recent response to "New Directions," Patricia Hill Collins observed that "definitions claiming that anyone can produce and develop Black feminist thought risk obscuring the special angle of vision that Black women [she specifies black American women] bring to the knowledge production process." Collins sees this special vision in black women's shared "legacy of struggle against racism and sexism." But I would argue that, while that struggle must surely set black women apart from their most immediate counterparts—black men, white women, white men—it can take a variety of forms, depending on the social positions of those in question. Further, it is by no means clear that such a struggle is root and branch of a sui generis critical position. Such would imply an aestheticized view of struggle and presuppose that black women have had a unanimous or univocal response to it, which they have then transliterated into the principles of a unique and unified poetics.

Avoiding the reductiveness of defining a critical position strictly as an identifying label applied on the basis of the critic's race and gender remains a challenge, one that Valerie Smith has taken up. In "Black Feminist The-

ory and the Representation of the 'Other,'" she quickly disposes of any notion that her intention is "to reclaim the black feminist project from those who are not black women." She uses "black feminist theory to refer not only to theory written (or practiced) by black feminists [biologically speaking], but also to a way of reading inscriptions of race (particularly but not exclusively blackness), gender (particularly but not exclusively womanhood), and class in modes of cultural expression."[40] Cheryl Wall notes, similarly, that for black women to make "our positionality explicit is not to claim a 'privileged' status for our positions. . . . Making our positionality explicit is, rather, a response to the false universalism that long defined critical practice and rendered black women and their writing mute."[41]

But, in the final analysis, the arguments and counter-arguments about the lack of definitional integrity of black feminist criticism quickly reach the point of gridlock. Although they possess an interest and an urgency of their own, they are ultimately not the only issues to be decided. In other words, it is not entirely to the point to say that black feminist criticism lacks the parameters of a clear theoretical position, for part of its value— both in its early articulations as well as now—lies in its illumination of particular social arrangements of academic life.

Suspending for the moment, then, appropriate and necessary questions about what it is and who has the authority to speak and write in its name, I would suggest that the pressing matter of this moment is not to determine once and for all whether black feminist criticism has validity as a discrete, coherent category of knowledge, but rather, to speculate about how that category has served, even when it has snagged, those who are self-described "black feminist critics." Such a speculation takes us into transgressive arenas in which we risk violating the "socialities" of academic protocol.

Both in the dedication to "Toward a Black Feminist Criticism"—"for all my sisters, especially Beverly and Demita"—and in the language of collectivity threaded throughout the essay, Barbara Smith expressed a yearning for a filial connection in a literary critical enterprise. She transported that language to the celebrated anthology But Some of Us Are Brave, *edited with Gloria T. Hull and Patricia Bell-Scott, using it to organize and title the pieces of the first section: "Searching for Sisterhood: Black Feminism." The lead essay of the section, Michele Wallace's "A Black Feminist's Search for Sisterhood," is a poignant memoir chronicling her experiences of exclusion and disconnection, one after another, from such black "revolutionary" organizations and institutions as the Black Power Movement, the National Black Theatre, Howard University—all leading her to conclude that the " 'new Blackness' was fast becoming the new slavery for sisters" (p. 9). No panacea was to be found, not even in the short-lived National Black Feminist Organization. Wallace's closing paragraph leaves no doubt about the urgent need for a black feminist collective.*

> *Black feminists . . . exist as individuals. . . . We exist as women who are Black who are feminists, each stranded for the moment, working independently because there is not yet an environment in this society remotely congenial to our struggle—because, being on the bottom, we would have to do what no one else has done: we would have to fight the world. (12)*

bell hooks echoes Wallace's concerns. Shortly after the publication of her Ain't I a Woman: Black Women and Feminism, *hooks wrote an essay about the trying process of writing the book and getting it published. The motivation to write it came from taking feminist classes from which material by and about black women was noticeably absent. She writes of feeling "estranged and alienated from the huge group of white women who were celebrating the power of 'sisterhood.' " Throughout the essay, hooks speaks repeatedly of "desperation," "urgency," "longing," to "find sources that would explain black female experience" and end her own estrangement.[42]*

It would clearly be a mistake (as well as an injustice) to argue that black feminist criticism emerged from some nebulous desire for "sisterhood" and can thus be reduced to this recurrent metaphor.[43] To allow this language of and yearning for "sisterhood," however, with all of its suggestions of emotional untidiness, to figure into any retrospective on the subject, is to approach an academic problem from a perspective that is seldom explored. Like so many critical stances of the late twentieth century, black feminist criticism is ripe for speculation about the relation between its emergence as a discourse formation and the shifting demographics in late-twentieth-century academic life, which produced, correspondingly, shifts in a variety of intellectual and institutional priorities. While such speculations cannot be undertaken here, it is instructive to consider Paul Gilroy's observations in light of the emergence of black feminist criticism. He argues that institutional life "aggregates people or disperses" them. Those who aggregate create a "solidarity from a sense of particularity." Following Gilroy, I would suggest that the category black feminist criticism, in its earliest formation, represented an attempt to foster just such an aggregate, to form what Abiola Irele calls "affective affiliations."[44] However utopian or ultimately illusory they proved to be, these affiliations became the basis for acting aga.nst the weight and power of an entrenched literary and critical tradition that had either excluded the writings of black women altogether or marginalized them within existing narratives about literary excellence and value, falsely perceived as transcendent categories.

But several questions arise here: Are such "affective affiliations" easily solidified and at what cost? Can a concept that derives, at least in part, from a yearning for affective association serve as the basis of a poetics? The tensions and disagreements among black women writers and intellectuals would suggest that black feminist criticism is an internally (and productively) fragmented discourse. Although this is not, in itself, a necessary obstacle to "affective affiliation," it makes such affiliations far from automatic.

Hazel Carby insists rightly that "black feminist criticism be regarded critically as a problem, not a solution, as a sign that should be interrogated, a locus of contradictions."[45] Any effort to neutralize these contradictions under the cover of a false unity would be misguided, would fail to take into account the fact that black women connect to each other along lines that extend far beyond race. As has become commonplace by now, the recognition of differences—of class, ethnicity, nationality, sexuality, etc.— among black women is at least as important as differences between them and white women, white men, and black men. And thus any assumption of an implied stability, an internal coherence of black feminist criticism, would have to be challenged. That category has always been simply incapable of describing and containing the diverse body of work generally collected under its banner. Such diversity lends vitality to this enterprise, if not challenges the validity of the terms of its existence. One of the most influential challenges has come from Alice Walker. Her attempt to articulate a "womanist" theory has found currency among many black women, particularly those in the fields of theology and sociology. Walker implicitly rejects the term "black feminist," objecting to any intellectual category that requires the affixation of a color to make it visible. "I wanted a word," she said, "that was visible in itself, because it came out of my own culture." Others, finding that Walker's position and her certainties about culture need more thorough interrogation, call for black women critics to refer to themselves simply as "feminist."

With all its problems, however, I would vote to preserve the category black feminist criticism, for I question the value of detaching "blackness" from feminism and the potential consequences of a move toward a re-universalization. Where then is the body in the text? This I ask, even as I understand that blackness is not reducible to physical characteristics, even as I understand that black people's bodies have been used to rationalize *their oppression. To strike out the "black" in "black feminist criticism" is to lend tacit support to a standard of "neutrality" according to which the "blemishes" of blackness would vanish. But to leave it there is to refuse to collaborate with this fiction of neutrality, which effectively requires that black women argue for their own invisibility. As Patricia Williams puts it, "to accommodate a race-neutral world view is to become an invisible black, a phantom black, by avoiding the label 'black' (it's all right to be black in this reconfigured world if you keep quiet about it). The words of race are like windows into the most private vulnerable parts of the self; the world looks in and the world will know, by the awesome, horrific of name."*[46]

We might ask here, for whom is the name horrific? and for whom does a black feminist critic write? In challenging the black feminist critic to be "constantly aware of the political situation of all Black women" (p. 164), Barbara Smith emphasized that black feminist criticism would be more than an academic discourse, more than a skill that any literate person could learn and then "apply." She thus established out front the sociopolitical basis of her critical position and pressed literary analysis into service as cultural critique. Although Smith tried to expand its bases and enlarge its reach, black feminist criticism remains an overwhelmingly academic enterprise tied to institutional arrangements and priorities of the corporate university. And at times, it strains under the pressure to reconcile and satisfy the often conflicting demands of political transformation, on the one hand, and disciplinary litmus tests, on the other.

For example, the salient particulars of a black feminist critical position have been difficult to reconcile, at times, with the influential verdicts of contemporary critical thought. For example, the assumption that the writer's medium is transparent, that there is an organic line of descent and connection from black women writers to black women critics to literary characters, and that "black women writers" "constitute an identifiable literary tradition" evident in the "innumerable commonalities" of language and theme that structure their work, would all be challenged as epistemologically suspect by the most salient claims of postmodernist thought. At present these claims exert perhaps the strongest hold on academic production in the literary marketplace, and it is in that realm that black feminist criticism has found its niche and widest appeal. Be that as it may, I agree with bell hooks that it is necessary for all feminist thought to "transcend the boundaries of the university setting," as well as the "printed page."[47] *The concept of a feminist theory "beyond words" embraces the multifarious systems of order, ways of giving meaning, interpreting or representing ideas that constitute the larger grammar of culture.*

And while the move to extend the conventional border of the "text" takes us productively outside the precincts of the university, we are not yet done with words, nor, for that matter, with the project of academic transformation.

For black feminist critics, a large part of that project has involved the work of canon formation, a process that many have faulted and harshly critiqued, charging that it assists rather than resolves this era's crisis in humanistic studies. Cornel West has argued, for example, that the effort on the part of Afro-American scholars to produce an Afro-American canon "reveals the worst of academic pluralist ideology."[48] While West raises pertinent questions about the limits and dangers of ideologies of canon formation, I would argue that they rest too comfortably on an assumption that we cannot entertain as final: that "literary studies" has totally lost all meaning as a functioning *unit of disciplinary organization and understanding. It hasn't.*

While postmodernist thinking has forcefully transformed our understanding of "disciplines" and how they function as accessories to "power" and "hegemony," that transformation has occurred mainly at the level of discourse. In other words, "disciplines" and "departments" are seldom blurred and transgressed at the level of institutional life. There are unarguably rich possibilities contained in bringing discourse and institutional practice into closer symmetry. The benefits to "local" knowledges—produced in disciplines and departments about authors, periods, "movements," etc.—of embedding their practices in structures beyond the local and the unitary cannot be overstressed. However, as long as the machinery of local knowledge production tools along, there is still a place for the literary focus of much black feminist criticism.

Susan Fraiman makes a point about the shift in the academy away from "women's studies" to "gender studies" that is useful in this context. She registers justified concern that this shift "with its emphasis on the 'larger picture' may cause us to abandon our recuperative work before it is finished, and while accounts of women are still susceptible to reerasure." Hers is not an alarmist concern. Her cautionary note acquires an even deeper sounding when we consider that even a book as popular and as controversial in the late 1970s as Ntozake Shange's for colored girls *is now out of print. Further, the pendulum of intemperate and partisan critical assessment of black women's writing, which Barbara Smith detailed in 1977, seems to be swinging this way again. Carol Iannone, nominated to the advisory council for the National Endowment for the Humanities, made the controversial remark that the award of the Pulitzer Prize to Alice Walker's* The Color Purple *and the American Book Award to Gloria*

Naylor's The Women of Brewster Place *may have been "less a recognition of literary achievement than some official act of reparation."*[49] *The nomination was defeated and its supporters registered their dismay by pillorying its "tyrannical" opponents for being "politically correct." Thinking of this situation returns me to perhaps the most glaringly naive aspect of my thinking ten years ago. Then I was fairly harsh in my judgment of the ideology in Barbara Smith's "Toward a Black Feminist Criticism." I faulted her for allowing ideology to inform critical analysis, but I now know that there is no criticism without ideology; there is nothing that ideology fails to touch. Smith knew then what we must know now: Any assumed separation between ideology and aesthetics is false, naive, and indefensible.*

Despite the power and appeal of Foucault, then, I would argue that it is not yet time to toll the death knell for the "author" or for "literary tradition," although we must proceed with more complicated definitions of "tradition" and how it functions, those such as Hortense Spillers describes in "A Hateful Passion, a Lost Love." In this essay, Spillers offers a departure from linear models of literary history and urges that we "not . . . accede to the simplifications and mystifications of a strictly historiographical time line." Abandoning linearity, she argues, offers "the greatest freedom of discourse to black people, to black women as critics, teachers, writers, and thinkers."[50] *I have abandoned that linearity here in the following studies of fiction by black women.*

PART II

Ideas of Tradition

Tradition. Now there's a word that nags the feminist critic.

—*Mary Helen Washington*

Traditions are not born. They are made. We would add that they are not, like objects of nature, here to stay, but survive as created social events only to the extent that an audience cares to intersect them.

—*Hortense J. Spillers*

2

Race of Saints

Four Girls at Cottage City[1]

Published in 1898, *Four Girls at Cottage City* appeared at the close of one of the most intense and productive decades in the history of Afro-American women writers and intellectuals, the decade that Frances E. W. Harper named the "woman's era." Maria Stewart, widely considered the first American-born woman—black or white—to give a public address, had inspired audiences as early as the 1830s with her fiery speeches. Her challenge to the "land of freedom" to "do away with tyranny and oppression" was issued by many blacks of the era. Heard perhaps less often were Stewart's particular appeals on behalf of black women. Her piercing question: "How long shall the fair daughters of Africa be compelled to bury their minds and talents beneath a load of iron pots and kettles?" was raised with renewed vigor and urgency in the 1890s. During that decade, such black women as Frances E. W. Harper, Anna Julia Cooper, Ida B. Wells-Barnett, and Pauline Hopkins recorded and protested against the era's most volatile and oppressive social issues confronting black Americans: the rising tide of lynching (understood as a terrorist weapon of social control) and the tightening strictures of Jim Crow. Most of these women were founding members of the National Association of Colored Women, a federation of club women who organized to combat racial oppression in these, its most virulent, forms. Much of their organizing was done on the pages of *The Woman's Era*, the official journal of the Woman's Era Club in Boston.

Although published in Boston in the midst of this fervid climate in which black female writers, intellectuals, and activists assumed uncompromising and determined stands against racism, *Four Girls at Cottage City* took a kind of retreat, making its setting—a fictionalized Oak Bluffs on Martha's Vineyard—rich with suggestion. In other words, the novel appeared during the same historical moment that produced not only Frances E. W. Harper's *Iola Leroy*, but also Ida B. Wells-Barnett's "Southern Horrors: Lynch Law in All Its Forms" (1892); Anna Julia Cooper's *A Voice from the South* (1892), in which she insisted on the higher education of women; and Pauline Hopkins's *Contending Forces* (1900), in which she urged black writers to "faithfully portray the inmost thoughts and feelings of the Negro."

In this lineup, Emma Dunham Kelley's novel seems naive and frivolous in its depiction of four carefree girls "in their pretty summer dresses" off for vacation at a Massachusetts resort. Vera, Jessie, Allie, and Garnet seem sprung from some halcyon days of yore. More importantly for considerations of Afro-American women's fiction, they are not what Alice Walker calls "black black women" (those unprotected by class and light-skinned privilege) in her essay "If the Present Looks Like the Past, What Does the Future Look Like?" Rather, two are "white skin[ned]" with "golden hair," and blue eyes, and though the other two have "rich complexions and dark eyes," they still have "rosy cheeks" and "rosy mouths." Their most severe confrontation with racial injustice is having to sit in "nigger heaven" when they go to the theater.

But to set Emma Dunham Kelley strictly apart from her black female contemporaries and to argue that she retreated from the reformist spirit of her age is to oversimplify and misrepresent the matter. In choosing to create heroines who are physically indistinguishable from white women, Kelley was no different from Frances Harper and Pauline Hopkins, both of whom wrote novels featuring heroines who could pass for white. Further, although *Four Girls at Cottage City* seems, on the surface, oblivious to the horrors of black life in the nineteenth century, it was no less a product of the woman's era. It simply chose a different mission. However "foreign" it might seem to the sensibilities of modern readers, that mission was as urgent in Kelley's day as organizing against lynching, rape, Jim Crow, and black disenfranchisement: the mission of spiritual uplift, alternately termed, spiritual feminism or domestic feminism. In fact, one of the most popular arguments of the nineteenth century held that only the elevation of the spirit would obliterate racism and other "earthly" injustices.

In *Four Girls at Cottage City*, Kelley combines conventions from spiritual autobiography with those from the sentimental novel to create a work that shows far more thematic affinities with what Nina Baym has labeled "woman's fiction" than with the novels of Kelley's black female contemporaries. As in the novels by white women, which Baym examines in her study *Woman's Fiction: A Guide to Novels by and about Women in America, 1820–1870* (1978),[2] Kelley's focus was interior and domestic; her aim, like theirs, was to show readers how they should live. As Baym notes, "these women authors envisioned themselves as lay ministers, their books as evangelical sermons that might spur conversion" (p. 44). That Kelley believed equally in the book as sermon is clear from the endless discussions the characters have about religion throughout the novel. In one such discussion, a character argues that, in writing novels, Dickens "was as well-employed as in preaching the gospel." These gospels, in fictional form, addressed what William Andrews calls the central question in spiritual autobiography in the Christian tradition: "the fate of the individual soul." In his introduction to *Sisters of the Spirit*, Andrews explains that the genre "chronicles the soul's journey not only from damnation to salvation, but also to a realization of one's true place and destiny in the divine scheme of things."[3]

Kelley announces her evangelical intentions early in the novel. When the girls stop at the first cottage that advertises rooms for rent, they are directed to an upper room "before a pair of very steep, very narrow stairs," which Vera stumbles down. Jokingly, she prophesies that, because of the cottage owner's treacherous steps, her place in the afterlife would be "in the lower regions." Leaving this cottage, the girls find more suitable lodging at Trinity Park. The cottage is right opposite the tabernacle. The spatial relationship between the cottage and the church signifies the "twinness" and inseparability of religiosity and domesticity, the sacred and the secular.

When the four girls journey, "happy light-hearted, careless and gay," to Cottage City, little do they know that their summer vacation will lead to a lifetime vocation: the struggle for salvation and the commitment to Christian service. Although scriptural passages and hymns abound in the novel, the hymn most often repeated and requested is "Nearer My God to Thee." While the girls begin their journey as a close-knit group of friends—reminiscent of Carole Smith-Rosenberg's description of relations between women in her essay "The Female World of Love and Ritual: Relations between Women in Nineteenth-Century America"[4]—they become "sisters of the spirit" and accept "the Savior" as their one true friend.

True to the generic conventions of sentimental fiction, "our girls," as the narrator refers to them, have guides along their spiritual journey: Charlotte Hood (an example of what Elizabeth Ammons terms the mother-savior)[5] and her ailing son, Robin. Both the mother-savior and the child are dominant character types in the sentimental novel with a spiritual focus. The role children played in nineteenth-century fiction—Harriet Beecher Stowe's Little Eva in *Uncle Tom's Cabin* is a prototypical example—has been well-documented. Believed to be innocent and uncorrupted, children, it was reasoned, were eminently well suited to assist in moral instruction. In addition to children, women, largely because they were excluded from male domains, were believed to be morally superior to men and thus better spiritual leaders. In "Women's Political Future," for example, Frances E. W. Harper echoed the age's widespread sentiments: "The world has need of all the spiritual aid that women can give for the social advancement and moral development of the human race." It is, Harper added, "the women of a country who help to mold its character and to influence if not determine its destiny."[6] *Four Girls* shares this ideology that arrogates to children and women (especially mothers) unique salvific powers.

Although all four girls are in need of spiritual assistance, Vera, described by turns as skeptical and haughty, a "flame of fire" and an "icicle cold [and] proud," stands most in need. Robin is the "taper that would light the path that Vera's young feet were to tread on their way to the 'better country,'" the "light that would guide her out of the night of doubt and uncertainty into the blessed day of light and glory." Though bedridden and paralyzed, Robin, together with his mother, teaches the girls a lesson in the virtues and transformative powers of suffering. Further, they teach the girls that gaining the kingdom of heaven is "long and weary work."

Appropriate to Kelley's evangelistic mission, Vera first sees Charlotte Hood in church and reads a "sermon" in her "pale radiant face," a face "lifted to heaven" and showing signs of "deep sorrow . . . passed through bravely." In one of the many coincidences and examples of awkward plotting in the novel, the girls meet the "sermonic" face at her cottage where she supports herself and her ailing son on her meager earnings as a laundress. The girls remark that Charlotte and Robin have suffered a cruel and unjust fate, but Charlotte interrupts in "thrilling tones" to declare her fate the workings of an "all-wise and . . . all-merciful God."

From this point, which is the novel's structural center, Charlotte Hood controls the point of view, telling her life story—a sermonic set piece—as inspiration and testimony. Her story conforms to the standard morphology of conversion: conviction of sin, inner doubt and struggle, repentance, salvation, and inner peace. Each day, from Robin's sickroom, Charlotte gives the girls the next installment of her life of suffering and her struggle for repentance and salvation. Despite her minister's urgings that she turn to God to assuage her suffering, neither he nor his male orthodoxy and moralism is ultimately able to console Charlotte and lead her along the path to salvation. Rather, she is saved by the experience of reading a woman's novel.[7] Here, the most interesting and suggestive features of *Four Girls at Cottage City* emerge, and the gendered inflections of its spiritual mission are made most apparent.

After losing her daughter, Margie, her "little white lamb," and her mother and two sisters in close succession, Charlotte sinks into the depths of despair. Falling into a deep sleep, she has the dream that "save[s] [her] soul from everlasting death." She likens her three-day journey in the dream to the scenes described in Elizabeth Stuart Phelps's novel *Beyond the Gates* (1883), one in Phelps's religious quartet that included the best-selling *The Gates Ajar* (1868), *The Gates Between* (1887), and *Within the Gates* (1901). *Beyond the Gates* offers an account of the afterlife with distinctly feminist suggestions.

In *The Life and Works of Elizabeth Stuart Phelps* (1983), Lori Kelley explains that Phelps successfully ministered in her novels to the needs of female Christians dissatisfied with the offerings of male orthodoxy and achieved, thereby, a "quasi-clerical status." Importantly, the religion she preached bypassed the formal church and its hierarchies. In the heaven created in these novels, Lori Kelley continues, "women receive the public acclaim and approval so long denied them in the male-dominated society of earth."[8]

Emma Dunham Kelley incorporates this feminist dimension of Phelps's novel of the afterlife into *Four Girls at Cottage City*. As God's medium, Charlotte assumes a quasi-clerical status in the novel. God moves her heart so that she, "through His guidance," will move the girls to accept "the Savior for [their] friend." Charlotte recounts the Judgment Day of her dream in which she is summoned to the throne of God, a figure described in terms that parallel earlier descriptions of Charlotte herself: Hers is a "pale radiant face" with blue eyes; his is a "fair face" with "eyes [of] deep blue." In the dream, God the Judge becomes God the gentle, loving, somewhat maternal parent who takes Charlotte on a tour to see other souls "working their way to Heaven." Although Charlotte's earthly minister figures in the dream, wearing an expression of "proud triumph," he is finally given no place near the throne. It is not he who stands at God's "right hand," but Hester, a "poor old woman" who is given a jewel from God's crown.

Just as Hester serves as inspiration and example to Charlotte in the dream, Charlotte becomes inspiration and example to Vera and the girls at Cottage City. She teaches them that their "beautiful little resort" on earth has an even more blissful counterpart in heaven, imaged in the dream as a "beautiful country! All light, and joy and music ... green hills, pleasant valleys ... men and women" all "lov[ing] one another with equal love."

This "heaven," which might be viewed as a feminist utopia, peopled by men and women who love each other as equals, could not be easily replicated on earth due largely to male dominance and the influence of masculine values. Together with the other literary "evangelists" of the nineteenth century, however, Emma Dunham Kelley imagined an antidote, an alternative earth that might be saved by maternal values. This world relegated men to the peripheries of women's daily lives.

There is no better example than the relationship between Mother and Father, the keepers of the cottage where the girls spend their vacation. When the girls arrive, Mother leads them to their room up a pair of "Christian stairs." The girls quickly surmise that she is the "ruling spirit" of the house, the "velvet hand in an iron glove." There are repeated references to her holding father "determinedly back" and to his "retir[ing] obediently." When they visit the girls' room, Mother blocks Father's entry, forcing him to stand outside the doorway, in the shadows of what is clearly represented as a "woman's room."

Although the girls spend much of their time with their two gentlemen callers, Fred and Erfort, Jessie complains that the men are too much underfoot. "When we came down here, I thought we four girls were going around together and have a good time. There is no fun when there's a parcel of men around." As is typical in sentimental novels, the heroines eventually do fulfill their traditionally expected roles as wives and mothers. In fact, the novel ends with a scene that features Vera as wife and mother. But despite that conventional narrative ending, marriage is depicted here, as in so many novels by women, as breaking the "link ... in the golden chain" of female communities, to borrow a passage from Kelley's first novel, *Megda* (1891).

These matrifocal communities, which valued relationships and connection, would be the era's answer to the corruption of masculine ideals and values of conquest and competition. But contemporary critics are not amiss in arguing that, women, because their sphere of influence and power was delimited to home and hearth, had no real power to effect lasting social change, a criticism that might well be leveled against *Four Girls at Cottage City*. Certainly, the reader leaves the novel wondering what, if any, power spiritual feminism holds for transforming society. The novel alludes to racial injustice (in the description of "nigger heaven") and to class inequities (in Jessie's criticism of a woman whose poodle is better provided for than Charlotte and her son). It even offers a model solution to the inequities of class by having the girls sacrifice personal pleasures and plans in order to finance the operation that will correct Robin's spinal injury.

For the most part, however, the narrative forgoes the dramatic possibilities that the material realities of race and class suggest, subsuming them under the larger spiritual vision that collapses all social distinctions in the interest of Christian egalitarianism. But the reader cannot easily ignore the implications of Kelley's decision to cast a white-skinned woman as mother-savior. This decision might be read by some as Kelley's capitulation to the era's race-prejudiced theology, which saw blackness as synonymous with evil and equated whiteness with grace. Kelley's intention is clearly not to embroil herself in theological controversy or to demonstrate how the lessons of spiritual journeying can be applied in the here-and-now for the betterment of humankind.

A contemporary feminist might hope that in the Schomburg Library of Nineteenth-Century Black Women Writers, this novel would attempt to formulate just such an application, to dramatize the relationship between spiritual elevation and social responsibility with respect to the conditions of Afro-Americans. But to note the novel's neutrality on racial concerns and the politics of theology that it reflects is not to argue that all literature by blacks must take up the racial banner in protest against injustice. Nor is it to pit Emma Dunham Kelley against other black women writers of her day in the interest of creating some literary hierarchy based on political ideology. It is, rather, much more fruitful to see her as one precursor of the spiritual feminism that is currently resonating throughout contemporary Afro-American women's fiction, as seen in such works as Ntozake Shange's *for colored girls who have considered suicide when the rainbow is enuf* (1977), Toni Cade Bambara's *The Salt Eaters* (1980), and Alice Walker's *Meridian* (1976) and *The Color Purple* (1982). Continuing the tradition of which *Four Girls at Cottage City* is a part, these contemporary black women writers see God as maternal, as a spiritual force within the female self, a force detached from the institutional, hierarchical, male-dominated church. But taking up where Kelley left off, their concern with female spirituality is firmly rooted in the material realities of black women's lives. Such retentions and transformations, such continuities and discontinuities, are the stuff of literary tradition.

1987

3

"The Changing Same"[1]

GENERATIONAL CONNECTIONS AND BLACK WOMEN NOVELISTS—*Iola Leroy* and *The Color Purple*[2]

As Iola finished, there was a ring of triumph in her voice, as if she were reviewing a path she had trodden with bleeding feet, and seen it change to lines of living light. Her soul seemed to be flashing through the rare loveliness of her face and etherealizing its beauty. Everyone was spellbound. Dr. Latimer was entranced, and, turning to Hon. Dugdale, said, in a low voice and with deep-drawn breath, 'She is angelic!' . . . 'She is strangely beautiful! . . . The tones of her voice are like benedictions of peace; her words a call to higher service and nobler life.'[3]

As soon as dinner over, Shug push back her chair and light a cigarette. Now is come the time to tell yall, she say.
Tell us what? Harpo ast.
Us leaving, she say.
Yeah? say Harpo, looking round for the coffee. And then looking over at Grady.
Us leaving, Shug say again. Mr. _____ look struck, like he always look when Shug say she going anywhere. He reach down and rub his stomach, look off side her head like nothing been said. . . .
Celie is coming with us, say Shug.
Over my dead body, Mr. _____ say.
You satisfied that what you want, Shug say, cool as clabber.
Mr. _____ start up from his seat, look at Shug, plop back down

again. He look over at me. I thought you was finally happy, he say. What wrong now?

You a lowdown dog is what's wrong, I say. It's time to leave you and enter the creation. And your dead body just the welcome mat I need.[4]

The character being *spoken about* in the first passage is Iola Leroy, the title character of Frances E. W. Harper's 1892 novel, thought, until recently, to be the founding text of a black women's tradition in the novel. A group of men are giving their approval of an impromptu speech that Iola has just delivered on the ennobling effects of suffering and the necessity for Christian service. They lay stress, simultaneously, on her physical beauty and saintliness.

In the second passage, from Alice Walker's 1982 novel, *The Color Purple,* Celie, the novel's central character *is speaking,* along with her spiritual guide and lover, the itinerant blues singer Shug Avery. Celie's, unlike Iola's, is an audience of hostile, disapproving men; nevertheless, with force and resoluteness, Celie announces her plans to move on in search of personal fulfillment and spiritual growth.

I cite these two passages as examples of two strikingly different images of black female character in black women's fiction—one "exceptional" and outer-directed, the other "ordinary" and inner-directed; two different approaches to characterization, one external, the other internal; and finally, two different narrative voices, one strained, stilted, genteel, and inhibited, the other spontaneous, immediate, fresh, and authoritative.[5]

Although the passages are different, the novels from which they are excerpted share important basic patterns. Both novels recount the problems of familial separation and reunion, of lost and found identities. More significantly, however, these novels represent the two most salient paradigms in the black female literary tradition in the novel. Although manipulated differently, depending on the author, these paradigms derive from a common center in black women's novels. Both revisionist in impulse, they are revealed, most graphically, in the depiction of black female characters. Borrowing from Susan Lanser's *The Narrative Act,* I call these paradigms, simply, public and private narrative fiction. I see them posed respectively and most dramatically in France E. W. Harper's *Iola Leroy* and Alice Walker's *The Color Purple.*[6]

Of necessity, I use these terms, not literally, but metaphorically, for as Lanser notes correctly, "obviously all fictional narration is 'public' in the sense that it was written to be published and read by an audience. What I am distinguishing here are fictional narrative acts designed for an apparently public readership [or one "outside" the text] and those narratives designed for reception only by other characters and textual figures."[7]

In the following discussion, I would like to adapt and modify Lanser's distinction between public and private point of view to posit a provisional distinction between public and private narrative fiction.[8] I wish to distinguish here between those novels by black women that seem to imply a public readership (or one outside the black cultural community) and those that imply a private readership or one within that cultural matrix.[9] Given the complexity and ambiguity inherent in questions about audience, one can only speculate about the audience for whom a specific text seems intended. To be certain, authors cannot determine conclusively who their actual readers are. Nevertheless, all writers begin by fictionalizing or imagining an audience. As Peter Rabinowitz notes, authors "cannot make artistic decisions without prior assumptions (conscious or unconscious) [stated or implied], about their audience's beliefs, knowledge, and familiarity with conventions," literary and/or social.[10] Each text, then, selects, encodes, and images its targeted audience—what Wolfgang Iser calls its "implied reader"—through the style, language, and strategies it employs. (That does not preclude, of course, its being read by those outside the targeted reading group.)

I have chosen character as a way of examining these paradigms even though the current wave of literary/theoretical sophistication calls into question "naive common-sense categories of 'character,' 'protagonist,' or 'hero,'"[11] and rejects the "prevalent conception of character in the novel" which assumes that "the most successful and 'living' characters are richly delineated autonomous wholes."[12] For, despite such positions, imaging the black woman as a "whole" character or "self" has been a consistent preoccupation of black female novelists throughout much of their literary history.[13] That these writers frequently use the *bildungsroman*—a genre that focuses primarily on the gradual growth and development of a "self" from childhood to adulthood—attests strongly to this preoccupation. It seems appropriate, therefore, to allow critical concerns of black women's novels to emerge organically from those texts, rather than to allow current critical fashion to dictate what those concerns should be.

In considering character in black women's fiction as a structure that reflects dominant paradigms in their tradition, other critical questions arise. Although the scope of this essay does not permit me to explore them in full and equal detail, the following interlocking questions are implied in my consideration of characterization. In that one of the most challenging aspects of characterization for any writer is the authentic representation of speech, what is the relationship between race/gender and literary voice?

In turn, what is the relationship between author and audience, for that relationship largely determines and explains, not only narrative voice, but also a range of artistic strategies and structures. What do the configurations and variations of character in black women's fiction reveal about patterns of literary influence among black women writers, about their literary history?[14]

But examining how black women writers approach characterization is not a purely aesthetic question, for in raising questions about this literary structure, one simultaneously confronts political and cultural questions that must be embedded in their historical context, not articulated solely in terms of our own. For black women novelists of the nineteenth century, character as aesthetic structure was tightly coupled to character as a complex of moral attributes, most clustered around sexuality.

Largely because of the negative construction of their sexual identity, black women novelists treated sexuality with caution and reticence. This pattern is clearly linked to the network of social and literary myths perpetuated throughout history about black women's libidinousness. It is well known that during slavery the white slave master helped to construct an image of black female sexuality that shifted responsibility for his own sexual passions onto his female slaves. They, not he, had wanton, insatiable desires that he was powerless to resist. The image did not end with emancipation. So persistent was it that black club women devoted part of their first national conference in July 1895 to addressing it,[15] thereby working to fulfill their motto, "Lifting as We Climb."[16]

Though myths about black women's lasciviousness were not new to the era, a letter from one J. W. Jacks, a white male editor of a Missouri newspaper, made them a matter of urgent concern to black club women. Forwarded to Josephine S. Pierre Ruffin, editor of *The Woman's Era*,[17] the letter attacked black women's virtue, supplying "evidence" from other black women. According to Jacks, when a certain Negro woman was asked to identify a newcomer to the community, she responded, "the negroes will have nothing to do with 'dat nigger,' she won't let any man, except her husband, sleep with her, and we don't 'sociate with her."[18]

Mrs. Ruffin circulated the letter widely to prominent black women and to heads of other women's clubs around the country, calling for a conference to discuss this and other matters of direct concern to black middle-class women. Given this historical context, it is not surprising that black women novelists of the nineteenth and early twentieth centuries dealt quietly with issues of black sexuality.

Of course, reticence about sexuality in literature during these periods was certainly not peculiar to black women writers; however, black women's unique psychosexual history in turn-of-the-century United States casts a different and important light on a more general cultural convention. Black women writers responded to the myth of black women's sexual licentiousness by insisting fiercely on their chastity. In attempting to overcome their heritage of rape and concubinage—a fight the club women waged—they stripped the characters they created of *all* sexual desire. In such works as Emma Dunham Kelley's *Megda* (1891), Frances E. W. Harper's *Iola Leroy* (1892), and Pauline Hopkins's *Contending Forces* (1900),[19] black heroines struggle to defend and preserve the priceless gem of virginity. Conscious of the fact that a reconstruction of black female sexuality was required, these writers assumed a revisionist mission in their work, one based on a belief that they could substitute reality for stereotype.[20] That substitution would assist a larger and related mission: to elevate the image of the entire black race. In so doing, they naively believed, they could eliminate caste injustices.

This impulse is, at once, the greatest strength and the greatest weakness of these early texts, for it results, without exception, in the creation of static, disembodied, larger-than-life characters. These early black heroines are sexually pure, invariably exemplary, characterized by their self-sacrifice and by their tireless labor for the collective good. Ironically, despite the early writers' efforts to revise homogenized literary images, they succeeded merely, and inevitably, in offering alternative homogenization; they traded myth for countermyth, an exchange consistent with their public mission. The countermyth dominates *Iola Leroy* and is evident most strikingly in Iola's conscious choice to glorify the virtues of motherhood and domesticity, the mainstays of the mid-nineteenth-century cult of true womanhood.[21]

Although this ideology of domesticity conflicted sharply with the majority of black women's lives, Harper, like the majority of black writers of her era—both men and women—ironically accommodated her "new" model image of black womanhood to its contours. As Barbara Christian observes, "Since positive female qualities were all attributed to the white lady," black writers of the nineteenth century "based their counterimage on her ideal qualities, more than on [those] of any real black women." The image of the Lady combined and conflated physical appearance with character traits. Immortalized particularly in the Southern antebellum novel, the image required "physical beauty [that is, fair skin] . . . fragility, refinement and helplessness." "The closest black women could come to such an ideal, at least physically," Christian continues, "would . . . have to be the mulatta, quadroon, or octoroon."[22]

Iola fulfills this physical requirement. "My! but she's putty," says the slave through whose eyes we first see her. "Beautiful long hair comes way down her back; putty blue eyes, and jis ez white ez anybody is dis place" (p. 38). This ideal dominates novels by black women in the nineteenth century, due, as Alice Walker argues reasonably, to a predominantly white readership "who could identify human feeling, humanness, only if it came in a white or near-white body." She concludes, "'Fairness' was and is the standard of Euro-American femininity."[23]

By giving Iola a role to play in the larger struggle for race uplift, Harper modified the image of the Southern lady, but it is important to note that Iola's role in the struggle is enacted within the boundaries of the traditional expectations of women as mothers and nurturers, expectations that form the cornerstone of the cult of true womanhood. According to Iola, "a great amount of sin and misery springs from the weakness and inefficiency of women." In "The Education of Mothers," one of the two public speeches she gives in the novel (public speaking being largely reserved for men in the text), she appeals for "a union of women with the warmest hearts and clearest brains to help in the moral education of the race" (p. 254).[24] Not only does the content of such speeches contribute to Iola's exemplary image, the style and language do also.

Ordinary or black folk speech has been historically devalued by the standard (white) English-speaking community, a devaluation that, as John Wideman maintains, "implies a linguistic hierarchy, the dominance of one version of reality over others."[25] That devaluation and all that it implies is especially pervasive in Harper's era, in which, notes Arlene Elder, "Blacks were ridiculed in white plantation and Reconstruction humor for the rough rhythms, slurred words, malapropisms, and quaint images in their language. In order to escape this degrading image, [early] black novelists sped to the other extreme of creating cultured mulattoes"[26] who used the elegant, elaborate, and artificial language found in much of the popular fiction of their day. At every point that Iola speaks in the novel, it is in the form of a carefully reasoned oration in defense either of her virtue or of some moral or social ideal. Even in conversations at home with family and friends, Iola expounds, as in the following example:

> To be the leader of a race to higher planes of thought and action, to teach men clearer views of life and duty, and to inspire their souls with loftier aims, is a far greater privilege than it is to open the gates of material prosperity and fill every home with sensuous enjoyment. (p. 219)

In significant contrast to Iola's formal oratory is the folk speech of the novel's secondary characters, captured particularly well in the opening chapter titled "Mystery of Market Speech and Prayer Meeting." The chapter describes the slaves' masterful invention of a coded language to convey information to each other, unsuspectedly, about battles won and lost during the Civil War. Their rich and imaginative language is self-consciously mediated in this chapter and throughout the novel by the stilted and pedantic voices of the narrator and the novel's major character. Nowhere is this pattern more strikingly illustrated in the novel than in the passage that describes the reunion between Iola's uncle, Robert, and his mother, from whom he was separated as a child. "Well, I'se got one chile, an' I means to keep on prayin' till I find my daughter," says Robert's mother. "I'm so happy! I feel's like a new woman!" (p. 183). In contrast, Robert responds: "My dear mother . . . now that I have found you, I mean to hold you fast just as long as I live. . . . I want you to see joy according to all the days wherein you have seen sorrow (p. 183).

In *Iola Leroy,* the propaganda motive, the hallmark of public discourse, largely explains these extreme differences of speech styles between the principal characters—all educated mulattoes—and the minor characters— all illiterate and visibly black servants and workers. The implications of such differentiations are clear: the speech of these secondary characters (which Iola finds "quaint," "interesting," and "amusing") must be mediated and legitimated by the more accepted language of the major characters.

In the course of *Iola Leroy,* as Iola fulfills her role as exemplary black woman, she comes to resemble a human being less and less and a saint more and more. We learn very little about her thoughts, her inner life. Nothing about her is individualized, nor does this seem to be Harper's chief concern, for she is creating an exemplary type who is always part of some larger framework. That larger framework is moral and social in *Iola Leroy,* and every aspect of the text, especially character, must be carefully selected to serve its purpose. All of the novel's characters are trapped in an ideological schema that predetermines their identities. Every detail of Iola's life, down to the most personal experiences of family life, is stripped of its intimate implications and invested with social and mythical implications. It is significant that of all the Old Testament types, she identifies with Moses and Nehemiah, for "they were willing to put aside their own advantages for their race and country" (p. 265).

Iola's role as social and moral exemplar is paralleled by the novel's role as exemplum. Like its title character, *Iola Leroy* is on trial before the world. It aims for a favorable verdict by choosing its models carefully. Harper's most recognizable model is Harriet Beecher Stowe's *Uncle Tom's Cabin,* the most popular novel of the mid-nineteenth century in America. Space does not permit me to detail the striking similarities of plot, theme, style, and characterization between the two novels. Although Harper makes slight modifications, echoes of the most salient episodes of *Uncle Tom's Cabin* are present throughout *Iola Leroy*.[27]

Harper's choice of *Uncle Tom's Cabin* as model is a logical and appropriate one, given the polemical and public role that she expected her novel to play, a role that Stowe's novel had played to unrivaled success with an audience comprised mainly of Northern white Christians. Harper addresses and appeals to this audience directly in the afternote of the novel:

> From threads of fact and fiction I have woven a story whose mission will not be in vain if it awakens in the hearts of our countrymen a stronger sense of justice and a more Christlike humanity in behalf of those whom the fortunes of war threw, homeless, ignorant and poor, upon the threshold of a new era. (p. 282)

Those Northern whites might be more inclined to lend their assistance to this homeless and displaced lot if the images of black life that Harper and her black contemporaries valued and affirmed accorded with that audience's horizon of social and literary expectations. In this respect, *Iola Leroy* is in company with a number of novels by black writers of its era, all dedicated to a public mission, all foundering on the shoals of two contradictory attempts: "to conform to the accepted social [and] literary . . . standards of their day and their almost antithetical need to portray their own people with honesty and imagination."[28]

The need to portray their people with honesty and imagination has been paramount for contemporary black women novelists. For many—Alice Walker, Toni Morrison, Gayl Jones, and Sherley Anne Williams, among others—that need has compelled them to transform the black female literary ideal inherited from their nineteenth-century predecessors. Although these recent writers have preserved the revisionist mission that inspired that ideal, they have liberated their own characters from the burden of being exemplary standard bearers in an enterprise to uplift the race. The result is not only greater complexity and possibility for their heroines, but also greater complexity and artistic possibility for themselves as writers. The writings of Alice Walker are suggestive examples of this paradigm shift.[29]

In "Beyond the Peacock," an essay in her collection *In Search of Our Mother's Gardens*, Walker writes, "each writer writes the missing parts to the other writer's story. And the whole story is what I'm after."[30] To Walker, a major, if not *the* major, missing part is the story of what she calls the "black black" heroine, described in the essay "If the Present Looks Like the Past." Unlike Iola Leroy and the other nineteenth-century black women characters that Walker surveys in the essay, the black black heroine can neither pass for white nor be protected by class privilege. While Walker isn't the only black female novelist to problematize the Iola Leroy type,[31] she has made a particularly suggestive and controversial attempt in the Celie letters of *The Color Purple*. These letters can be read as Walker's effort to write the missing parts of *Iola Leroy* and other black women's texts in its tradition. In other words, Celie is a revision of a revision of black female character, an unvarnished representation.

Whereas Iola Leroy as character is largely indistinguishable from the Southern Lady and is devoted to the mission of middle-class racial "uplift," Celie is a poor, visibly black, barely literate drudge devoted simply to avoiding and surviving the brutalities inflicted on her by every man with whom she comes into contact. Unlike Iola, no ornate and elevated speeches come trippingly to Celie's tongue. She speaks in black folk English, and, unlike Harper, Alice Walker provides none of the self-conscious assurances to the reader—apostrophes, contractions, corrections from more "well-spoken" characters—that she knows the "standard."

But perhaps Celie's most striking distinction from Iola is her sexual experience. Iola survives attempted rape; Celie does not. Celie is unable to fend off attacks on her virtue by predatory men as her very first letter makes starkly clear: "You gonna do what your mammy wouldn't. First he put his thing up gainst my hip and sort of wiggle it around. Then he grab hold my titties. Then he push his thing inside my pussy" (p. 11). Although Celie's introduction to sexuality is rape, as her narrative unfolds, she, unlike Iola, discovers how vital healthy sexual experiences are to the development of her self-esteem and her creative powers. Significantly, the only form of sexuality that aids that process is expressed with a woman, one of the few lesbian relationships explored in black women's literature.[32]

Iola and Celie reflect their authors' divergent approaches to characterization as well. Whereas Harper approaches Iola's character largely from the outside through her physical characteristics and through what others say about her, Walker reveals Celie's character completely from the inside. Everything we learn about Celie is filtered through her own consciousness and rendered in her own voice.

In *Iola Leroy*, self is sacrificed to the collective mission and the result is a static symbol rather than a dynamic character. In *The Color Purple*, the collective mission, as imaged by Harper, is sacrificed to the self, and the result is the creation of a character in process, one more complex and thoroughly realized than Iola Leroy.[33]

Iola's energy is invariably directed outside of herself, and the narrative's action is correspondingly social and public in emphasis. Celie's energy, on the other hand, is primarily directed inward, and the narrative action of *The Color Purple* is correspondingly psychological, personal, and intimate in emphasis.

Like *Iola Leroy, The Color Purple* fits primarily into the private paradigm, suggested by its choice of the epistolary mode—by definition, personal and private—and the finite focus of the Celie letters. One of their most striking features is the conspicuous absence of any reference to the "outside" world. Except for an occasional reference to Macon, Memphis, and one to World War I, the world is shut out.[34] Instead, like epistolary novels generically, *The Color Purple* emphasizes the psychological development of character.

Celie begins her story at age 14, in the form of letters to God, the only one who can hear her, she thinks. Feeling isolated and ashamed, she tells Him of her life of brutality and exploitation at the hands of men. Writing is all-important to Celie; her last resounding word to her sister, Nettie, before they separate is, "Write" (p. 26).

While Celie's letters are an attempt to communicate with someone outside herself, they also reveal a process of self-examination and self-discovery in much the same way the letter functioned for the protagonists in Richardson's *Clarissa* and *Pamela*. In other words, Celie's growth is chartable through her letters to God, which are essentially letters of self-exploration, enabling her to become connected to her thoughts and feelings. That connection eventually liberates her from a belief in a God outside herself, whom she has always imaged as "big and old and tall and graybearded and white" (p. 176), and acquaints her with the God inside herself.

The spiritual dimension of Celie's discovery of the God-in-self has striking implications for her experience as a writer—for a writer she is, first and foremost. A self-reflexive novel, *The Color Purple* explicitly allegorizes much about the process and problematics of writing. It dramatizes the relationship between writer and audience and its effect on narrative authority and autonomy, to forceful voice. *The Color Purple* makes clear that the black woman writer has written primarily without an audience capable of accepting and appreciating that the full, raw, unmediated range of the black woman's story could be appropriate subject matter for art.[35]

The Celie letters addressed to God indicate her status as a writer without an audience, without a hearing, a predicament she recognizes only after discovering that her husband has intercepted and hidden in a trunk letters her sister Nettie has written to her from Africa over a thirty-year period.

As Celie recovers from the shock, she announces to Shug that she has ceased to write to God, now realizing that "the God I had been praying and writing to is a man, and just like all the other mens I know. Trifling, forgitful, and lowdown." When Shug cautions Celie to be quiet, lest God hear her, Celie responds defiantly, "Let 'im hear me, I say. If he ever listened to poor colored women the world would be a different place" (p. 175).

Celie's decision to cease writing to God and to begin writing to her sister, Nettie, marks a critical point in both her psychological development and in her development as a writer. Significantly, before Celie discovers that God is not listening, her letters to him record passive resignation, silence, and blind faith in his benevolence. She can suffer abuses in this life, she confides to Sofia, because "[it] soon be over. . . . Heaven last all ways" (p. 47). In these letters, she identifies with Squeak who speaks in a "little teenouncy voice" (p. 83). She "stutters," "mutters," her "throat closes" (p. 86), and "nothing come[s] out but a little burp" (p. 115). Celie admits that she "can't fix [her] mouth to say how [she] feel[s]" (p. 88). Appropriately, these letters record a distinct split between what she thinks and what she feels and says. For example, when Nettie leaves for Africa, she expresses sadness at leaving Celie to be buried by the burden of caring for Mr. ——— and his children. Celie writes, "It's worse than that, I think. If I was buried, I wouldn't have to work. But I just say, Never mine, never mine, long as I can spell G-o-d I got somebody along" (p. 26). Similarly, when Celie thinks she sees her daughter, Olivia, at the drygoods store in town, she strikes up a conversation with the woman who has custody of the child. The woman makes a joke about the child's name, and Celie writes: "I git it and laugh. It feel like to split my face" (p. 24). The image of the split functions here, as in so many novels by women, as a sign of the character's tenuous sense of self, of identity, if you will.[36] The image objectifies the split between Celie's outer and inner selves that will ulti- mately be made whole as the novel develops.

It is further significant that none of the letters addressed to God is signed. In their anonymity, their namelessness, the letters further under- score Celie's lack of individuality. When she begins to write to Nettie, however, her inner and outer selves become connected. Her thoughts are fused with her feelings, her actions, her words, and the letters assume a quality of force and authority, at times, of prophecy, as seen in Celie's conversation with Mr. ——— before she leaves for Memphis:

Until you do right by me, everything you touch will crumble.
He laugh. Who you think you is? he say. You can't curse nobody. Look

at you. You black, you pore, you ugly, you a woman. Goddam, he say, you nothing at all.

Until you do right by me, I say, everything you even dream about will fail. (p. 187)

Celie concludes: "I'm pore, I'm black, I may be ugly and can't cook. . . . But I'm here" (p. 187). Thus these letters addressed to Nettie are alternately signed, "Your sister, Celie" and "Amen," an expression of ratification, of approval, of assertion, of validation. The suggestion is clear: Celie is now ratifying, asserting, and validating her own words, her own worth, and the authority of her own experience. Celie's validation of her linguistic experience is central to that process.

Celie's story underscores sharply, as Iola's does not, the argument of many students of language that "ordinary" discourse can be continuous with "poetic," or "literary" discourse, and that any assumed distinctions between the two are unsupported by linguistic research.[37] For considerations of African American literature that argument is especially critical, for if both forms of discourse can be continuous with each other, the need for an external and legitimating filter is eliminated.[38]

In wanting to teach her to "talk correctly," Jerene and Darlene, Celie's helpers in her Folkspants, Unlimited, enterprise, imply the popular belief that ordinary black speech must be "corrected" in order to have literate status, but Celie comes to understand that "only a fool would want you to talk in a way that feel peculiar to your mind" (p. 194).

The narrative links Celie's refusal to talk in a manner peculiar to her mind with a change in audience. That refusal—the mark of psychic wholeness as well as of narrative authority and autonomy—is licensed and buttressed by the sympathetic audience she imagines. Significantly, Celie directs her letters away from God, a "public" and alien audience outside herself and toward her sister, Nettie, a private, familial, familiar, and receptive audience. The qualitative differences between the letters to God and those to Nettie imply a causal connection between a receptive audience (imaged as one with "kinship" ties to the writer) and the emergence of a forceful, authoritative, and self-validating narrative voice.[39]

The question that immediately arises, however, is, given this connection, what explains the comparative lack of force and authority in Nettie's letters? How do they serve the narrative? Early reviewers of *The Color Purple* rightly saw Nettie's letters as lackluster and unengaging compared to Celie's. While Nettie's letters advance the narrative line, they disrupt the immediacy and momentum of Celie's. That notwithstanding, Nettie's letters do function to unify the narrative by repeating its central images and concerns. Most significantly, they continue and expand its commentary on the act of writing and the role that context and circumstances play in the creative process.

But the Nettie letters have perhaps the most striking and intriguing suggestions for Alice Walker as a writer, for her discovery of her own voice. For Walker, as for so many women writers, the process of that discovery begins with thinking back through and reclaiming her female ancestors. While much has been made (with Walker's encouragement) of Walker's obvious debt to Zora Neale Hurston, there has been virtually no acknowledgment that she owes an equal, though different, debt to black women writers before Hurston. In "Saving the Life That Is Your Own: The Importance of Models in the Artist's Life," Walker admits that her need to know the oral stories *told* by her female ancestors, stories that Hurston transcribed in her folklore and writing, was equal to her need to know the stories *written* by nineteenth-century black women.[40] Even if they had to be transformed or rejected altogether, the experiences that these earlier writers recorded were crucial to Walker's development as a writer.

In an interview with Gloria Steinem, Walker remarks that "writing *The Color Purple* was writing in my first language" in its "natural, flowing way."[41] In the novel, that language is Celie's, not Nettie's, indicating that Walker identifies her own writing voice with Celie's. However, that identification does not require that she reject Nettie's. Both the oral and the literate are parts of her literary ancestry and she conjoins them in the Celie and Nettie letters, respectively, reinforcing one of the novel's central themes: female bonding. Together their letters form a study of converging contrasts that are homologous with the relationship between Frances E. W. Harper and Alice Walker.

As their letters reveal, the correspondences between the sisters' experiences are striking, even strained and over-determined. Much of what Nettie writes to Celie describing the situation in Africa—the breakdown of male/female relationships, the power of male domination, and the bonding between women—is replicated in Celie's experiences in the rural South. Nettie writes to Celie of the paved roads in Africa; Celie, to her, of those in Georgia. Nettie describes her round and windowless African hut; Celie, Shug's difficulty including windows in her plans for a round house in Memphis.

While the sisters' experiences converge at these critical points, they diverge at others, perhaps most importantly in the voice, content, and style of their epistles. While Celie's letters are written in black folk English and record her personal trials and near defeat, Nettie's, written in more formal language, record the trials and decimation of a people and their culture. Nettie's personal relationships with Samuel, Corinne, and their children seem dwarfed and insignificant compared to the destruction of the Olinka culture. In other words, while the majority of Celie's letters can be said to represent the private paradigm of the African American female tradition in the novel, the majority of Nettie's letters can be said to represent the public paradigm. I say "majority" because Nettie's letters to Celie are, significantly, in two distinct linguistic registers. Her first letters to Celie focus on personal matters and are largely indistinguishable from Celie's letters:

> Dear Celie, the first letter say,
> You've got to fight and get away from Albert. He ain't no good.
> When I left you all's house, walking, he followed me on his horse. When we was well out of sight of the house, he caught up with me and started trying to talk. You know how he do. . . . (p. 119)

The next letter reads: "I keep thinking it's too soon to look for a letter from you. And I know how busy you is with all Mr. ——— children . . ." (p. 120). Shortly after these letters, Nettie writes to Celie of the events leading to her decision to go to Africa as a missionary, explaining her agreement to help build a school in exchange for furthering her education. That letter reads:

> . . . When Corinne and Samuel asked me if I would come with them and help them build a school . . . I said yes. But only if they would teach me everything they knew to make me useful as a missionary. . . . They agreed to this condition, and my real education began at that time. (p. 124)

From this point on, Nettie's letters shift from the personal to the social, the political, the historical. They assume the quality of lecture and oration, losing the intimacy more appropriate in correspondence to a sister. Nettie's has become an educated imagination, shaped by the context within which she moves as well as by her function as a missionary in a colonizing enterprise.

Although Celie and Nettie are separated by an ocean, by their life-styles—one ordinary, the other exceptional—and by the style of their epistles—oral and literate—these separate realities become integrated in the novel and held in sustained equilibrium. Each sister is allowed to exist as an independent entity; each, through her letters, is allowed to speak in her own voice without apology, mediation, or derision.

While one might expect it, there is no apology, mediation, or derision on Walker's part for her predecessor, Frances E. W. Harper, the impulses of whose work she incorporates in the voice and experiences of Nettie. Reminiscent of Iola, Nettie guards her virginity. Her self-conscious and ambiguous description of her developing passion for Samuel brings to mind Iola's reticence about sexuality. In one letter Nettie recounts to Celie her "forward behavior" with Samuel. As she and Samuel embraced, Nettie writes, "concern and passion soon ran away with us," and "I was transported by ecstasy in Samuel's arms" (pp. 210–11).

But the more important resemblance between Nettie and Iola is their sacrifice of personal needs and wishes for a larger social purpose. Nettie is swept up in a social movement and energized by its unofficial motto: "OUR COMMUNITY COVERS THE WORLD" (p. 208). She is, in her words, working for the "uplift of black people everywhere" (p. 127). The concept of racial uplift, of corporate mission, so central to *Iola Leroy,* is explicit in Nettie's letters and acts as counterpoint to Celie's more private and personal concerns. Further, together these letters objectify the pattern of intertextual relations among black women writers, a pattern which departs from what Harold Bloom describes in *The Anxiety of Influence* and *A Map of Misreading.*[42] Bloom's linear theory of the oedipal war between literary fathers and sons does not hold among black women writers, many of whom reverently acknowledge their debts to their literary foremothers. Unlike Bloom, I see literary influence, to borrow from Julia Kristeva, in the intertextual sense, each text in dialogue with all previous texts, transforming and retaining narrative patterns and strategies in endless possibility.[43]

This pattern of literary influence from Harper to Walker departs in significant ways from that among black men.[44] Henry Gates's description of intertextuality in his discussion of Richard Wright, Ralph Ellison, and Ishmael Reed, for example, characterizes the formal relations between them as largely adversarial and parodic.[45] While there is certainly much to parody in Harper's *Iola Leroy*—most notably, the uplift concept and the excesses of formality that generally attended it—Walker refrains from doing so, and perhaps, therein, lies a fundamental distinction between African American male and female literary relations. We might argue that Walker has transformed and updated the concept of "uplift," associated almost exclusively with Harper and her generation, for a kind of uplift functions metaphorically in *The Color Purple.* The novel elevates the folk forms of rural and southern blacks to the status of art. In a similar fashion, it takes the tradition of letters and diaries, commonly considered a "female" tradition (and therefore inferior), from the category of "non-art" and elevates it to art.

But while Walker retains uplift as metaphor in *The Color Purple,* she rejects the burden it imposes on the writer, a burden that black writers have shouldered to their detriment throughout their literary history in service to a corporate mission. Certainly a major consequence of that mission for the writers of Harper's generation was a homogenized literary era that inhibited the writers' discovery of their unique voices.

The Color Purple is rich with images of voice, of singing, that complement and comment upon the novel's controlling metaphor of writing as seen in Celie's description of an exchange between Shug and Mary Agnes, a.k.a. Squeak:

> Shug say to Squeak, I mean, Mary Agnes, You ought to sing in public
> Mary Agnes say, Naw. She think cause she don't sing big and broad like
> Shug nobody want to hear her. But Shug say she wrong.
> What about all them funny voices you hear singing in church? Shug say.
> What about all them sounds that sound good but they not the sound you
> thought folks could make? What bout that? (p. 111)

Mary Agnes does go on to become a blues singer in her own right, singing in her own unimitative voice. Moreover, the narrative clearly implies that she can sing in public only when she discovers her own name (Mary Agnes, not Squeak) and her own "private," unique voice.

The Color Purple underscores the regrettable fact that black writers have not been permitted the freedom to discover and then to speak in their unique voices largely because they have been compelled to use their art for mainly propagandistic (public) purposes. Ntozake Shange makes that point in her collection of poems *nappy edges:* "We, as a people, or as a literary cult, or a literary culture / have not demanded singularity from our writers, we could all sound the same, come from the same region, be the same gender, born the same year." She adds, "we assume a musical solo is a personal statement / we think the poet is speakin for the world, there's something wrong there, a writer's first commitment is to the piece itself, then comes the political commitment."[46]

The work of Frances E. W. Harper implies no such choice. Her age demanded the reverse. The morality of black women was being rampantly impugned; black people were suffering rank injustices, when they were not being lynched in teeming numbers. Without question, the writer lifted the pen in an act of political intervention.[47]

Walker sacrifices the impulse to uplift the race, if that means sanitizing it, although hers, no less than Harper's, is a project whose aim is cultural transformation. She envisions a new world—at times utopian in dimension—in which power relations between men and women, between the colonizers and the colonized, are reconfigured to eliminate domination and promote cooperation. Further, in the structural arrangement of the letters—Celie's first, then Nettie's, then alternation of the two—she shows that self-development and corporate mission are not mutually exclusive but can be consonant with each other.

The Color Purple reflects Walker's awareness that the literary manifestations of racial uplift (or any social movement for that matter) are explained, in part, by the relationship between writer and audience. Unlike Harper, Walker could choose to ignore the fact that her audience was predominantly white, a choice strongly influenced, as was Harper's, by the social realities and literary circumstances of her place and time.

We might pinpoint specifically the emergence of black nationalism in the 1960s and 70s and the rise of the women's movement that followed closely on its heels. During this period, the writers and critics who formed the cultural arm of the larger political movement became convinced, as Houston Baker notes, that "their real audience, like the nation to come, was black." Accordingly, they directed "their energies to the creation of a new nation and their voices to an audience radically different from any [they] had ever conceived of," a black audience which would include, as never before, ordinary blacks from ghetto communities.[48] They fashioned a critical methodology, termed the "black aesthetic," a "system of isolating and evaluating the artistic works of black people which reflect the special character and imperatives of black experience."[49]

Like the black aestheticians, those women in the vanguard of the women's movement's second wave called for women's release from unreal and oppressive loyalties. Feminist criticism became one literary manifestation of that political stance. Similar in spirit and methodology to the largely male-dominated black aesthetic movement, feminist critics likewise repudiated and subverted what they considered alien, male-created literary standards, and began to describe and analyze a female aesthetic that reflected women's unique culture.

It is necessary to note that, ironically, in their earliest formulations, the objectives and practices of both the black aesthetic and feminist criticism often came dangerously close to insisting on a different and no less rigid set of aesthetic orthodoxies. Despite their own prescriptive leanings, however, these two modes of critical inquiry must be credited with opening up unprecedented possibilities for black and women writers. In isolating and affirming the particulars of black and female experience, they inspired and authorized writers from those cultures to sing in their different voices and to imagine an audience that could hear the song.

The narrative strongly implies that that audience is comprised mainly of Walker's "sisters," other black women. Its structure and plot—two black sisters writing to each other—lend this reading some support. It is not that Walker can or even desires to exclude readers outside this group; it is simply that she addresses her letters to them.

I am all too aware that this suggestion raises at least two glaring empirical paradoxes: the novel has been enormously successful with a very diverse readership, a large part of which is white, while often criticized by those to whom it seems addressed.[50] However, the premise is recommended and supported by a major thread in the novel's plot: the act of reading letters that are written and intended for other eyes.

Just as the novel's letters lend themselves to Walker's reflexive depiction of the act of writing, they simultaneously lend themselves to her reflexive depiction of the act of reading. They offer a compelling model of the relationship Walker implies between herself and her readers, her own correspondents, her audience of "kissin' friends" who enter by the "intimate gate," to borrow from Zora Neale Hurston. In choosing them as her auditors and their experiences as her story, she has made the private public, and, in the process, created a new literary space for a black and a female idiom against and within a traditionally Eurocentric and androcentric literary history.

1984

It is a commonplace of current critical discourse to acknowledge that ideas of literary history or "tradition" are most appropriately read as narratives, the details of which are often selected in the interest of etching unitary and coherent story lines. By turns, these stories ignore discontinuities, explain them away, or assimilate them into existing narratives, all the while prompting readers to accept certain textual priorities and reading protocols. For these reasons, many look with suspicion, if not scorn, on ideas of tradition, even finding the very term tradition, a "critical fable intended to encode and circumscribe an inner and licit circle of empowered texts."[51] Within dominant narratives of African American literary history, the circle of empowered texts have tended to include few by women and fewer still by those from the nineteenth century. Many fault the dominant plot of racial protest and the reading codes and priorities it established— both derived mainly from texts by men—with obscuring, until recently, the texts of a "black women's tradition."

Positing such a category as a clear and uncomplicated entity rests on no less powerful a fable, complete with its own textual consecrations and reading codes. But more importantly, constructing that category as a separate and "alternative" entity leaves intact and unexamined the reigning critical paradigm against which women writers are inevitably judged. What I call the racial recognizability quotient, or the "blackness" factor, constitutes the critical center of gravity of that paradigm, which circles ceaselessly around variations on two interlocking questions: What is the relationship between race and color? What is the relationship between color and emancipatory narrative strategies? The priority that nineteenth-century black women writers placed on "whiteness," which Molly Hite reads rightly as "the most overused element of characterization,"[52] has thrown into question the credentials of nineteenth-century novels by black women as "black" texts, a dispute resting on the widely accepted equation: race = color. Anticipating the passing novels that dominated the 1920s and '30s, many of these nineteenth-century works can seem to be nudging readers in a different, if you like, a modernist, direction by implying vexing questions about race: How do we recognize "blackness" and assign it a value in the social order in the absence of the visible mark of color?

In preparing the introduction to Four Girls at Cottage City, *the questions I posed indicated that I could only recognize "blackness" as it had already been constructed throughout Afro-American literary history: What is "black" about this book? How does it alter existing assumptions about nineteenth-century literature by* black *women? What formal and thematic features, what narrative strategies give these books a black woman's signature? Because this list of questions derived from the existing critical framework that assumes tautologically that blackness is always and self-evidently about itself, they ricocheted back on me. A different set of questions must be posed here, questions alert to the nuances of textual detail and narrative moment that distinguish this text and others like it from those with which it is invidiously compared.*

According to conventional critical grids and the hierarchies of "race consciousness" they inscribe, the writings of Emma Dunham Kelley are read as "race neutral" and thus apolitical foils to the more political and "race conscious" works of Ida B. Wells-Barnett, Frances E. W. Harper, and Anna Julia Cooper on one side and, say, Charles Chesnutt, on the other. Such zero-sum dichotomies are even more relentlessly pursued by critics unconditioned and opposed to the religious vocabularies that animate Kelley's work, which sits squarely in the discourse of spiritual writings and the tradition of religious movement: These provide the most logical contexts for reading her work, which is less an aberration in one stream of post-Reconstruction African American writing than might at first appear.

Mrs. A. E. Johnson's Clarence and Corinne is a text that compares favorably to Four Girls at Cottage City. In her introduction to the Schomburg edition of Clarence and Corinne, Hortense Spillers urges readers who "smuggle in race" to be mindful of how the "narrative's subtitle insinuates its own supplementary meanings. God's Way renders the other theme of the work."[53] That the novel was published by the American Baptist Publication Society establishes up front its evangelical designs, against which contemporary reading audiences are conditioned. The what and how of Johnson's writing, Spillers continues, are altogether less significant than the fact that she wrote: "the very act of writing itself is far more important than any particular outcome (p. xxix)." She concludes that "even though Clarence and Corinne does not answer any of the expectations of a postmodernist reading protocol, it is a type of story that we must learn to read again for precisely that reason" (p. xxxvi). Spillers's defense of Johnson generalizes easily to Emma Dunham Kelley and amounts to a recertification of her work. But however much we strain to read writers like Kelley and Johnson "in their own write," to quote Henry Louis Gates,[54] they are inevitably subordinated in a linear logic of progress, by what Susan Sontag terms the relentless "rhythm of advent and supersession,"[55] which controls our understanding of literary history in many of its details.

In juxtaposing Frances E. W. Harper's Iola Leroy and Alice Walker's The Color Purple, I attempted to transcend that logic, implied in the popular notion that fiction by black women gets "better and better" with each generation, especially in its delineation of black female character. But a supersessional logic emerged nonetheless in the essay's reading strategies, which show a tendency to privilege twentieth-century over nineteenth-century texts, even while calling for non-hierarchical ways of considering them together. That tendency is reflected in my decision to evaluate Iola Leroy as character and text in terms of Celie and The Color Purple, the latter representing in my mind some kind of high-water mark in writing fiction with political intent. The essay associates emancipatory narrative strategies almost exclusively with a contemporary moment of literary production and thus uses its values and critical codes as the yardstick for measuring the failings and achievements of nineteenth-century texts. These codes constitute the "key words," to borrow from Raymond Williams, the generic vocabulary of critical terms for literary study on African American women: COLOR, CLASS, STEREOTYPE, and SEXUALITY. These key concepts converge in easily the most studied issue in the recent past: the representation of "black womanhood," especially the mulatta.

Critics have long been locked in a fierce struggle over just how to read the representation of the middle-class mulatta in turn-of-the-century fiction by black women, over just how to resolve the range of cultural tensions around race and gender/race and class attached to this figure. Their debates have been fueled by a fundamental question: Does the mulatta figure serve or subvert dominant ideologies of race and gender?

Influenced by Alice Walker's engaging discussion of race and color in nineteenth-century fiction by black women ("If the Present Looks Like the Past"), I concluded that the "past" should look like the "present." In other words, in all matters central to the literary representation of black womanhood, Iola Leroy *should resemble* The Color Purple, *a strategy destined to overlook the possible ways in which Walker's ideologies of race, gender, sexuality, and class, which she locates in a literary utopia, might not only be open to some dispute, but might also be seen as the contemporary counterpart of the idealism associated strongly with her nineteenth-century precursors.*[56]

While many share Walker's concern to explain the pervasiveness of the mulatta in nineteenth-century black fiction, they have gone astray in reading this figure as an unequivocal capitulation to dominant beliefs in the "rightness" and superiority of whiteness. Hazel Carby offers a more constructive and complicated conceptualization of the function of the mulatta in black women's fiction of the era. Against the popular critical perspective that the mulatta functions as a "gesture of acquiescence to a racist social order" and is thus "politically unacceptable," Carby argues that the mulatta acts as a "mediating device." As such, she continues, the mulatta enabled an exploration of both the sexual and social relations between the races, relations proscribed under Jim Crow laws and customs.[57]

Carby's rereading of the mulatta enables a reconsideration of sexuality in Iola Leroy. *In reading both* The Color Purple *and* Iola Leroy, *I proceeded from a reificaton of "sexuality." I resorted to the modern tendency to view sexual expression as inherently liberating, rather than governed by relations of power in a steadily changing and complicated cultural field. Such a reification is most glaring in my treatment of* Iola Leroy *and probably results from providing an overly "literary" context for evaluating Harper's work, work that was a vital part of what Hazel Carby terms an "autonomous black feminist movement" that exploded in the 1890s. That wider political context enabled Harper to achieve the popular success as a writer that she might not have otherwise.*

If the context for reading Harper's work is enlarged to take the goals and strengths of this movement into account, then my reading of how and why sexuality functions as it does in Iola Leroy *must be completely rethought. Appropriating standard opinions of nineteenth-century fiction, I argued that in order to counter the widespread assumption that black women were sexually immoral, nineteenth-century black women "wanted to be remembered as upholders of puritan morality," hence, much of their work involved "encourag[ing] . . . masses of black women to accept the sexual morality of the Victorian bourgeoisie."[58] However valid such an explanation might be, removed from historical context, even a reconstructed context, it oversimplifies the complex ways racialist (and racist) ideologies shaped and continue to shape black women's sexual choices. The sexual habits of turn-of-the-century women appear considerably less "prudish" when we consider the sexual dimensions in constructions of race that operated, then and now, to separate "good" sexual practices from "bad"[59] and to construct black sexuality as the deviant alternative to more culturally prescribed sexual norms. The alleged sexuality of black women, defined against the so-called purity of white women, was the fulcrum on which racialist sexual ideologies turned. This discursive construction found practical enforcement and consequences in the uncontainable rush of lynchings—sexually motivated weapons of terrorist control— that swept across the South during the 1890s.*

If we take this context into account, then, for black women to defend themselves at the level of discourse against racist allegations of their sexual immorality, did not "represent some misguided bow to outmoded Victorian sexuality," as Elizabeth Ammons is correct to note. Rather, their self-defense "represented an essential part of their life-and-death struggle as women against lynching in the U.S." As Ammons goes on to say, black women's sexual history "did not consist of the right to be more sexual. It consisted of the right to be less *sexual, the right even to be* unsexual.*" Therefore, Ammons concludes, "Harper's heroine is characterized as a moral paragon—linked to an elevated Victorian image of womanhood— to demonstrate the vicious untruth of the "wanton theory underlying rape-lynch mythology."[60]*

Foregrounding this rape-lynch mythology further strengthens the thematic connections I tried to press between Walker and Harper. One could argue that The Color Purple *self-consciously re-enacts a form of rape in a significant feature of its plotting: stolen letters. As Ruth Perry suggests, "reading the letters written and intended for other eyes is the most reprehensible invasion of privacy and consciousness in epistolary fiction. These are overtones of sexual invasion—of mind rape—in the intercepting or "violating" of another's words. This experience is suggestive for the audience as well since they are reading letters not intended for public consumption. The most unholy thing in these books is uninvited access to another's inner life." Perry goes on to describe the marketing of such letters by booksellers who "advertised the fact that a set of letters had not been intended for publication because privacy, like virginity, invites violation."*

The ever-present threat of violation served Frances E. W. Harper's construction of a counter-mythology through representing marriage as a social program geared toward black self-determination. According to twentieth-century feminist reading strategies, marriage is an unambiguous capitulation to the status quo—meaning the oppression of women—but in a persuasive argument, Claudia Tate suggests a way to recuperate marriage for more transgressive ends and aims. She argues that a masculinist discourse of unconditional freedom (and here she might have added a feminist discourse as well), construes marriage as freedom's antithesis. This reading formation has dominated criticism of African American culture in the twentieth century and explains why contemporary readers construe marriage as a loss of freedom.

Against the hegemony of these reading formations, Tate proposes that nineteenth-century novels by black women be read with the understanding that "exercising the civil right to marry . . . was as important to the newly freed black population as exercising" the right to vote. For black people of that era, she continues, "to vote and to marry . . . were two civic responsibilities that nineteenth-century black people elected to perform: they were twin indexes for measuring how black people collectively valued their civil liberties." Thus, for the women writers who represented that group experience, "marriage and family life were not the culminating points of a woman's life but the pinnacle of a people's new beginning."[61] The value of Tate's reconsideration of these nineteenth-century writers lies precisely in its attempt to historicize their narrative choices and to read their plots according to the specific contours of racial formation pervasive in their time.

These recent reevaluations of nineteenth-century fiction by black women have done much to reorient our thinking about the most vexing aspects of their work. Recuperating the figure of the mulatta as a component of a larger interventionist strategy disturbs many of the critical complacencies surrounding this perennial subject of critical controversy. But however welcome such recuperations might be, they still leave some matters yet unsettled. That Emma Dunham Kelley, Frances E. W. Harper, and their contemporaries, despite their best intentions and political motivations, could both fight and reproduce dominant racialist ideologies around color cannot be denied. Color-based social stratification within the race was real. Though not the only basis for divisions in black communities, color-consciousness was real and pervasive and found subtle, perhaps uncon-

scious, expression in strategies of nineteenth-century black fiction and overt expression in the structures of everyday life that affected those who wrote it. To acknowledge this is not to detract from the power these writers command as cultural critics, but rather, to caution ourselves against the limits and dangers of hyper-idealization and -correctness. Lacking a critical vocabulary that could encompass these nineteenth-century writers, we have erred outlandishly in trying to fit them into a twentieth-century world picture. In our zeal to correct that error, we have remade these writers into aesthetic ideals and granted them an artistic and political self-consciousness that re-homogenizes them, even as it insists on their "difference." We have made our corrections by drawing on the necessary discipline of "historicism" and contextualism, but one that frequently and falsely implies a notion of both history and of context in need of its own corrections. We assume that our twentieth-century world picture is itself clear of the film and residues of "history," and that context can be retrieved as a whole cloth. As Jonathan Culler argues, "the notion of context frequently oversimplifies rather than enriches discussion" and overlooks the workings of semiotics, which render contexts in equal need of elucidation.[62] Or as Dominick LaCapra puts it, "contexts are [not] ipso facto explanatory," nor do they "escape involvement in a relational network."[63] In other words, what we know of context we have made. But to make this observation is not, in the final analysis, to invalidate our recent efforts to reconstruct the pieces of a nineteenth-century past; it simply requires that we be alert to the "new" critical complacencies they might engender.

PART III

Undercover: Passing and
Other Disguises

4

On Face

The Marks of Identity in Jessie Fauset's
Plum Bun or Getting Read in the
Harlem Renaissance

The place of color-based stratification *within* "the race" has been at the heart of critical interpretations of Jessie Fauset's fiction and largely accounts for the disparaged position she has long occupied among African American writers. While all of Fauset's novels comprehend the extent to which social hierarchies are color-coded, both within and between the races, a coding that interacted with America's basic attitudes toward racial intermixture, such comprehension should not be mistaken for endorsement. Critics have consistently ignored the subtle function of class, race, and color in her work, while insisting that it should only be noted for being a curious eddy in the swirling currents of literary change.

The canonical word is that Fauset wrote traditional novels of manners of the black middle class, the refined intelligentsia, to prove one thesis and one thesis only: except for the biological accident of color, blacks are no different from whites and should therefore enjoy all the rights and privileges of U.S. citizenship that whites enjoy. When her contemporary Alain Locke reviewed Fauset's first book, *There is Confusion* (1924), he described it as the novel "the Negro intelligentsia has been clamoring for."[1] Locke praised her second novel, *Plum Bun*, for avoiding "the swift muddy waters of the Negro underworld and the hectic rapids and cataracts of Harlem."[2] But by the time he reviewed her last novel, *Comedy, American Style* (1933), Locke had come to express much more ambivalence about Fauset's "higher" reaches. In one of his famous retrospectives for *Opportunity* magazine, he wrote that "Negro fiction would be infinitely poorer without the persevering and slowly maturing art of Miss Fauset and her almost single-handed championship of upper- and middle-class Negro life as an important subject for fiction." But in the final analysis Locke thought Fauset's style was too "mid-Victorian for moving power today."[3]

Among Fauset's contemporaries, Locke's opinions were fairly typical. For example, while Claude McKay commended Fauset's generosity as literary editor of *The Crisis,* his general opinion was that "she was away over on the other side of the fence" with "that closed decorous circle of Negro society, which consists of persons who live proudly like the better class of conventional whites." Using a highly belittling metaphor, he likened Fauset and her novels to the "fastidious and precious" primroses of Morocco which "spread themselves across the barren hillsides before the sudden summer blazed over the hot land."[4]

In reconstructing the history of Fauset's critical reception, one is struck immediately by the essential sameness in readers' responses. With noticeably few exceptions they mindlessly reproduce the domestic and diminutive metaphors, the general stock of ideas contained in earlier critical assessments. With faint echoes of McKay, David Littlejohn compares her novels to "vapidly genteel lace curtain romances," none "rising above the stuffy, tiny-minded circulating-library norm." Robert Hemenway sees in them "the trials of domestic society"—"housekeeping, dressmaking, flirtations, and dinner engagements."[5] In *The Negro Novel,* for example, Robert Bone groups Fauset invidiously with the writers he terms the "Rear Guard" or those "who lagged behind," clinging to established literary traditions. The "Rear Guard" were considered the "imitative" black writers who drew their source material from the black middle class in an effort "to orient Negro art toward white opinion" and "to apprise educated whites of the existence of respectable Negroes." Bone adds that Fauset's emphasis on the black middle class results in novels that are "uniformly sophomoric, trivial and dull."[6]

Such surface oppositions have been produced and reproduced, with minimal variation, in an impregnable case of critical mimesis, which re-evaluations of Fauset's work have done little to dislodge. Even in the work of otherwise sensitive feminist readers, Fauset's novels are considered, at best, ideologically conservative in the contest over the terms of black representation being waged among Harlem Renaissance writers,[7] and, at worst, "bad fairy tales,"[8] written by an author unconscious of "her own internal-ized race prejudice," wedded to an encoded "hierarchy based on color" and determined to "convince whites that blacks are like them."[9]

It is not difficult to find in Fauset's novels those faults that readers have consistently isolated. Without a doubt her novels focus mainly on the trials of middle-class mulattoes, and they do deploy a range of generic conventions—the romance, novel of manners, fairy tales—and cultural codes that seem to underwrite a traditional social order. Like Emma Dun-ham Kelley's *Megda* and *Four Girls at Cottage City,* Fauset's books are mainly novels of female socialization, though without the evangelical mis-sion. Much like the female protagonists who dominate Kelley's novels and Harper's *Iola Leroy,* those in Fauset's achieve the culminating sign of cultural value and order for women: marriage. It is to these features that critics refer when arguing that Fauset's writing is dated and mid-Victorian.

My aim here is not to refute the weight of such critical opinions point for point, but rather to submit the most salient categories and assumptions in analyses of her work to closer scrutiny. It is far more useful to view her literary choices as less an incontestable sign of her attachment to black middle-class values than as a function of a complicated set of relationships: cultural, social, economic, and political. That Fauset shared specific liter-ary conventions and cultural values with her nineteenth-century predeces-sors is clear, but it would be a mistake to argue that her fiction follows theirs in a straight and uncomplicated line of organic descent.

While vestiges of their plot structures can be found in her novels, Fauset exhibited a far more ambivalent stance than her predecessors toward the program of racial uplift, an ambivalence made especially clear in *Plum Bun* (1929), her second and most artistically engaging novel. She structures this ambivalence mainly in the opposition between Angela Murray, the protagonist, and her sister, Jinny, between whom the narrative divides its sympathies. Jinny adopts the language and program of racial uplift, be-lieving, in a fashion reminiscent of Iola Leroy, that "there are some things which an individual might want, but which he'd just have to give up forever for the sake of the more important whole" (p. 69). Angela scorns such ideals because they require "inevitable sacrifices for the race; the burnt offering of individualism for some dimly glimpsed racial whole" (p. 117). The personal sacrifice that Angela is ultimately unwilling to make is represented in the novel as a desire for power and opportunity, both distributed solely on the basis of skin color and class. As a mulatta, Angela stands a greater chance of fulfilling her desires, even if it means rewriting her racial origins and sacrificing the collective good.

Harper and her contemporaries maintained the viability both of the collective good and the racial whole, despite differences of class and color. Through the figure of the mulatta, for example, Harper tried to resolve the problematical relation between the physical body and racial identity. The product of miscegenation, the mulatta stood as a "bodily challenge to the conventions of reading the body," to borrow from Karen Sanchez-Eppler. However, novels like *Iola Leroy* insisted that "the body is a sign of identity," even as they undermined "the assurance with which that sign [could] be read."[10]

Jessie Fauset's first two novels, *There Is Confusion* and *Plum Bun*, likewise undermine that assurance, but they dramatize more effectively than either Kelley's or Harper's books *the* compelling question: What happens when the sign of the body is *recognized* as white and is thus free of the barriers to opportunity that "race" imposes? In dramatizing that question, Fauset, like her contemporary Nella Larsen, raised the specter of miscegenation that was as threatening in her day as it was in Harper's and Kelly's. *Plum Bun* appeared at the end of a decade in which both lynchings and urban uprisings accelerated in the United States and in which theories and ideologies of race, especially race "purity," proliferated. While many of these theories were motivated by a desire to restrict immigration on racial grounds, they were appropriated as well by agents of white supremacy in racist campaigns targeted specifically at black citizens.[11]

While Fauset is alert to the failures and entrapments of "reading" the racial body, she is also alert to the difference it makes when that body is female and not male. The latter introduces into the equation of racial identity the necessary inflections and complications of gender.

Reminiscent of both Harper and Kelley, Fauset structures marriage into the geometry of each of her novels, but her response to that institution takes the form of both conformity and critique. In her work marriage seems on the one hand to be linked to issues of sexual respectability and preservation of the status quo. But on the other hand, after her first novel, *There Is Confusion* (1924), she questions whether sexual expression for women should be attached to the moorings of marriage, especially since it was no guarantor of female respectability. Further, she understood that "respectability" was weak currency indeed in a society that reduced women to sexual commodities in the marriage marketplace. She brings these issues to full expression in *Plum Bun*. While her attachment to the priorities of liberal reform struck many readers, then as now, as an insular and thus inadequate strategy of social change, we might say that Fauset chose the terms of her enclosure, avoiding the finality and fixity of racial classification as well as the class and caste of gender and genre alike.

On face *Plum Bun* is just another novel of racial passing.[12] It has all the outward generic features of the passing novel: a mulatta protagonist, seeking to avoid the constraints of color prejudice in the United States, decides to cross the color line and pass for white, a deception fraught with anxieties and frequently discovered. After learning that life on the other side is not without its difficulties, she develops an appreciation of black life and culture and returns "home," psychically if not physically, to the black community and embraces its values.

But while *Plum Bun* certainly displays the most salient features of the novel-of-passing, to read it simply as such is to miss its complex treatment of the intersections of gender, racial, and class oppressions, as well as to miss the irony and subtlety of its artistic technique. *Plum Bun* is a richly textured and ingeniously designed narrative, comprised of plots within plots and texts within texts that refer to and comment upon one another in multiple and intricate combinations. In this rich tapestry, the passing plot is just one thread, albeit an important one, woven into the novel's frame, the *bildungsroman,* or novel of development.

While the passing plot constitutes a major stage in Angela Murray's coming-of-age, in the narrative's configuration and economy, that plot cannot be separated from the marriage plot, which constitutes the structural core of the novel. Angela's obsessions with getting married are frustrated and complicated by the realities of sex-role stereotyping, the politics of sexuality, and the limitations of her own romantic assumptions. Although she is making plans to marry at the novel's end, it is not because she believes marriage to be "the most desirable end for a woman," but rather because she has developed from the adolescent crippled by romantic assumptions about marriage to a woman who questions these assumptions. In that the *bildungsroman* frequently combines elements of fantasy and romance with social realism, it is an appropriate genre through which to chronicle such a development.

The conjunction of passing and marriage—dual plots in a novel of female development—is a clever artistic choice and one that well serves Fauset's controlling theme: the unequal power relationships in U.S. society. These two plots (which we might designate "racial" and "female," respectively) could not be more fitting in a narrative about power asymmetries, for both passing and marriage are attempts—at times naive and fantasy-ridden—by blacks and women to overcome the structural inequalities that disempower them. In other words, both passing and marriage are the means by which these two disenfranchised groups, respectively, hope to gain access to power. In the world of the narrative, however, their expectations are frequently unfulfilled.

This tension between expectation and fulfillment is introduced in the epigraph that both titles the novel and structures its five sections ("Home," "Market," "Plum Bun," "Home Again," and "Market is Done"):

> To Market, To Market,
> To Buy a Plum Bun;
> Home again, Home again,
> Market is done.

The unmarked speaker of the nursery rhyme expects and fulfills her/his objective to buy a plum bun at the market, a fulfillment in ironic contrast to the foiled expectations of Angela Murray, who is marked and thwarted by her class and gender if not her "race." Thus, we must read the epigraph as part of the white male narrative of optimism and fulfillment, of "political and economic opportunism," for "the only character in the novel who actually buys much of anything . . . is Roger Fielding. The verse is thus sexually as well as racially ironic."[13]

The opening of the narrative complements the epigraph in invoking the generic conventions of the classic fairy tale, appropriate in a novel of female development. Filtered largely through Angela's eyes, the ironic opening describes Opal Street where she lives on an "unpretentious little street lined with unpretentious little houses, inhabited . . . by unpretentious little people. . . . In one of these houses dwelt a father, a mother and two daughters." Continuing a pattern she began in an early novella, "The Sleeper Wakes,"[14] Fauset focuses on the powerful role fairy tales play in conditioning women to idealize marriage and romantic love as the source of their completeness as well as their material well-being.[15]

Reading fairy tales to Angela and her sister, Virginia, their mother adds, "'And they lived happily ever after, just like your father and me.'" But her mother must emend and *mark* the conventional fairy tale plot: Angela and her sister must become "schoolteachers and independent" so as to escape the degrading and exploitative conditions she once suffered as a ladies' maid. But for much of the narrative, this practical imperative, based on the realities of most black women's lives, wars with Angela's frenzied pursuit of a different and dominant cultural fantasy in which women are rescued by wealthy men and share in their power secondarily.[16]

Nowhere is this more strikingly illustrated than in the following passage:

> She remembered an expression "free, white and twenty-one"—this was
> what it meant then, this sense of owning the world. . . . "If I were a man,"
> she said, "I could be president," and laughed at herself for the "if" itself

proclaimed a limitation. But that inconsistency bothered her little; she did not want to be a man. *Power,* greatness, authority, these were fitting and proper for men; but there were sweeter, more beautiful gifts for women, and *power* of a certain kind too. Such a *power* she would like to exert in this glittering new world, so full of mysteries and promise. If she could afford it she would have a salon, a drawing room where men and women should come and pour themselves out to her sympathy and magnetism. To accomplish this she must have money and influence; indeed since she was so young she would need even protection; perhaps it would be better to marry . . . a white man. The thought came to her suddenly out of the void; she had never thought of this possibility before. . . . She knew that men had a better time of it than women, coloured men than coloured women, white men than white women. . . . It would be fun, great fun to capture *power* and protection in addition to the freedom and independence which she had so long coveted and which now lay in her hand. (pp. 87–88, emphasis added)

This passage captures vividly the novel's central concern with the forms and sources of power and domination, which are gender-, race-, and class-specific. While white men can become president, wielding the power and authority that office affords, women must settle for a second-hand form of power, experienced vicariously through their husbands. And to say that these husbands are white is superfluous and is to underscore the naivete of such a fantasy for black women. The passage hints, moreover, at what will be a developing connection in the narrative: the causal link between money and power and the white male prerogative to monopolize both. Angela realizes these relations of power and fantasizes about enjoying her share by marrying. She fantasizes about the "great fun" it would be to "capture power and protection." What she will actually encounter in her relationship with Roger Fielding, her wealthy white man, is a replay of the racial prehistory of concubinage and sexual exploitation that has long characterized black women's relationships with white men.[17] Angela leaves the memory of that history behind her in Philadelphia.

As passing constitutes a rewriting of origins, Angela's behavior is guided by a "new world" innocence. Soon after her arrival in New York, the narrator draws an implicit comparison between her and Benjamin: "No boyish stowaway on a ship had a greater exuberance in going to meet the unknown than" had Angela (p. 93). But her attempts at fulfillment with Roger in New York—imaged as a war and contest of wills—illuminate glaringly how unmatched she is and reveal his decided advantage in this conflict. Ironically, while Angela fights valiantly to reach her goal, unknown to her is that Roger is not after marriage, but rather "free love."[18]

In other words, Angela's and Roger's trips to the market are for two different plum buns. For her the plum bun is power and influence attainable only through marriage to a wealthy white man. For him, the plum bun is sex, a consumable to be bought, used up, and expended. Put another way, Angela's game play for marriage is Roger's foreplay for sex. But finally and ironically, Angela tries to "buy" in a society that only allows her to "sell."

The novel's critique of the relations between money, sex, and power gathers force in its core chapters, "Market" and "Plum Bun," in which marriage is imaged as an economic system. Juxtaposed to each other, in both chapters commercial and sexual imagery dominates. There are repeated references to withholding and giving, terms with both sexual and material/economic connotations. Martha cautions Angela not to "withhold too much and yet to give very little" (p. 145). As she negotiates this delicate balance, Angela imagines her "life . . . rounding out like a fairy tale" (p. 131), and her relationship with Roger becoming "the finest flower of chivalry and devotion." She is confident that Roger "love[s] her and would want to marry her, for it never occurred to her that men bestowed such attentions on a *passing* fancy" (emphasis added).

Angela's relationship with Roger exemplifies Nancy Hartsock's description of the nature of the commodities exchange in the courtship market: "sexual gratification and 'firm commitments' (presumably marriage)." In this arrangement, Hartsock continues, "conflicting interests are present, as in any exchange, since the girl is interested in keeping the price of her sexual favors high in order to strengthen her position, whereas the boy wants to obtain sexual gratification at the lowest possible price. She withholds sex to create a scarcity, and, assuming demand remains constant . . . the price will then rise. . . . [I]n order to safeguard the high price of her affection, [she] must be ungenerous in expressing it; it must be a prize not easily won."[19]

To gain his desired end, sex, Roger uses his wealth. "Anything . . . that money can buy, I can get and I can give," he tells Angela. This proposition elicits a counter-proposition from Angela who, despite her sexual fastidiousness, considers resorting to using the only weapon she has: sex, the power of the "weak." She reasons that "men paid a big price for their desires. Her price would be marriage." Of course, Angela soon discovers her powerlessness to command that price. The novelty of their passion worn off, Roger ends the relationship, and Angela thus becomes one of the scores of heroines throughout literary history seduced and then abandoned by their lovers.

In dramatizing Angela's story it is significant that her racial background is never revealed to Roger. Thus Fauset substitutes class for race as an explanation for the failed relationship between Angela and Roger, a strategy that supports the narrative's effort to question an arbitrary system of racial classification. It also highlights the sexual inequalities in heterosexual romance and reinforces the narrative's representation of marriage as, at base and at best, an economic arrangement. The latter point is illustrated graphically in Angela's last exchange with Roger when he returns to her with the long-awaited marriage proposal. Angela asks, "Why is it that men like you resent an effort on our part to make our *commerce* decent? . . . Theoretically, 'free love' or whatever you choose to call it is all right. Actually, it's all wrong. . . . Marriage was good enough for my mother, it's good enough for me" (p. 320, emphasis added). The accumulating ironies of this passage are clear: "commerce" signals at once sexual intercourse and the selling of commodities, a system of exchange into which Angela has willingly, if naively, inserted herself. Thus, raw economics compromises and ironizes any code of "decency" or "respectability" to which Angela or any other woman might aspire.

Fauset captures the subtle tension between sexual pleasure and restraint but detaches it from the realm of morality, thus giving narrative license to Angela's desires, even as it describes them euphemistically as "the forces of nature," the "impulses" and "yearnings" antedating social conventions. In the face of awakening desire, Angela comes to regard these conventions as "prudish and unnecessary." Though she decides to control her sexual desires, it is strictly because "in the light of the great battle which she was waging for pleasure, protection, and power, it was inexpedient" (p. 200). For her, marriage is the sign of that battle won, the provision of "safety" and "assurance" she desires, but the novel imposes one barrier after another, postponing the fulfillment of Angela's desire, a deferral that grants no priority to marriage in the process of Angela's development.

Despite Angela's best efforts to marry, she is thwarted until she makes independence as important a goal as marriage, an independence uncovered and maintained, significantly, by work. That work leads Angela to a new understanding of the nature of power. While all of her experiences with power to this point have involved a dialectic of dominance and submission, after her affair with Roger ends, power becomes associated in her mind with individual capacity or "power" to act independently, making decisions about her own life. It is significant, then, that Angela's process of autonomy begins in earnest when she becomes gainfully employed as a designer for a fashion journal while continuing to refine her portrait painting.

Consistent with the romantic conventions on which it draws, the novel ends as Angela is planning to marry, but she has developed a sense of independence and autonomy that needs ratification from neither men nor marriage. In the words of the narrative, she is now ripe to enter the most ideal marriage, in which both partners are "strong individualists, molten and blended in a design which fail[s] to obscure their emphatic personalities" (p. 113).

After sustaining her critique of the institution of marriage throughout the novel, its promise at the end seems a betrayal of that critique. It certainly bespeaks a clear ambivalence, evident moreover in the narrative's double closure. For all practical purposes the novel ends twice: first when Angela returns "home" to Philadelphia and next when she is reunited with Anthony in Paris. The journey back home, the return to the source, constitutes a kind of primal scene in African American fiction. It is evident in *Iola Leroy* in the form of Iola's search for her mother and ironized bitterly in Nella Larsen's *Quicksand* in Helga's return to the South. But in *Plum Bun* this nostalgic return to origins is failed. When she tries to visit her old family home, the "coloured" woman who now lives there refuses Angela entry and calls her "poor white trash." This scene not only refuses the "happy ending" of a family reunion, but in its staging of racial and class conflict it extends the narrative's dramatization of the shifting categories and patterns of exclusion and domination. Here Angela is without color and is thus, in terms of U.S. racial semantics, without "race," but the black woman assigns her a race and marks her with the stigma of a degraded class.

The introduction of class difference into a racial confrontation saves both the scene and the novel from being reducible to simple black/white confrontation. In *Plum Bun,* scenes and situations of race, class, color, and sex relations keep shifting, underscoring the fact that divisions of power are constantly redrawn and realigned. So effectively does this scene of Angela's "re-marking" compress and round out the novel's concerns with the various cultural assignments and classifications and the power inequities they create, that it could well have ended the novel, but in an appended transatlantic crossing, the novel ends on Christmas Day in a Paris pension.

Actually the narrative closes on what can be read as a faint metaphor of commerce woven into a pseudo "happy ending" of Angela's and Anthony's imminent fulfillment in romance. Anthony has traveled from the States to be Angela's Christmas present in France. She receives him downstairs in the drawing room (instead of her bedroom), and the book ends with his first words to her: "There ought to be a tag on me somewhere." That

Anthony wears the tag constitutes another of Fauset's reverse constructions—this time gendered—but with the tag she preserves the link, if only faintly, between money and romance/marriage.

We could also invoke Anthony's words, "There ought to be a tag on me somewhere," to account for this implausible ending. In other words, Fauset must have thought that there ought to be a tag on *Plum Bun,* for this ending is clearly tacked on, underscoring not only Fauset's technical deficiencies throughout her career, but also her difficulties with resolving the relation between ideology and form. In this regard, she was not alone among writers who inherited nineteenth-century forms (including the "happy ending") but could not stretch them to accommodate their "modernist" ambivalences about marriage and the nuclear family, both staples of nineteenth-century narration.[20] Fauset conveniently disposes of Angela's parents in the novel's first sixty pages, an act that dissolves the family in the process. Further, Angela's return "home," as we have seen, is not a family reunion but a turning out of doors, a resolution that parallels and rounds out the corrosive tone that Fauset sounds through much of the "Home" section.[21]

Although writing specifically about Victorian fiction, D. A. Miller offers observations that can be generalized to Fauset's patterns of closure in *Plum Bun.* The inadequacy of closure, notes Miller, "can now be understood—not in the old-fashioned way, as a failure of organic form, nor even in the new-fashioned way, as the success of a failure of organic form— but in the broader context of institutional requirements and cultural needs."[22] In other words, narrative resolutions are not strictly formal, a point self-evident in Fauset's case. Not only sexualized ideologies of race, but also the patronage system and publishing trends dominant during the Harlem Renaissance, which helped to construct those ideologies, formed a piece of this "broader context" that explained her formal patterns.

From the very beginning of her career Fauset had insisted that the U.S. publishing system had helped to shape dominant ideologies of race in fiction and nonfiction alike, a situation that called urgently for black writers to portray black people. She was skeptical as to whether whites could "write evenly on the racial situation in America" and admitted to an interviewer that she began to write fiction in earnest when T. S. Stribling's novel *Birthright* failed, in her estimation, to depict blacks with balance and complexity. Fauset asserted confidently: "Here is an audience waiting to hear the truth about us. Let we who are better qualified to present that truth than any white writer try to do so." But Fauset's calculations could not have been more off the mark, and her inability to prevail against the tide of publishing about blacks during the Harlem Renaissance shows the error of her miscalculations in sharp relief.

No examination of the Harlem Renaissance is complete without a consideration of the economics and politics of the literary marketplace at that time, without a consideration, in particular, of the complex arrangement that often obtained between black writers and their publishers and patrons. Because these writers were so new to the commercial arts, "they were necessarily dependent; they had no force or leverage [either] within the publishing or the critical establishments," as Nathan Huggins rightly notes. "Opinion was against black artists," he continues, and thus "they needed supporters and advocates, defense and encouragement from those who were supposed to know." Just "whose sensibilities, tastes, and interests were being patronized?"[23] however, was the question that hovered around and tainted all such arrangements. Since they had the money, it is obvious that the sensibilities of white patrons and publishers were being patronized. It was difficult for any writer during the period to ignore the patronage system, though few actually benefited from it.

One of the most famous artist/patron relationships was that between Langston Hughes and Mrs. Rufus Osgood Mason. The power plays in their relationship capture the typical dynamics of such relationships. Mrs. Mason demanded of Hughes what many powerful whites of the era demanded: satisfaction of their jungle fantasies. As Hughes put it in his autobiography *The Big Sea*, "concerning Negroes, [Mrs. Mason] felt that they were America's great link with the primitive, and that they had something very precious to give to the Western world." He went on to say, "she wanted me to be primitive and know and feel the intuitions of the primitive. But, unfortunately, I did not feel the rhythms of the primitive surging through me, and so I could not live and write as though I did."[24]

Hughes was not the only black writer who felt this pressure, nor was the patronage system the only place it was applied.[25] Even those who refused to submit to the pressures for the primitive debated the issue in literary reviews and symposia throughout the period, maintaining implicitly that the demand for the treatment of primitive exotics was, pure and simple, the demand for a depiction of the black "underworld" and a desire for white control over black representation. One such symposium ran in *The Crisis* from March to December 1926, titled, "The Negro in Art: How Shall He Be Portrayed?" The questions posed by the editor, W. E. B. Du Bois, implicitly equated the publishing industry's demand for the "primitive/exotic" with the demand for the depiction of the black "underworld," for sex and sensationalism. A variety of writers—both white and black—were asked to respond to such questions as: "Is not the continual portrayal of the sordid, foolish and criminal among Negroes convincing the world that this and this alone . . . is really and essentially Negroid . . . and preventing white artists from knowing any other types and preventing black artists from daring to paint them?" "Is there not a real danger that young colored writers will be tempted to follow the popular trend in portraying Negro character in the underworld rather than seeking to paint the truth about themselves and their own social class?"

Jessie Fauset responded, arguing emphatically that following the popular trend of portraying the black "underworld" was a "grave danger" for black writers. If they followed the crowd, she added, they risked creating "a literary insincerity both insidious and abominable."[26] In choosing not to pander to this branch of popular taste, Fauset exercised remarkable courage and integrity and remained faithful to her own artistic objectives, objectives with very little currency in a publishing industry that was itself involved in selling black sex and sensationalism for high profits.

For verification, we need look no further than the commercial success of Carl Van Vechten's novel *Nigger Heaven* (1926) and Claude McKay's *Home to Harlem* (1928). While each of these books attempted to strike a balance between the black "intelligentsia" and the black "underworld," their harshest critics argued that the latter dominated and accounted for the books' high sales. *Nigger Heaven* sold 100,000 copies immediately, went through thirteen reprints and was translated into French, Swedish, Russian, and Japanese. Widely considered the first and most popular novel to depict the "lower strata" of the black race, *Nigger Heaven* allegedly created the demand in the publishing industry for works by and about blacks with a similar emphasis. Though McKay denied the influence of Van Vechten's novel on his own, *Home to Harlem,* its emphasis on the sexual abandon and primitive exoticism to be found in the Harlem cabaret scene has linked the novel in critics' minds to *Nigger Heaven.* The fact that *Home to Harlem* reached the *New York Herald Tribune* best-seller list amounted to "literary prostitution," according to Marcus Garvey. To Du Bois, the novel catered to that "prurient demand" in "a certain decadent section of the white American world" for black characters given to "lascivious sexual promiscuity."[27]

In this book market, black writers had few options: they could do the bidding of publishers and patrons or encounter great difficulties getting published, as did Fauset, who, when she ventured publication outside the pages of *The Crisis,* met with censorship and rejected manuscripts. She criticized publishers for not being "better sport[s]" about work that did not capitulate to current fashion. Most, she argued, had an *"idée fixe,"* adding that "they even more than the public . . . persist in considering only certain types of Negroes interesting and if an author presents a variant they fear that the public either won't believe it or won't stand for it."[28] Fauset was right. "White readers just don't expect Negroes to be like this," wrote the first publisher to see and reject the manuscript of her first novel, *There Is Confusion*. Other publishers followed suit. Only a promised preface by the white writer Zona Gale persuaded the Frederick Stokes Company to publish Fauset's third novel, *The Chinaberry Tree*.

Despite rejections and difficulties, Fauset refused to satisfy the demands of the publishing establishment, although she knew that it reserved the power to pass judgments on her work. That Jessie Fauset had matters of asymmetrical power relations firmly in mind when she wrote *Plum Bun* seems clear. Although the novel is no simple-minded allegory, it is altogether reasonable to suppose that the novel responds in part to this rigidity of patrons and publishers alike, a speculation that gains power when we consider that Angela is cast as an artist figure. It is significant that, early in her artistic career, Angela considers becoming a portrait painter, but she resists the thought because "she hated the idea of the position in which she would be placed, fearfully placating and flattering possible patrons, hurrying through with an order because she needed the cheque, accepting patronage and condescension" (p. 111).

Through Angela's experiences as an artist, Fauset comments not only on the commodification of artistic production, but also on the commodification of blackness, which could not be detached from the construction of sexuality. That *Plum Bun* attempts to intervene in a discourse on black women's sexuality seems clear from the very beginning of the novel, where Fauset confronts the racialist mythology head on. Angela's mother, Mattie, described working as a lady's maid for a white actress who felt Mattie to be like "all coloured people": "thickly streaked with immorality" and "naturally loose" (p. 29). The narrative struggles to contravene this stereotype through a series of reversals that project all "loose" (meaning outside matrimony and thus "out of control") sexual activity onto white women. All those women who kiss their lovers openly in the doorways of apartment buildings or who invite them in for casual sex are white. While they subscribe to the principles of "free love," black women hold out for marriage and "respectability," although the economics of the institution that Fauset has so deftly drawn compromise and ironize any such goal. Fauset's strategy here amounts to a simple reversal and re-racialization of the salient terms of Western cultural sexual mythology and thus carries no weight against their formative power, but the effort bears remarking nonetheless. While she knew that the power to pass judgments on her work rested with the white male literary establishment, she refused to fulfill their expectation. In the process, she had fun, at least in *Plum Bun,* flirting with and teasing them.

Although there are no explicitly sexual scenes in the novel, it brims with sexual winks and innuendoes. Fauset capitalizes on the multivalent sexual implications of the title *"Plum Bun."* The suggestions in "bun" or "tail," vulgar terms for sexual intercourse, are clear, as are those in Roger's name, a noun for penis as well as a verb for copulation. Fauset must have heard the classic blues singers of the 1920s—Gertrude "Ma" Rainey and Bessie Smith, for example, who sang openly of sexual relationships, of sugar bowls and deep sea divers—whose double-entendres were hard to miss. Perhaps the most common metaphor in these classic blues lyrics is likening sexual activity to food. In particular, the vagina is likened to baked goods and confections—biscuits, cornbread, and especially jelly rolls, as in the following popular lyric:

> Jelly roll, jelly roll ain't so hard to find,
> There's a baker shop in town bakes it brown like mine,
> I got a sweet jelly, a lovin' sweet jelly roll,
> If you taste my jelly it'll satisfy your worried soul.

While none of the sexual suggestions of plum bun seem lost upon Fauset, she by-passes their salacious suggestions and offers instead a delicate examination of the politics of sex that extends well beyond the novel. Those readers going to the literary market expecting their plum bun—sex and sensationalism Van Vechten style—were unfulfilled.

The "Van-Vechtenites" were not the only readers whose expectations were unfulfilled. While the genre of passing helped to mask Fauset's digs at the publishing industry, the fairy tale and romance helped, similarly, to mask her criticism of the image of women and the idealization of romantic love that these genres privilege and prop. The audience for books idealizing romantic love was as strong as always, easily rivaling the market for books wallowing in sex and sensationalism. Thornton Wilder's Pulitzer Prize–winning novel, *The Bridge of San Luis Rey,* paralleled Van Vechten's *Nigger Heaven* and McKay's *Home to Harlem* in commercial success and popular appeal. Within ninety days of its publication, the novel had sold 100,000 copies, becoming the most popular book of 1928. While Van Vechten and McKay sold the "new Morality" to readers, Wilder sold the idealization of romantic love.

I am not suggesting that Fauset's is a specific critique of Wilder or his novel but, rather, of the cultural valorization of romance that it embodied.

If read closely, the novel's evocation of the fairy tale and the romance, which socialize women to expect the prince, will inevitably seem designed for satiric purposes. For example, stunned at Roger's offer to set her up in a "lovenest," Angela thinks, "So this was her castle, her fortress of protection, her refuge" (p. 182). He finally seduces her in front of the fireplace on a stormy evening, complete with a driving rain and beating wind—all the trappings of romantic seduction. "He swept her up in his arms, cradling her in them like a baby with her face beneath his own. 'You know that we were meant for each other, that we belong to each other!'" Such stock language and scenes recur and are undercut and satirized in the novel. The narrative uses such stylizations to work the contrasts between these "normalizing" conventions and its efforts to transgress them.

There are repeated references to various generic conventions.[29] For example, we learn that, as children, Angela and Jinny "had been forbidden to read the five and ten cent literature of their day. But somehow a copy of a mystery story entitled 'Who killed Dr. Cronlin?' found its way into their hands, a gruesome story . . . full of bearded men, hands preserved in alcohol, shadows on window curtains. . . . Every page they hoped would disclose the mystery, but their patience went unrewarded for the last sentence still read: 'Who killed Dr. Cronlin?'" (p. 318). Similarly, when Roger returns tendering a marriage proposal, Angela notes "in books the man who often returned beaten, dejected, even poverty-stricken, but Roger . . . seemed as jaunty, as fortunate, as handsome as ever" (p. 318). In these and other passages Fauset seems aware of the power of generic conventions and seems to want to reshape them, particularly those like the fairy tale and the romance that are a part of the arsenal of women's gender construction. She invokes these conventions to reconfigure them, if not *pass* beyond them altogether.

The history of criticism of Fauset's work has missed this strategy, perhaps because it is so indirect. An inherently self-reflexive novel, *Plum Bun,* like the protagonist whose story it tells, is passing. It "passes" for just another novel of passing and for the age-old fairy tale and romance. While white skin is Angela's mask, these safe and familiar literary genres and conventions are the narrative's mask. The passing plot afforded Fauset a subtle vehicle through which to wage her critiques against these genres. In revising their conventions, Fauset fits into a pattern that audience-oriented critics describe: authors' use of familiar and normative conventions or "horizons of expectation" in unfamiliar and unconventional configurations in order to point up the deficiencies of those norms. In so doing, writers alter, expand, and possibly transform the reader's expectations to allow for what was formerly unexpected and unacceptable. *Plum Bun* baits the reader with a range of familiar expectations of women and of blacks, found both in and out of literature, but then refuses to fulfill them, particularly those that conform to the culturally coded exegeses of race and gender.

And thus we can say that, while Fauset employs "traditional" features of popular fiction, she uses them to forward a nontraditional agenda. She employs the tradition of romance not for purposes of valorization, but for purposes of critique. Aware that the romance is a narrative of power play, she criticizes the way it idealizes love and marriage and solidifies traditional and repressive gender arrangements. More importantly, she dares to open the taboo question of how generic conventions of romantic form are inadequate to meet the demands of an interracial love plot, which can only be assimilated to issues of class conflict.

Examined in the context of the Harlem Renaissance and the popular literature of the 1920s in general, Fauset's conventions seem less the signature of a hidebound traditionalist with prudish mid-Victorian habits and more the mark of an artist delineating and negotiating the complex field of cultural production and ideology in 1920s and 1930s America.

1984

5

The "Nameless . . . Shameful Impulse"

Sexuality in Nella Larsen's *Quicksand* and *Passing*[1]

> Ann had perceived that the decorous surface of her new
> husband's mind regarded Helga Crane with . . . intellectual
> and aesthetic appreciation . . . but that underneath that
> well-managed section, in a more lawless place . . . was
> another, a vagrant primitive groping toward something
> shocking and frightening to the cold asceticism of his reason
> . . . that *nameless . . . shameful impulse* . . . [emphasis
> added]
>
> —*Quicksand*[2]

> Irene . . . was trying to understand the look on Clare's face
> as she had said goodbye. Partly mocking, it had seemed,
> and partly menacing. *Something else for which she could find no
> name.* [emphasis added]
>
> —*Passing*

Based on her treatment of the black middle class and her examination of
the dynamics of racial passing, Nella Larsen is usually paired with Jessie
Fauset in studies of the Harlem Renaissance,[3] though most critics rightly
find Larsen a more gifted writer than Fauset.[4] Larsen demonstrates a
poised facility with writing, a knowledge and mastery of the elements of
fiction—especially narrative economy, effective language, focused characterization, unity, point-of-view—not always evident in Fauset's novels.
While critics have commended these features of Larsen's writing since the

beginning of her career, they have consistently criticized the endings of *Quicksand* (1928) and *Passing* (1929). Both novels obviously reveal Larsen's difficulty with rounding off stories convincingly, a problem she shared with her contemporaries Jessie Fauset and Zora Neale Hurston. For example, the tension between ideology and form, which characterizes the ending of *Plum Bun,* is even more pronounced in Fauset's first novel, *There Is Confusion* (1924), which closes as the heroine renounces her successful stage career to marry, accepting "as a matter of course" that her husband "was the arbiter of her own and her child's destiny."[5] More disappointing, given the enthusiastic claims critics make about her feminism, is Zora Neale Hurston's Missy May in her story, "The Gilded Six Bits" (1933), who proudly boasts to her husband, "if you burn me, you won't get a thing but wife ashes." At the story's end, weak from bearing her husband a "lil boy chile," she crawls to pick up the silver dollars that he is throwing through the door.[6] Or, finally, there is Arvay Henson in Hurston's last and problematical novel, *Seraph on the Suwanee* (1948), who retreats from the brink of independence and self-realization and returns to her verbally abusive husband, resolved that "he was her man and her care" and "her job was mothering. What more could any woman want and need? . . . Yes, she was serving and meant to serve. She made the sun welcome to come on in, then snuggled down again beside her husband."[7]

While these endings are unsatisfactory and unsettling, in that they sacrifice strong and emerging independent female identities to the more acceptable demands of literary and social history, they seem far less unsettling in comparison to those of *Quicksand* and *Passing.* Though both novels feature daring and unconventional heroines, in the end, they sacrifice these heroines to the most conventional fates of narrative history: marriage and death, respectively. In *Quicksand* the cultured and refined Helga Crane marries a rural southern preacher and follows him to his backwoods church to "uplift" his parishioners. At the end of the novel, she is in a state of emotional and physical collapse from having too many children. In *Passing* the defiant and adventurous Clare, who flouts all the social rules of the black bourgeoisie, falls to her death under melodramatic and ambiguous circumstances.

It is little wonder that critics of Larsen have been perplexed by these abrupt and contradictory endings. But if examined through the prism of black female sexuality, not only are these resolutions more understandable, they also illuminate the peculiar pressures on Larsen as a woman writer during the male-dominated Harlem Renaissance. They show her grappling with the conflicting demands of her racial and sexual identities and the contradictions of a black and feminine aesthetic. Although the endings of *Quicksand* and *Passing*, like the resolution of *Plum Bun*, seem to be concessions to the dominant ideology of romance—marriage and motherhood—viewed from a feminist perspective, they are much more radical and original efforts to acknowledge a female sexual experience most often repressed in both literary and social realms.

To be writing about black female sexuality within this conflicted context, then, posed peculiar dilemmas for Larsen: How could she write about black female sexuality in a literary era that often sensationalized it and pandered to the stereotype of the primitive exotic? How could she give a black female character the right to healthy sexual expression and pleasure without offending the proprieties established by the spokespersons of the black middle class? The answers to these questions for Larsen lay in attempting to hold these two virtually contradictory impulses in the same novel. We might say that Larsen wanted to tell the story of a black woman with sexual desires, but was constrained by a competing desire to establish black women as respectable in black middle-class terms. The latter desire committed her to exploring black female sexuality obliquely and, inevitably, to permitting it only within the context of marriage, despite the strangling effects of that choice both on her characters and on her narratives.

In their reticence about sexuality, her novels look back to their nineteenth-century predecessors; but in their simultaneous flirtation with female sexual desire, they are solidly grounded in the "liberation" of the Freudian 1920s, the Jazz Age of sexual abandon and "free love"—when female sexuality, in general, was acknowledged and commercialized in the advertising, beauty, and fashion industries. Larsen and Jessie Fauset, among the most prolific novelists of the decade, lacked the daring of their contemporaries, the black female blues singers such as Bessie, Mamie, and Clara Smith (all unrelated), Gertrude "Ma" Rainey, and Victoria Spivey. These women sang openly and seductively about sex and celebrated the female body and female desire as seen, for example, in a stanza from Ma Rainey's "It's Tight Like That": "See that spider crawling up the wall . . . going to get his ashes hauled. / Oh it's tight like that." Or Clara Smith's "Whip It to a Jelly": "There's a new game, that can't be beat / You move most everything 'cept your feet / Called whip it to a jelly, stir it in a bowl / You just whip it to a jelly, if you like good jelly roll."[8]

Behind the safe and protective covers of traditional narrative subjects and conventions, Jessie Fauset and Nella Larsen could only hint at the idea of black women as sexual subjects. Although their heroines are not the paragons of chastity that their nineteenth-century predecessors created, we cannot imagine them or their creators singing along with Bessie Smith,

"I'm wild about that thing," or "You've got to get it, bring it, and put it right here." Rather, they strain to honor the same ethics of sexual conduct called for by a respondent to a 1920s symposium titled "Negro Womanhood's Greatest Needs." Conducted by some of the same leading black club women who had organized around J. W. Jacks's libelous attack on black women's virtue, the symposium ran for several issues in *The Messenger,* one of the black "little magazines" of the period. The writer lamented what she called the "speed and disgust" of the Jazz Age, which created women "less discreet and less cautious than [their] sisters in years gone by." These "new" women, she continued, were "rebelling against the laws of God and man." Thus, she concluded that the greatest need of Negro womanhood was to return to the "timidity and modesty peculiar to pure womanhood of yesterday."[9]

Such appeals to the virtues of "pure womanhood" were clearly not new, but as standards of sexual morality shifted and relaxed, greater vigilance of black women's sexual expression resulted. *The Negro Woman's World,* a kind of conduct book for black women, was just as rigid as the club women in prescribing ideologies of sexual morality. As one contributor put it,

> Today the barriers are down between the sexes. In the old days man attempted to force morality by compelling the woman to be pure, while he went his lightsome way. Today there is a call to woman to observe certain restrictions in the light of elemental reason. Lenin, the apostle of the new Russia, where sexual liberty reaches its zenith, in addressing the young women of his country said, "no man cares to drink from a soiled glass." Chastity as the pure devotion between one man and one woman establishes the ideal family. This one pure love irradiates the whole existence.[10]

The blues lyrics, the club women's symposium, and the magazine editorial capture the dialectics of desire and fear, pleasure and danger that define women's sexual experiences in male-dominated societies. As Carole Vance maintains, "Sexuality is simultaneously a domain of restriction, repression, and danger as well as a domain of exploration, pleasure, and agency."[11] For women, and especially for black women, sexual pleasure leads to the dangers of domination in marriage, repeated pregnancy, exploitation, and loss of status.

Both *Quicksand* and *Passing* wrestle simultaneously with this dialectic between pleasure and danger. As with *Plum Bun,* the ideological ambivalences of Larsen's novels were rooted in the artistic politics of the Harlem Renaissance regarding the representation of black sexuality, especially black female sexuality. In the power relations of the period, Fauset's allegiances seemed clear-cut and straightforward compared to Larsen's. We might say that, in the battleground over black representation at this historical moment, Larsen was indeed caught between the proverbial rock and hard place. On the one side was her friend, Carl Van Vechten, roundly excoriated, along with his "followers," by many members of the black middle-class intelligentsia. He was responsible for introducing *Quicksand* to Knopf, and perhaps Larsen showed her gratitude by dedicating *Passing* to him and his wife, Fania Marinoff. On the other side, Larsen was herself a member of the black intelligentsia whom Van Vechten had criticized for failing to exploit the fresh, untapped material in Harlem, a criticism he inserted in *Nigger Heaven,* using the character Russett Durwood as his mouthpiece. Durwood advises Byron Kasson, the black would-be writer, to abandon the old clichés and formulas and write about what he knows— black life in the raw. Harlem is "overrun with fresh, unused material," he tells Kasson. "Nobody has yet written a good gambling story; nobody has touched the outskirts of cabaret life; nobody has gone into the curious subject of the *diverse tribes of the region*" [emphasis added]. He ends by predicting that if the "young Negro intellectuals don't get busy, a new crop of Nordics is going to spring up . . . and . . . exploit this material before the Negro gets around to it."[12] Van Vechten was one such Nordic whose sounds are echoed in a review of *Quicksand* that described the novel as "a harmonious blending of the barbaric splendor of the savage with the sophistication of the European." In depicting such black bourgeois intellectuals as Robert Anderson and James Vayle in *Quicksand,* Larsen would seem to share some of Van Vechten's opinions of that class. But as much as she could poke fun at their devotion to "racial uplift," she belonged, blood and breath, to that class, and must have found it extremely difficult to cut her ties with it.

The contradictory impulses of Larsen's novels are clear in the psychic divisions of her characters, divisions especially apparent in Helga Crane of *Quicksand.*[13] Most critics locate the origins of that dualism in Helga's mixed racial heritage.[14] Classifying her as the classic "tragic mulatta," alienated from both races, critics see Helga defeated by her struggle to resolve the psychic confusion created by this mixed heritage. The argument that Helga's is a story of the "tragic mulatta" is clearly supported by the novel's epigraph from Langston Hughes's poem "Cross," which treats the problem of racial dualism as seen in the last two lines: "I wonder where I'm gonna die, / Being neither white nor black?" But the epigraph suits *Quicksand* only partially, for it touches only indirectly the issue of sexuality that dominates the novel. In other words, in focusing on the problems of the "tragic mulatto," readers miss the more urgent problem that Larsen tried to explore: the pleasure and danger of female sexual experience.

Helga is divided psychically between a desire for sexual fulfillment and a longing for social respectability. The pressures of the divisions intensify to the point that she wonders "Why [she] couldn't . . . have two lives?" (p. 93). The novel works out this tension between sexual expression and repression in both thematic impulse and narrative strategy. Helga's psychic struggle seems the same war fought by Nella Larsen between narrative expression and repression of female sexuality as literary subject. The novel, like its protagonist, would seem to want two lives as well: as female sexual confession and novel of racial uplift.

Helga's sexual repression is understandable, given her "illegitimate" origins and her proper upbringing. The Naxos academic community, the setting in which the novel opens, is rigidly stratified, emphasizing "ancestry and connections" above all. More than a mythical allusion, Naxos is an anagram of Saxon, suggesting the school's worship of everything Anglo-Saxon.[15] At Naxos, attitudes about the sexual conduct of a single woman are rigidly conservative and upheld by the "humorless" and "prim" Miss MacGooden, the dormitory matron. "Prid[ing] herself on being a 'lady' from one of the best families" in the South, she explains her reasons for never marrying: "There were things in the matrimonial state . . . entirely too repulsive for a lady of delicate and sensitive nature to submit to." Though others strain to follow Miss MacGooden's example, becoming "ladies-in-making," Helga finds it "altogether negative" (p. 12).

Larsen captures these conflicts between Helga and Naxos through the iconography of clothing.[16] Like Fauset she maps Helga's subjectivity through the articles of her dress. The dull sobriety of Naxos considers "bright colors . . . vulgar," requiring "black, gray, brown, and navy blue." In sharp conflict with this dress code, Helga's elaborate clothes are in "dark purples, royal blues, rich greens, deep reds in soft, luxurious woolens or heavy, clinging silks" suggesting her passionate intensity and sexuality (pp. 17–18).[17]

Leaving this repressive environment, Helga goes, appropriately, to Harlem, which, at least in Harlem Renaissance mythology, is the site of sexual freedom and abandon; even here, however, her dress is conspicuous and outlandish. At a dinner party, for example, Helga decides to wear a "cobwebby black net [dress] touched with orange," even though she is aware that it is too "decollete" (p. 56). The cut and color of the dress suggest warmth and passion, but, significantly, the lure of sexuality is trapped in a net. Here, unlike at Naxos, Helga's conflicts are not with a repressive environment, but rather with herself.

Helga's internal conflicts find their most complete expression in the Harlem cabaret scene where she observes an assortment of semibarbaric, exotic people, the "essence of bodily motion," all moving to the syncopated beat of jungle tom-toms. Here her impulses of attraction/repulsion, pleasure/danger reach a near deadlock. Simultaneously excited and arrested by the music, "when suddenly [it] died, she dragged herself back to the present with a conscious effort; and a shameful certainty that not only had she been in the jungle but that she had enjoyed it, began to taunt her. She wasn't, she told herself, a jungle creature" (p. 59).

Throughout the novel, Helga retreats from these sexual feelings. Wanting to avoid them, she leaves Harlem, the mecca of the exotic, the primitive, and escapes to Copenhagen. The split between black and Scandinavian is an extreme duality of hot/cold, dark/light, south/north, resonating with and reflecting the divisions in Helga. Copenhagen does not relieve Helga's dilemma, because, ironically, the Danes transform and reduce her to a "veritable savage," a "decoration," a "curiosity, a stunt at which people came and gazed" (pp. 69, 73, 71).

The Danes' transformation of Helga into a sexual object continues the familiar pattern in the novel in which Helga is alternately defined by others (primarily men) as a "lady" or a "Jezebel." Neither designation captures her as a sexual subject, but simply as an object. She is not allowed to choose the terms and the objects of sexual desire. She leaves Naxos because Dr. Anderson calls her a "lady" with "dignity and breeding" (p. 21). While looking for work in Chicago, men—white and black alike—mistake her for a prostitute.[18] Finally, when Helga wanders into a church wearing a clinging red dress, the church women call her a "scarlet 'oman," a "pore los' Jezebel" (p. 112).

Axel Olsen, the Danish artist, presumes to identify Helga's contradictions when she refuses his insulting sexual proposition, adding, "in my country the men of my race, at least, don't make such suggestions to decent girls" (p. 86). Helga expresses an awareness of her legacy of rape and concubinage at the hands of white men, a legacy that compels her to decline both Olsen's sexual proposition and his marriage proposal, and in so doing, to remove herself as the silent object of his gaze.

Though Olsen's remarks are insulting, they act as a catalyst for Helga's determination to reconcile the "suspensive conflict[s]" (p. 83) of her life and to release her pent-up desires for sexual freedom. Significantly, up to and through Copenhagen, Helga has been the sexual object pursued, while after Copenhagen, she becomes the subject pursuing. It is appropriate that the field of her pursuits is Harlem where, again in mythical terms, sexual freedom and unrestraint ostensibly abound. But ironically, Helga seeks release with Dr. Anderson, who has already designated her a "lady," and therefore a being without sexual desires. Further, Anderson himself is the very embodiment of sexual conflict and repression. He makes "ascetic protest[s] against the sensuous, the physical," though underneath his "decorous surface" lurked a "more lawless place," a "nameless" and "shameful" (pp. 94–95) place that must be repressed. Though he kisses Helga passionately at a party, he is loathe to follow through on the overture. His apology to her leaves Helga disconcerted and haunted by "voluptuous visions." "Desire . . . burned in her flesh in uncontrollable violence" (p. 109).

The sexual desires, pent-up throughout the novel, finally explode in Helga's primitive, passionate religious conversion, the description of which unambiguously simulates sexual excitement and orgasmic release:

> Little by little the performance took on an almost Bacchic vehemence. Behind her, before her, beside her, frenzied women gesticulated, screamed, wept. . . .
> And as Helga watched and listened gradually a curious influence penetrated her; she felt an echo of the weird orgy resound in her own heart; she felt herself possessed by the same madness; she too felt a brutal desire to shout and to sling herself about. . . . She grasped at the railing, and with no previous intention began to yell like one insane, drowning every other clamor, while torrents of tears streamed down her face. . . . Those who succeeded in getting near to her leaned forward to encourage the unfortunate sister, dropping hot tears and beads of sweat upon her bare arms and neck. The thing became real. A miraculous calm came upon her. Life seemed to expand, and to become very easy. Helga Crane felt within her a supreme aspiration toward the regaining of simple happiness, a happiness unburdened by the complexities of the lives she had known. About her the tumult and the shouting continued, but in a lesser degree. Some of the more exuberant worshippers had fainted into inert masses, the voices of others were almost spent. Gradually the room grew quiet and almost solemn, and to the kneeling girl time seemed to sink back into the mysterious grandeur and holiness of far-off simpler centuries. (pp. 113–14)

Larsen dramatizes the fine line between sexual and religious ecstasy, often said to be characteristic of fundamentalist religious sects, further underscoring the ambiguity of Helga's motives in her marriage to the Rev. Green, a fundamentalist preacher.[19]

The question still remains as to why the refined Helga, who "took to luxury as the proverbial duck to water" (p. 67), participates in a religious orgy, is seduced, then marries a man whose "fingernails [are] always rimmed with black," and who smells of "sweat and stale garments" (p. 121). Why not marry James Vayle to whom she was engaged at Naxos or another of the upwardly mobile men like him who "danced attendance on her"? One explanation is that the James Vayles and the Robert Andersons are largely responsible for constructing and upholding the contradictory sexual images of women that Helga has resisted throughout the novel. Further, their conflicting attitudes are mirror images of Helga's own internal attitudes, which Larsen's echoing descriptions reinforce. Just as Anderson's sexual attraction to Helga is "nameless" and "shameful," so was hers for James Vayle, her former fiancé. "The idea that she was in but one nameless way necessary to him filled her with a sensation amounting almost to shame" (p. 8).

The only condition under which sexuality is not shameless is if it finds sanction in marriage. Further, because she was born out of wedlock, Helga is preoccupied with the issue of "legitimacy." Marriage to a preacher, then, is legitimacy redoubled. Although she "question[s] her ability to retain, to bear, this happiness at such cost as she must pay for it[,] [t]here was, she knew, no getting around that. [The Rev. Green's] agitation and sincere conviction of sin had been too evident, too illuminating" (p. 116).

The price that Helga must pay for this sexual "happiness" is far greater than she imagined, for the three children that she bears in rapid succession are the hidden price she had not foreseen. Closing the novel on this note, Larsen openly castigates the dual price—marriage and pregnancy/ childbearing—that women pay for sexual expression. The novel's images of suffocation culminating in the title, "Quicksand," reinforce the point.

Like so many novels by women, Quicksand likens marriage to death for women.[20] Larsen attacks the myth that marriage elevates women in the social scale, suggesting that, for them, the way up is, ironically and paradoxically, the way down. Helga's marriage and the children that issue from it "use her up" (p. 123) and freeze her development, not even leaving time for laboring "in the vineyard of the Lord" (p. 118). The aftermath of the birth of her fourth child is likened to a death and burial (she "go[es] down into that appalling blackness of pain") followed by a symbolic resurrection when she "return[s] to earth" (p. 128). But Helga's is a mock resurrection, for she rises from the dead only to be reentombed.[21] At the novel's end, she is in labor with her fifth child.

The ending completes the structural opposites on which the novel has turned. Whereas it opens on Helga in an elegantly furnished room, dressed in a "vivid green and gold negligee," the picture of "radiant, careless health" (p. 2) and sexual energy, it closes on her trapped in the "four rooms of her ugly brown house" with "white plaster walls" and naked "uncovered painted floors" (p. 121). Though near the novel's end she is pictured in a "filmy crepe" negligee, "a relic of her prematrimonial days" (p. 129), it is clear that Larsen wants to stress the reality that "legitimate" sex, for women, is harnessed to its reproductive consequences, for Helga wears this negligee while she is in labor with her fourth child. Though she initially accepts the social script that marriage makes sex moral in the eyes of the law and the church, Helga comes to regard it as "immoral" (p. 134). Appropriately, she requests that the nurse read Anatole France's "The Procurator of Judea" to her as she recovers from the birth of this child, for its blasphemous, anti-Christian views parallel Helga's own belated insight into the role of Christianity in her oppression.

Larsen's sympathies seem to lie with Helga, who is powerless to resist these binding and suffocating institutions that deny her the right to define the terms of her own sexuality. But in the end she undercuts her own critique through her images of Helga's desire. However much Larsen criticizes the repressive standards of sexual morality upheld by the black middle class, she is finally unable to escape them. Significantly suggesting moral degradation, sexuality is linked throughout the novel to imagery of descent and animalism.[22]

The structure of the novel is a vertical line downward, a movement reinforced by several echoing scenes. In the Harlem cabaret, for example, Helga and her party "[descend] through a furtive, narrow passage into a vast subterranean room . . . characterized by the righteous as hell." The church into which Helga stumbles near the end is a former stable. There the "frenzied women" crawl over the floor "like reptiles," "tearing off their clothing."[23]

Just before her "religious conversion" Helga is literally thrown, "soaked and soiled," "into the gutter." Finally, as if to atone for these "transgressions," Helga goes to the deep South where she is buried alive.[24]

Perhaps this resolution was as unsatisfying for Larsen as it has remained for her readers, and may well explain her decision to return in her next novel to the complex issue of black female sexuality in order to pose a different resolution. In other words, in *Quicksand,* Larsen stakes her exploration of female sexuality in the narrative zone that women writers have traditionally used: within the genre of the romance in which sex for women is enacted and legitimated within marriage and harnessed to motherhood. But in *Passing,* she leaves the "safety" of that familiar domain.

> She wished to find out about this hazardous business of
> "passing," this breaking away from all that was familiar and
> friendly to take one's chance in another environment.

Larsen reopens the question of female sexuality in *Passing* with much bolder suggestions. While in *Quicksand* she explores these questions within the "safe" and "legitimate" parameters of marriage, in *Passing* she takes many more risks, calling more boldly into question the heterosexual priorities maintained by the program of bourgeois uplift. Although Clare and Irene—the novel's dual protagonists—are married, theirs are sexless marriages. In Clare's case, the frequent travels of her financier husband and her fear of producing a dark child explain this situation. In Irene's case, her own sexual repression is at fault. It is significant that Irene and her husband sleep in separate bedrooms (he considers sex a joke) and that she tries to protect her sons from schoolyard discussions about sex. Having established the absence of sex from the marriages of these two women, Larsen can flirt, if only obliquely, with the idea of a lesbian relationship between them.

It is no accident that critics have failed to notice the novel's flirtation with this idea, for many are misled, as with *Quicksand,* by the epigraph.[25] Focusing on racial identity or racial ambiguity and cultural history, the epigraph invites the reader to place race at the center of any critical interpretation. Interestingly, Larsen uses the almost romantic refrain of Countee Cullen's poem "Heritage" as the novel's epigraph—"One three centuries removed / From the scenes his fathers loved, / Spicy grove, cinnamon tree, / What is Africa to me?"—foregoing the more dramatic and provocative suggestions of the poem's ending:

> All day long and all night through,
> One thing only must I do:
> Quench my pride and cool my blood,
> Lest I perish in the flood.
> Lest a hidden ember set
> Timber that I thought was wet
> Burning like the dryest flax,
> Melting like the merest wax,
> Lest the grave restore its dead.

Not only does the epigraph mislead the reader, but Irene, the central consciousness of the narrative, does as well. It is largely through her eyes, described appropriately as "unseeing," that most of the narrative's events are filtered, significantly, in retrospect and necessarily blurred. The classic unreliable narrator, Irene is confused and deluded about herself, her motivations, and much that she experiences. It is important, therefore, to see the duplicity at the heart of her story. As Beatrice Royster rightly observes, "Irene is an ideal choice as narrator of a tale with double meanings. She tells the story as the injured wife, betrayed by friend and husband; she tells it as a confession to clear her conscience of any guilt in Clare's death."[26]

Irene paints herself as the perfect, nurturing, self-sacrificing wife and mother, the altruistic "race woman," and Clare as her diametrical opposite. In Clare, there was "nothing sacrificial." She had "no allegiance beyond her own immediate desire. She was selfish, and cold and hard," Irene reports (p. 144). Clare had the "ability to secure the thing that she wanted in the face of any opposition, and in utter disregard of the convenience and desires of others. About her there was some quality, hard and persistent, with the strength and endurance of rock, that would not be beaten or ignored" (p. 201). Irene describes Clare as "catlike," suggesting that she is given to deception, to furtive, clandestine activity. Concluding her observations with an attitude of smug self-satisfaction, Irene declares that she and Clare are not only "strangers . . . in their racial consciousness," but also "strangers in their ways and means of living. Strangers in their desires and ambitions" (p. 192).

As is often typical of an unreliable narrator, Irene is by turns hypocritical and obtuse, not always fully aware of the import of what she reveals to the reader. Ironically, detail for detail, she manifests all that she abominates in Clare. Despite her protestations to the contrary, Irene, with a cold, hard, exploitative, and manipulative determination, tries to protect her most cherished attainment—security. She equates this security with marriage to a man in a prestigious profession and the accoutrements of middle-class existence—children, material comfort, and social respectability. Moreover, Irene resorts to wily and covert tactics to ensure that illusion of security. After persuading her husband to abandon his dream of leaving racist Harlem to practice medicine in Brazil, Irene rationalizes that she had done this, "not for her—she had never really considered herself—but for him and the boys" (pp. 186–87).

Even Irene's work with racial uplift programs, such as the Negro Welfare League, betrays her. Although she deludes herself that this work is proof of her racial consciousness, it is actually self-serving. The social functions that Irene arranges to aid the "unfortunate" black masses are so heavily attended by prominent whites that her husband, Brian, fears that "'Pretty soon the colored people won't be allowed in at all, or will have to sit in Jim Crowed sections.'"

Not only does Larsen undercut Irene's credibility as narrator, but she also satirizes and parodies the manners and morals of the black middle class that Irene so faithfully represents. That parody comes through in the density of specificity in the novel, as seen in the description of a typical morning in Irene's household:

> They went into the dining-room. [Brian] drew back her chair and she sat down behind the fat-bellied German coffeepot, which sent out its morning fragrance mingled with the smell of crisp toast and savoury bacon in the distance. With his long, nervous fingers he picked up the morning paper from his own chair and sat.
>   Zulena, a small mahogany-coloured creature, brought in the grapefruit. They took up their spoons. (p. 184)

The description of the endless tea and cocktail parties and charity balls satirizes the sterility and banality of the bourgeoisie.

> There were the familiar little tinkling sounds of spoons striking against frail cups, the soft running sounds of inconsequential talk, punctuated now and then with laughter. In irregular small groups, disintegrating, coalescing, striking just the right note of disharmony, disorder in the big room, which Irene had furnished with a sparingness that was almost chaste, moved the guests with that slight familiarity that makes a party a success. (p. 219)

Although Irene is clearly deluded about her motives, her racial loyalty, her class, and her distinctness from Clare, the narrative suggests that her most glaring delusion concerns her feelings for Clare.

Though, superficially, Irene's is an account of Clare's racial passing and the related issues of racial identity and loyalty, underneath the safety of that surface is the more dangerous story—if not named explicitly—of Irene's awakening sexual desire for Clare. The narrative traces this developing eroticism in spatial terms. It begins on the roof of the Drayton Hotel (with all the suggestions of the sexually illicit), intensifies at Clare's tea party, and, getting proverbially "close to home," explodes in the intimate space of Irene's own bedroom. Preoccupied with appearances, social respectability, and safety, however, Irene tries to force these feelings underground. The narrative dramatizes that repression effectively in images of concealment and burial.

Significantly, the novel's opening image is an envelope (a metaphoric vagina) that Irene hesitates to open, fearing its "contents would reveal" an "attitude toward danger" (p. 143). Irene tries to preserve "a hardness from feeling" (p. 217), at times even "driv[ing] back her ... anger" (p. 189). Unable to explain her feelings for Clare, "for which she could find no name," Irene dismisses them as "just somebody walking over [her] grave" (p. 176). The narrative suggests pointedly that Clare is the body walking over the grave of Irene's buried sexual feelings.

Lest the reader miss this eroticism, Larsen employs fire imagery—the conventional representation of sexual desire—introducing and instituting it in the novel's opening pages. Irene begins her retrospective account of her reunion with Clare, remembering that the day was "hot," the sun "brutal" and "staring," its rays "like molten rain." Significantly, Irene, feeling "sticky and soiled from contact with so many sweating bodies" (pp. 146–47), escapes to the roof of the Drayton Hotel, where she is reunited with Clare after a lapse of many years. (Irene is, ironically, "escaping" to the very thing she wants to avoid.)

From the very beginning of their reencounter, Irene is drawn to Clare like a moth to a flame. (Suggestively, Clare is frequently dressed in red.) The "lovely creature" (p. 151) "had for her a fascination, strange and compelling" (p. 161). When the two are reunited, Irene first notices Clare's "tempting mouth"; her lips, "painted a brilliant geranium-red, were sweet and sensitive and a little obstinate." Into Clare's "arresting eyes" "there came a smile and over Irene the sense of being petted and caressed" (p. 161). At the end of this chance encounter, "[s]tanding there under the appeal, the caress, of [Clare's] eyes, Irene had the desire, the hope, that this parting wouldn't be the last" (p. 162).

When Irene has tea at Clare's house, she notices that Clare "turned on . . . her seductive caressing smile" (p. 169). Afterwards, a "slight shiver [runs] over [Irene]" when she remembers the mysterious look on Clare's "incredibly beautiful face." "She couldn't, however, come to any conclusion about its meaning. . . . It was unfathomable, utterly beyond any experience or comprehension of hers" (p. 176).

The awakening of Irene's erotic feelings for Clare coincides with Irene's imagination of an affair between Clare and Brian. Given her tendency to project her disowned traits, motives, and desires onto others, it is reasonable to argue that Irene is projecting her own developing passion for Clare onto Brian, although in "all their married life she had had no slightest cause to suspect [him] of any infidelity, of any serious flirtation even." (p. 223). The more her unsettling feelings develop, the more she fights them, for they threaten the placid surface of her middle-class existence as a doctor's wife. "Safety and security," Irene's watchwords, crop up repeatedly in the novel after Clare arrives and explain Irene's struggle to avoid her.

Undeterred, however, Clare visits Irene's house unannounced, coming first to the bedroom where she "drop[s] a kiss on [Irene's] dark curls," arousing in Irene "a sudden inexplicable onrush of affectionate feeling. Reaching out, she grasped Clare's two hands in her own and cried with something like awe in her voice: 'Dear God! But aren't you lovely, Clare!'" (p. 194). Their conversation in this scene has a sexual double edge, heightened by Irene's habitual gesture of lighting cigarettes.

Clare scolds Irene for not responding to her letter, describing her repeated trips to the post office. "I'm sure they were all beginning to think that I'd been carrying on an illicit love-affair and that the man had thrown me over." Irene assures Clare that she is concerned simply about the dangers of Clare's passing in Harlem, the risks she runs of being discovered by "knowing Negroes." Clare's immediate response is "You mean you don't want me, 'Rene?" Irene replies, "It's terribly foolish, and not just the right thing." It's "dangerous," she continues, "to run such silly risks." "It's not safe. Not safe at all." But "as if in contrition for that flashing thought," "Irene touched [Clare's] arm caressingly" (p. 194–95).

Irene's protestations about racial passing are suspicious and not altogether warranted by the situation, especially since she passes occasionally herself. Further, they function in the same way that Helga's response to Axel Olsen functions: as a mask for the deeper, more unsettling issues of sexuality. Irene tries to defuse the feelings by absorbing herself in the ritual of empty tea parties, but "it was as if in a house long dim, a match had been struck, showing ghastly shapes where had been only blurred shadows" (p. 218). At one such party, near the narrative's end, Clare is, in typical fashion, an intruding presence, both at the party and in Irene's thoughts. "Irene couldn't remember ever having seen [Clare] look better." Watching "the fire roar" in the room, Irene thinks of Clare's "beautiful and caressing" face (p. 220).

In the final section of the novel, Clare comes to Irene's house before they go to the fateful Christmas party. Coming again into Irene's room, "Clare kisse[s] her bare shoulder, seeming not to notice a slight shrinking" (p. 223). As they walk to the party, Clare at Brian's side, Irene describes a "live thing pressing against her" (p. 237). That "live thing," represented clearly as full-blown sexual desire, must be contained, and it takes Clare's death to contain it. Significantly, in Irene's description of the death, all of the erotic images used to describe Clare throughout the novel converge.

Gone! The soft white face, the bright hair, the disturbing scarlet mouth, the dreaming eyes, the caressing smile, the whole tortured loveliness that had been Clare Kendry. That beauty that had torn at Irene's placid life. Gone! The mocking daring, the gallantry of her pose, the ringing bells of her laughter. (p. 239)

Although the ending is ambiguous and the evidence circumstantial, I agree with Cheryl Wall that, "Larsen strongly implies that Irene pushes Clare through the window," and, in effect, becomes "a psychological suicide, if not a murderer."[27]

To suggest the extent to which Clare's death represents the death of Irene's sexual feelings for Clare, Larsen uses a clever objective correlative: Irene's pattern of lighting cigarettes and snuffing them out. Minutes before Clare falls from the window to her death, "Irene finished her cigarette and threw it out, watching the tiny spark drop slowly down to the white ground below" (p. 238). Clearly attempting a symbolic parallel, Clare is described as "a vital glowing thing, like a flame of red and gold" who falls from (or is thrown out of) the window as well. Because Clare is a reminder of that repressed and disowned part of Irene's self, she must be banished, for, more unacceptable than the feelings themselves is the fact that they find an object of expression in Clare. In other words, Clare is both the embodiment and the object of the sexual feelings that Irene banishes.

In effect, Larsen commits a banishing act as well. Put another way, the idea of bringing sexual attraction between two women to full narrative expression is, likewise, too dangerous a move for Nella Larsen, which helps to explain why critics have missed this aspect of the novel. Larsen's clever narrative strategies almost conceal it. In *Passing,* she uses a technique commonly found in narratives by African American and women novelists with a "dangerous" story to tell: "safe" themes, plots, and conventions are used as a protective cover, underneath which lie more dangerous subplots. Larsen envelops the subplot of Irene's developing, if unnamed and unacknowledged, desire for Clare in the safe and familiar plot of racial passing.[28]

Put another way, the novel's clever strategy derives from its surface theme and central metaphor—passing. Like *Plum Bun,* it takes the form of the act it describes. Implying false, forged, and mistaken identities, the title functions on multiple levels: thematically, in terms of the racial and sexual plots, and strategically, in terms of the narrative's disguise.

The structure of the novel complements and reinforces this disguise. Neat and symmetrical, *Passing* is composed of three sections, with four chapters each. The order and control which that tight organization suggests are a clever cover for the unconventional subplot in the novel's hiding places.

In *Passing* Larsen performs a double burial: the erotic subplot is hidden beneath its safe and orderly cover and the radical implications of that plot are put away in disposing of Clare. Although she is the center of vitality and passion, these qualities, which the narrative seems to affirm, are significantly and conveniently contained by the narrative's ending. And Clare becomes a kind of sacrificial lamb on the altar of social and literary convention.

Clare suffers the fate that many a female character has suffered when she has had what Rachel Blau DuPlessis terms an "inappropriate relation to the 'social script.'" Death results, she continues, when "energies of selfhood, often represented by sexuality . . . are expended outside the 'covert' of marriage or valid [generally spelled heterosexual] romance."[29] While Larsen criticizes the cover of marriage, as well as other social scripts for women, she is unable in the end to extend that critique to its furthest reaches.

In ending the novel with Clare's death, Larsen repeats the narrative choice that *Quicksand* makes: to punish the very values the novel implicitly affirms, to honor the very value system the text implicitly satirizes. The ending, when hidden racial identities are disclosed, functions on the ideological as well as the narrative level. Larsen performs an act of narrative "dis"-closure, undoing or reversing the promises of the narrative. Or, to borrow from *Quicksand,* Larsen closes *Passing* "without exploring to the end that unfamiliar path into which she had strayed" (p. 106).

Both *Quicksand* and *Passing* are poised between the tensions and conflicts that are Western culture's stock ambivalences about female sexuality: lady/Jezebel or virgin/whore. Larsen sees and indicts the sources of this ambivalence: the network of social institutions—education, marriage, and religion, among the most prominent—all interacting with each other to strangle and control the sexual expression of women. But, like her heroine Helga, Larsen could "neither conform nor be happy in her nonconformity" (p. 7).

Considering the focus of both her novels on black female sexuality, one naturally wonders if Nella Larsen would have taken still more risks had her short, but accomplished, literary career been extended. However oblique and ambivalent Larsen's treatment of black female sexuality, because she gave her characters sexual feelings at all, she must be regarded as something of a pioneer in the African American female literary tradition. To be sure, her novels only flirt with the idea of female sexual passion. We might say that they represent the desire, the expectation, the preparation of eroticism that contemporary black women's novels are attempting to bring to franker and fuller expression. In such novels as Gayl Jones's *Corregidora* (1975) and *Eva's Man* (1976), Toni Morrison's *Sula* (1976), Alice Walker's *The Color Purple* (1982), Ntozake Shange's *Sassafras, Cypress, and Indigo* (1982), Gloria Naylor's *The Women of Brewster Place*

(1982), and Ann Allen Shockley's *Loving Her,* among others, black women are creating sexual subjects, rather than objects of male desire. And thus, they are naming what at least one stream of Larsen's imagination and her literary milieu deemed a "nameless," "shameful impulse."

1986

To argue that the endings of Quicksand *and* Passing *illuminate much about narrative constructions of race, gender, and sexuality during the Harlem Renaissance is to target a point of economical access to the novels, but then to critique the endings as somehow failing to deliver on a sexual promise in their plots is inherently contradictory. Such a contradiction arises from a view of sexuality as an autonomous drive or force or instinct abstracted from a dense and complex social field. Recent work on the history of sexuality has challenged this traditional notion, substituting in its place a view of all desire—sexual desire included—as historically contingent and constructed.*

Such a view simultaneously challenges the concept of "repression" that derives logically from a belief in an autonomous sexuality. And thus, we must conclude that the cause of Helga's frustration and aimlessness and Irene's devious machinations is irreducible to the merely sexual. Both Helga and Irene are the victims of, not only bourgeois constraints on sexual morality and expression, but also a whole network of repressive forces that structure bourgeois society. The sexual is only one site and source of their oppression, which must not obscure the sites with which the sexual interacts. For example, the ways that gender and sexuality interact with race in the construction of identity in a libidinal economy is lost in a focus on sexuality qua *sexuality. At a second glance, then, both novels seem not so much to subordinate gender and sexuality to race, but to be acutely aware of the fact that Irene laments: she was "caught between two allegiances, different, yet the same. Herself. Her race. Race: the thing that bound and suffocated her. . . . A person or the race . . . she was unable to disregard the burden of race" (p. 225). Nor, for that matter, can she disregard the burden of class, which, for blacks, is generally conflated with race and regarded as synonymous with libidinousness in the imagination of the dominant culture.*

The epigraph to Quicksand, *a stanza from Langston Hughes's poem "Cross," compresses questions about class, racial identity, heritage, and sexuality in a poem about miscegenation:*

> *My old man died in a fine big house*
> *My ma died in a shack.*

I wonder where I'm gonna die,
Being neither white nor black?

These intersecting identities *have a way of converging neatly in the narrative regime of racial passing.*

A reconsideration of the ideology of Nella Larsen's narrative strategies must follow from these reconsiderations of racial and sexual identity formation. To critique the fates of the heroines is to repeat the utopian political drives of an early stage of feminist criticism that worked off the assumption that a "feminist text" should manifest itself as such by an explicit liberation of a central protagonist at the moment of closure. "Liberation," according to this reasoning, is often falsely construed to mean the triumph of sexual autonomy and individual will over repressive structures—marriage being chief among them. However useful such critiques might be, they fall short of perceiving that "the plots of women's literature," as Nancy Miller points out, "are not about 'life' and solutions in any therapeutic sense, nor should they be. They are about the plots of literature itself."[30] And thus we might suspend the certainty of a closed judgment about the sexual and textual politics of closure or at least reopen the question. Continuing with Miller, we might ask, "What does [a] 'strange' and implausible ending tell us about reading for the plot of women's fiction?" (p. 86) In pursuing that question we might discover that "even the 'old plot' rewritten by women also supplies a critique of the available cultural solutions" (p. 127). The critique in Quicksand *lies in its refusal to underwrite the available cultural conventions of the racial uplift novel. In fact, we could say that* Quicksand *is a comment on the closure of* Iola Leroy. *Helga's "young joy and zest for the uplifting of her fellow men" meet with little enthusiasm in this tiny Alabama town. Her plans to "'subdue' the clearly scrubbed ugliness of her own surroundings to soft offensive beauty," to help the other women with their clothes, to instruct their wild children in the "ways of gentler deportment" fail to materialize. To this community Helga is an "uppity, meddlin' No'thenah" (p. 119) who remains the lesser antithesis of Clementine Richards, a better match for the Reverend Green. Described in a fashion that evokes familiar photographs and descriptions of Ma Rainey, Clementine is a "strapping black beauty of magnificent Amazon proportions . . . of awesome appearance. All chains, strings of beads, jingling bracelets, flying ribbons, feathery neck-pieces, and flowery hats" (p. 119). But in matching the Reverend Pleasant Green with Helga and not Clementine, the narrative also supplies a critique of the conventional symmetry of closure that brings an ideal* couple together in a blissful union. This "imperfect" match mocks the very idea of a perfect match.

Such a mockery continues in Passing, which transgresses conventions of middle-class sexual norms altogether, even if it does so only metaphorically. But just because the narrative resorts to a rhetoric of metaphor and innuendo does not mean that it is silent on the question of sex, especially if we accept Foucault's assertion that "silence itself—the things one declines to say, or is forbidden to name . . . is less the absolute limit of discourse, the other side from which it is separated by a strict boundary, than an element that functions alongside the things said, with them and in relation to them within overall strategies" (p. 27). Thus, given the difficulty of racial self-representation, given the difficulty of sexual self-naming, Larsen has gone pretty far down that "unfamiliar path" and must be seen as much a victim as Helga, Irene, or Clare. In other words, without suggesting that Larsen's characters are mere proxies for her, Larsen's literary dilemma, generated by racism and indicated by implied homology with her characters, was an actual social dilemma: how to express female sexual desire, especially the lesbian desire, without becoming an icon of racist projection. Whatever Larsen's ultimate narrative limits, she is exploring the Catch-22s of black female sexual desire and expression—social, psychological, political. In showing how America entraps that desire she is indeed naming the unnameable.

PART IV

The Reader in the Text

What besides a proper name could hold
the self together once it were radically
split into discontinuities . . . a
totality that compels into integration
the parts that thereby "compose" it. It
is as though each character were governed
by a principle of majority rule that ne-
cessitates diversity and simultaneously
dominates it.

—*D. A. Miller,* Narrative and the Police

The question is, what kind of reader? . . .
We may call him [sic], for want of a
better term, the implied reader. He
embodies all those predispositions
necessary for a literary work to exercise
its effects. . . . The implied reader . . .
has his roots firmly planted in the
structures of the text: he is a construct
and in no way to be identified with any
real reader.

—*Wolfgang Iser,* The Act of Reading

6

Boundaries

Or Distant Relations and Close Kin—*Sula*[1]

What shall we call our "self"? Where does it begin? Where
does it end? It overflows into everything that belongs to us.
—Henry James, *Portrait of a Lady*

She had clung to Nel as the closest thing to both an other
and a self, only to discover that she and Nel were not one
and the same thing.
—Toni Morrison, *Sula*[2]

In "Negro Art," an essay published in *The Crisis* in 1921, W. E. B. Du
Bois described the desire of blacks for idealized literary representation.
"We want everything said about us to tell of the best and highest and
noblest in us . . . . we fear that evil in us will be called racial, while in
others, it is viewed as individual."[3] Concerned because blacks were being
"continually painted at their worst and judged by the public as they [were]
painted," Du Bois organized a write-in symposium called "The Negro in
Art: How Shall He Be Portrayed?" that ran from March to December in
The Crisis magazine. The subject of intense debate, the symposium elicited
applause and condemnation alike from its respondents. Though not an-
swering the questionnaire directly, Langston Hughes voiced his skepticism
and *The Crisis'* image campaign in "The Negro Artist and the Racial
Mountain," an essay first published in the *Nation*. There he blasted the

"Nordicized Negro intelligentsia" for demanding the black artists "be respectable, write about nice people, [and] show how good [black people] are."[4]

Roughly fifty years later, those in the vanguard of the Black Aesthetic movement, faithful to a paradigm focused almost exclusively on race, loitered at the corner where the psychological "self" and the literary subject meet and often collide. They formulated a discourse that turned on the rhetorical polarities "Positive" and "Negative" to fulfill another part of their mission: to grant racial image awards. Many demanded that black writers inscribe the "positive" racial self in Afro-American literature. Addison Gayle was a prototypical example. In his 1977 essay "Blueprint for Black Criticism," Gayle appealed specifically for literary characters modeled upon men and women such as Sojourner Truth, Harriet Tubman, Martin Delaney, H. Rap Brown, and Fannie Lou Hamer—a kind of Plutarch's *Lives* of the black race, if you like. In that they offer images of "heroism, beauty, and courage," Gayle continues, these men and women are "positive" characters, functional "alternatives to the stereotypes of blacks," and thus warriors in the "struggle against American racism."[5]

In the roughly ten years since Gayle issued his blueprint, African American literary criticism has finally seen the beginnings of a paradigm shift, one that has extended the boundaries and altered the terms of its inquiry. Falling in step with recent developments in contemporary critical theory, some critics of African American literature have usefully complicated many unexamined, common assumptions about the SELF and about race as a meaningful category in literary study and critical theory.[6] These recent developments have made it difficult, if not impossible, to posit with any assurance a "positive" black SELF, always already unified, coherent, stable, and known.

And yet, despite these important and sophisticated developments, Afro-American critics of Afro-American literature, in both the popular media and academic journals, continue to use the yardstick that measures the "positive" racial SELF, resisting any work that does not satisfy the nebulous demand for exemplary images. At no time has such resistance been more stubborn and determined and judgments more harsh than now, when diehard critics, reducing contemporary black women writers to a homogenized bloc, have alleged that their portrayal of black male characters is uniformly "negative."

A full inquiry into this debate,[7] which has escaped the pages of literary journals and essay collections and spilled over into the privileged organs of the literary establishment—(*The New York Times Book Review* and *The New York Review of Books*)—is not possible here, although it is in urgent need of address. But allow me to use Mel Watkins's comments from his June 1986 essay, "Sexism, Racism, and Black Women Writers," published in *The New York Times Book Review,* to represent the insistent refrain. Watkins argues that in the great majority of their novels, black women indicate that "sexism is more oppressive than racism." In these works, black males are portrayed in an "unflinchingly candid and often negative manner," almost without exception, "thieves, sadists, rapists, and ne'er-do-wells." In choosing "black men as a target," Watkins continues, "these writers have set themselves outside a tradition" devoted to "establishing humane, positive images of blacks".[8]

It is useful here to pause and extrapolate the interlocking assumptions of Watkins's essay most relevant to my concerns here. These assumptions are the struts of the dominant Afro-American critical paradigm in which: (1) the world is neatly divided into black and white; (2) race is the sole determinant of being and identity, subsuming sexual as well as all other forms of difference; (3) identity is preexistent, coherent, and known; and (4) literature has the power to unify and liberate the race. This paradigm pivots on a set of interchangeable and uncomplicated oppositions—black/white, positive/negative, self/other.

The overarching preoccupation with "positive" racial representation operates in tandem with a static view of the nature of identification in the act of reading. One result of this arrangement is an inflexible demand for literary characters who are essentially figurations of myth, akin to Alice Walker's description: "I am black, beautiful, and strong, and almost always right."[9] This is the SELF with which our hypothetical Afro-American critic, desperately seeking flattery, is likely to identify. To put the material in its baldest and most simplistic form, this SELF is uniformly "positive" and "good" and defined in contradistinction to its OTHER, uniformly "negative" and "bad."

As feminist theorists have consistently and emphatically argued, the opposition of SELF to OTHER, as well as its analogues, is gendered and hierarchical, tending to reproduce the more fundamental opposition between male and female. Man is SELF, and woman, OTHER.[10] And in this configuration, as Shoshana Felman eloquently puts it, echoing the dutiful terms of the dominant Afro-American paradigm, woman is "the negative of the positive."[11]

While these observations are commonplace in feminist discourse, their usefulness to students of Afro-American literary studies has not been fully interrogated. Preventing such interrogation is an almost exclusive focus on race in Afro-American literary discourse, which is often tantamount to a focus on maleness. That black women are subordinated (if not absolutely smudged out) in discourses on blackness is infrequently acknowledged. The black SELF has historically been assumed male, and thus Gloria Hull, Patricia Bell-Scott, and Barbara Smith do not engage in cheap and idle rhetoric in titling their landmark anthology: *All the Women Are White, All the Blacks Are Men.* If we restrict ourselves to literary studies alone, we have ample evidence to support this observation.[12] In constructions that dominate standard accounts of an Afro-American literary canon, the "face" of the race, the "speaking subject," is male.[13]

Black feminists are helping to redraw these limited boundaries and to move the discourses on blackness to terrains beyond those whose topographies keep us locked in opposition and antagonism. Toni Morrison's novel *Sula* (1974) is rife with liberating possibilities. It frustrates the race and image conscious critic at every turn by transgressing the rhetoric of opposition that excludes women from creative agency. Although the novel teases the reader with various oppositions—good/evil, virgin/whore, self/other—it avoids the false choices they imply and dictate. As Hortense Spillers eloquently puts it, when we read *Sula*, "no Manichean analysis demanding a polarity of interest—black/white, male/female, good/bad [and I might add, positive/negative, self/other]—will do."[14]

The narrative insistently blurs and confuses these and other binary oppositions, blurs the boundaries they create, boundaries separating us from others and rendering us "others" to ourselves. *Sula* glories in paradox and ambiguity, beginning with the prologue, which describes the setting, the Bottom, situated spatially in the top. We enter a new world here, a world in which we never get to the "bottom" of things, a world that demands a shift from a dialectical either/or orientation to one that is dialogical or both/and, full of shifts and contradictions, particularly shifting and contradictory conceptions of the SELF.

The novel questions assumptions about the SELF of Afro-American literature, opposes historical demands for the representation of a beau ideal, and offers a different set of options to critics and novelists alike. Coming significantly on the heels of the Black Power movement that rendered black women prone or the "queens" of the male warrior—an updated version of a familiar script—the narrative invites the reader to imagine a different script for women that transcends the boundaries of social and linguistic convention. Finally, *Sula* complicates the process of identification in the reading process, denying the conventional Afro-American critic a reflection of her or his ego ideal.

> Day and night are mingled in our gazes. . . . If we divide
> light from night, we give up the lightness of our

mixture. . . . We put ourselves into watertight
compartments, break ourselves up into parts, cut ourselves
in two. . . . We are always one and the other, at the same
time.

—Luce Irigaray[15]

To posit, as does *Sula,* that we are always one and the other at the same time is to effectively challenge a fundamental assumption of Western metaphysics that has historically operated in Afro-American literature and criticism: "the unity of the ego-centred individual self"[16] defined in opposition to an other.

Morrison begins by questioning traditional notions of SELF as they have been translated into narrative. She implicitly critiques such concepts as "protagonist," "hero," and "major character" by emphatically decentering and deferring the presence of Sula, the title character. Bearing *her* name, the narrative suggests that she is the protagonist, the privileged center, but her presence is constantly deferred. We are introduced to a caravan of characters—Shadrack, Nel, Helene, Eva, the Deweys, Tar Baby, Hannah, and Plum—before we get any sustained treatment of Sula. Economical to begin with, then, the novel is roughly one-third over when Sula is introduced, and it continues almost that long after her death.

Not only does the narrative deny the reader a "central" character, but it also denies the whole notion of character as static *essence,* replacing it with the idea of character as *process.*[17] Whereas the former is based on the assumption that the SELF is knowable, centered, and unified, the latter is based on the assumption that the SELF is multiple, fluid, relational, and in a perpetual state of becoming. Significantly, Sula, whose eyes are "as steady and clear as rain," is associated throughout with water, fluidity. Her birthmark, which shifts in meaning depending on the viewer's perspective, acts as metaphor for her figurative "selves," her multiple identity. To Nel, it is a "stemmed rose"; to her children, a "scary black thing," a "black mark"; to Jude, a "copperhead" and a "rattlesnake"; to Shadrack, a "tadpole." The image of the tadpole reinforces this notion of SELF as perpetually in process. Sula never achieves completeness of being. Sula dies in the foetal position, welcoming this "sleep of water," in a passage that clearly suggests she is dying yet aborning (p. 149). Morrison's reconceptualization of character has clear and direct implications for Afro-American literature and critical study, for if the SELF is perceived as perpetually in process, rather than a static entity always already formed and known, it is thereby difficult to posit its ideal or "positive" representation.

Appropriately for this conception of character as process, the narrative employs the double, a technique related, as Baruch Hoffman has observed, to the "rupturing of coherence in character."[18] It positions Nel and Sula in adolescence, a state of becoming when they are "unshaped, formless things" (p. 53) "us[ing] each other to grow on," finding "in each other's eyes the intimacy they were looking for" (p. 52). As doubles Sula and Nel complement and flow into each other, their closeness evoked throughout the narrative in physical metaphors. Sula's return to the Bottom, after a ten-year absence, is, for Nel, "like getting the use of an eye back, having a cataract removed" (p. 95). The two are likened to "two throats and one eye" (p. 147).

But while Sula and Nel are represented as two parts of a self, those parts are distinct; they are complementary, not identical. Although Sula and Nel might share a common vision (suggested by "one eye"), their needs and desires are distinct (they have "two throats").[19] Sula comes to understand the fact of their difference, as the epigraph to this essay suggests: "She clung to Nel as the closest thing to an *other* and a *self* only to discover that she and Nel were not one and the same thing." The relationship of OTHER to SELF in this passage, and throughout the narrative, must be seen as "different but connected rather than separate and opposed," to borrow from Carole Gilligan.[20]

Sula's understanding of her relationship to Nel results from self-understanding and self-intimacy, a process that Nel's marriage to Jude interrupts. Like so many women writers, Morrison equates marriage with the death of the female self and imagination. Nel would be the "someone sweet, industrious, and loyal, to shore him up . . . the two of them would make one Jude" (p. 83). After marriage she freezes into her wifely role, becoming one of the women who had "folded themselves into starched coffins" (p. 122). Her definition of self becomes based on the community's "absolute" moral categories about "good" and "bad" women, categories that result in her separation from and opposition to Sula.

The narrative anticipates that opposition in early descriptions of Nel and Sula. Nel is the color of "wet sandpaper," Sula is "heavy brown" (p. 52), a distinction that can be read as patriarchy's conventional fair lady/dark woman, virgin/whore dichotomy, one reflected in Sula's and Nel's separate matrilineages.

Sula's female heritage is an unbroken line of "manloving" women who exist as sexually desiring subjects rather than as objects of male desire. Her mother, Hannah, "ripple[s] with sex" (p. 42), exasperating the "good" women of the community who call her "nasty." But that doesn't prevent her from taking her lovers into the pantry for "some touching every day" (p. 44). In contrast, Nel's is a split heritage. On one side is her grandmother, the whore of the Sundown House, and on the other, her great-grandmother, who worshiped the Virgin Mary and counseled Helene "to be constantly on guard for any sign of her mother's wild blood" (p. 17). Nel takes her great-grandmother's counsel to heart, spending her life warding off being "turn[ed] to jelly" and "custard" (p. 22). Jelly and pudding here function as they do in Jessie Fauset's *Plum Bun,* as metaphors of sexuality drawn from the classic women's blues lyrics.

Nel's sexuality is not expressed in itself and for her own pleasure, but rather for the pleasure of her husband and in obedience to a system of ethical judgment and moral virtue, her "only mooring" (p. 139). Because Nel's sexuality is harnessed to and only enacted within the institutions that sanction sexuality for women—marriage and family—she does not own it.[21] It is impossible for her to imagine sex without Jude. After she finds him and Sula in the sex act, she describes her thighs—the metaphor for her sexuality—as "empty and dead . . . and it was Sula who had taken the life from them." She concludes that "the both of them . . . left her with no thighs and no heart, just her brain raveling away" (p. 110).

Without Jude, Nel thinks her thighs are useless. Her sexuality is harnessed to duty and virtue in a simple cause/effect relationship, as is clear from the plaintive questions she puts to an imaginary God after Jude leaves:

> even if I sew up those old pillow cases and rinse down the porch and feed
> my children and beat the rugs and haul the coal up out of the bin even
> then nobody. . . . I could be a mule or plow the furrows with my hands if
> need be or hold these rickety walls up with my back if I knew that
> somewhere in this world in the pocket of some night I could open my legs
> to some cowboy lean hips but you are trying to tell me no and O my
> sweet Jesus, what kind of cross is that? (p. 111)

Sula, on the other hand, "went to bed with men as frequently as she could" (p. 122) and assumed responsibility for her own pleasure. In her first sexual experience with Ajax—significantly, a reenactment of Hannah's sexual rituals in the pantry—Sula "stood wide-legged against the wall and pulled from his track-lean hips all the pleasure her thighs could hold" (p. 125). This is not to suggest that Sula's sexual expression is uncomplicated or unproblematic, but rather, that unlike Nel's, it is not attached to anything outside herself, especially not to social definitions of female sexuality and conventions of duty. Although initially she "liked the sootiness of sex," liked "to think of it as wicked" (p. 122), she comes to realize that it was not wicked. Further, apart from bringing her "a special kind of joy," it brought her "misery and the ability to feel deep sorrow" and "a stinging awareness of the endings of things" (p. 122, 123), a feeling of "her own abiding strength and limitless power" (p. 123). [In other words, Sula's sexuality is neither located in the realm of "moral" abstractions nor expressed within the institution of marriage that legitimates it for women. Rather, it is in the realm of sensory experience and in the service of the self-exploration that leads to self-intimacy.]After sex, Sula enters that "post-coital privateness in which she met herself, welcomed herself, and joined herself in matchless harmony" (p. 123).

Unlike Nel, Sula has no ego and therefore does not feel the ego's "compulsion . . . to be consistent with herself" (p. 119). In describing her, Morrison notes that Sula "is experimental with herself [and] perfectly willing to think the unthinkable thing."[22] For Sula, "there was only her own mood and whim," enabling her to explore "that version of herself which she sought to reach out to and touch with an ungloved hand," "to discover it and let others become as intimate with their own selves as she was" (p. 121).

Not only is sexual expression an act of self-exploration, but it is also associated throughout the narrative with creativity, as seen in the long prose poem Sula creates while making love to Ajax. But, significantly, that creativity is without sufficient outlet within her community. According to Morrison, "If Sula had any sense she'd go somewhere and sing or get into show business," implying that her "strangeness," her "lawlessness" can only be sanctioned in a world like the theater.[23] Because of her community's rigid norms for women, Sula's impulses cannot be absorbed. Without an "art form," her "tremendous curiosity and gift for metaphor" become destructive (p. 121). Without art forms, Sula is the artist become her own work of art.[24] As she responds defiantly to Eva's injunction that she make babies to settle herself, "I don't want to make somebody else. I want to make myself" (p. 92).

Because she resists self-exploration, such creativity is closed to Nel. She has no "sparkle or splutter," just a "dull glow" (p. 83). Her imagination has been driven "underground" from years of obeying the normative female script. She "belonged to the town and all of its ways" (p. 120). The narrative strongly suggests that one cannot belong to the community and preserve the imagination, for the orthodox vocations for women—marriage and motherhood—restrict, if not preclude, imaginative expression.

Obedience to community also precludes intimacy with self for women. Nel rejects this intimacy that involves confronting what both Sula and Shadrack have confronted: the unknown parts of themselves. In turning her back on the unknown, Nel fails to grow, to change, or to learn anything about herself until the last page of the novel. She thinks that "hell is change" (p. 108). "One of the last true pedestrians" in the Bottom, Nel walks on the road's shoulder (on its edge, not on the road), "allowing herself to accept rides only when the weather required it" (p. 166).

Nel fits Thomas Docherty's description of the type of character who is "fixed and centred upon one locatable ego," blocking "the possibility of authentic response, genuine sentiment." According to this ego-centered schema, "the self can only act in accord with a determined and limited 'characteristic' response" (*Reading (Absent) Character,* p. 80). Whereas Sula is an ambiguous character with a repertoire of responses along a continuum and thus cannot be defined as either totally "good" or "bad," Nel's is a limited response: "goodness," "rightness," as her name, "Wright," suggests. As it is classically defined for women, "goodness" is sexual faithfulness, self-abnegation, and the idealization of marriage and motherhood.

After years of nursing the belief that Sula has irreparably wronged her and violated their friendship, Nel goes to visit Sula on her deathbed as any "good woman" would do. "Virtue," "her only mooring," has hidden "from her the true motives for her charity" (p. 139). Their conversation, after years of estrangement, is peppered with references to good and evil, right and wrong. Nel protests, "I was good to you, Sula, why don't that matter?" And Sula responds in her characteristically defiant way: "Being good to somebody is just like being mean to somebody. Risky. You don't get nothing for it." Exasperated because "talking to [Sula] about right and wrong" (pp. 144–45) was impossible, Nel leaves, but not before Sula has the last word. And significantly, that last word takes the form of a question, an uncertainty, not an unambiguous statement of fact or truth:

> "How you know?" Sula asked.
> "Know what?" Nel still wouldn't look at her.
> "About who was good. How you know it was you?"
> "What you mean?"
> "I mean maybe it wasn't you. Maybe it was me." (p. 146)

In the space of the narrative Nel has another twenty-five years to deflect the contemplation of Sula's question through desperate acts of goodness: visits to "the sick and shut in," the category on the back page of black church bulletins that pull on the cords of duty. But on one such mission to visit Eva, Nel is confronted with not only the question but Eva's more unsettling suggestion that Nel's guilt in Chicken Little's death as well as her kinship to Sula.

> "Tell me how you killed that little boy."
> "What? What little boy?"
> "The one you threw in the water . . ."
> "I didn't throw no little boy in the river. That was Sula."
> "You, Sula. What's the difference?" (p. 168)

After years of repression, Nel must own her complicity in Chicken Little's drowning, a complicity that is both sign and symbol of the disowned piece of herself. She recalls the incident in its fullness, remembering "the good feeling she had had when Chicken's hands slipped" (p. 170) and "the tranquillity that follow[ed] [that] joyful stimulation" (p. 170). That remembrance makes space for Nel's psychic reconnection with Sula as friend as well as symbol of that disowned self. Significantly, that reconnection occurs in the cemetery, a metaphor for Nel's buried shadow. The "circles and circles of sorrow" she cries at narrative's end prepare her for what Sula strained to experience throughout her life: the process of mourning and remembering, remembering and mourning, that leads to intimacy with self, the root and source of intimacy with others. And the reader must mourn as Nel mourns, must undergo the process of development that Nel undergoes.[25] And as with Nel, that process begins with releasing the static and coherent conception of SELF and embracing what Sula represents: the SELF as process and fluid possibility. That embrace enables an altered understanding of the nature of identification in the reading process.

Recent theories of the act of reading have enriched and complicated—for the good—our understanding of what takes place in the act of reading. They have described the reading process as dialogical, as an interaction between a reader (a SELF) and an OTHER, an interaction in which neither remains the same.[26] In light of this information, we can conceive the act of reading as a process of self-exploration that the narrative strategies of *Sula* compel. What strategies does the narrative employ to generate that process? It deliberately miscues the reader, disappointing the very expectations that the narrative arouses, forcing the reader to shift gears, to change perspective. Though these strategies might well apply to all readers, they have specific implications for Afro-American critics.

Sula threatens readers' assumptions and disappoints their expectations at every turn. It begins by disappointing the reader's expectations of a "realistic" and unified narrative documenting black/white confrontation.

The novel's prologue, which describes a community's destruction by white greed and deception, gestures toward "realistic" documentation, and leads the reader to expect familiar black/white confrontation. But that familiar and expected plot is backgrounded. Foregrounded are the characters whose lives transcend their social circumstances. They laugh, they dance, they sing, and are "mightily preoccupied with earthly things—and each other" (p. 6). The narrative retreats from linearity privileged in the realist mode. Though dates title its chapters, they relate only indirectly to its central concerns and do not permit the reader to use chronology to interpret the novel's events in any simple cause/effect fashion. In other words, the story's forward movement in time is deliberately nonsequential and without explicit reference to "real" time. The narrative roves lightly over historical events, dates, and details, as seen in the first chapter. Titled "1919," the chapter begins with a reference to World War II, then refers, in quick and, paradoxically, regressive succession, to National Suicide Day, instituted in 1920, then backwards to Shadrack running across a battlefield in France in World War I.

In addition, the narrative forces us to question our readings, to hold our judgment in check, and to continually revise it. Susan Blake is on the mark when she says that "the reader never knows quite what to think" of characters and events in *Sula:* "whether to applaud Eva's self-sacrifice or deplore her tyranny, whether to admire Sula's freedom or condemn her heartlessness."[27] The narrative is neither an apology for Sula's destruction nor an unsympathetic critique of Nel's smug conformity. It does not reduce a complex sex of dynamics to a simple opposition or choice between two "pure" alternatives.

Among the strategies Morrison uses to complicate choice and block judgment are the dots within dots (. . . .) in the narrative that mark time breaks and function as stop signs. They compel the reader to pause, think back, evaluate the narrative's events, and formulate new expectations in light of them, expectations that are never quite fulfilled.[28]

The Afro-American critic, wanting a world cleansed of uncertainty and contradictions and based on rhetorical polarities—positive and negative— might ask in frustration, "Can we ever determine the right judgment?" The narrative implies that the answer can only come from within, from exploring all parts of the SELF. As Nel asks Eva in the scene mentioned earlier, "You think I'm guilty?" Eva whispers, "Who would know that better than you?" (p. 169).

Not only does the narrative disappoint the reader's expectations of correct answers and appropriate judgment, but it also prevents a stable and unified reading of the text, though I have fabricated one here by tracing a dominant thread in the narrative: the relationship between SELF and OTHER. But in exploring this relationship, Morrison deliberately provides echoing passages that cancel each other out, that thwart the reader's desire for stability and consistency. You will recall the passage, "She clung to Nel as the closest thing to both an other and a self, only to discover that she and Nel were not one and the same thing." But the following passage, which comes much later in the narrative, effectively cancels this passage out: Sula learned that "there was no other that you could count on . . . [and] there was no *self* to count on either."

The novel's fragmentary, episodic, elliptical quality helps to thwart textual unity, to prevent a totalized interpretation. An early reviewer described the text as a series of scenes and glimpses, each "written . . . from scratch." Since none of them has anything much to do with the ones that preceded them, "we can never piece the glimpses into a coherent picture."[29] Whatever coherence and meaning reside in the narrative, the reader must struggle to create.

The gaps in the text allow for the reader's participation in the creation of meaning in the text. Morrison has commented on the importance of the "affective and participatory relationship between the artist and the audience," and her desire "to have the reader work *with* the author in the construction of the book." She adds, "What is left out is as important as what is there."[30]

The reader must fill in the narrative's many gaps; for instance: Why is there no funeral for either Plum or Hannah? What happens to Jude? Where *was* Eva during her eighteen-month absence from the Bottom? What really happened to her leg? How does Sula support herself after she returns from her ten-year absence?[31] The reader's participation in the meaning-making process helps to fill in the gaps in the text, as well as to bridge the gaps separating the reader *from* the text. This returns us full circle to the problem posed at the beginning of this essay: the boundary separating some Afro-American readers from the black text that opposes a single, unified image of the black SELF.

As Norman Holland and others have noted, each reader has a vision of the world arising from her/his identity theme. In the act of reading, the reader tries to recreate the text according to that identity theme. As we read, Holland continues, we use the "literary work to symbolize and finally to replicate ourselves, to reflect ourselves, to affirm ourselves by denying or demeaning the other."[32] But, writing in a different context, Holland usefully suggests that "one of literature's adaptive functions . . . is that it allows us to loosen boundaries between self and not self."[33]

Transgressing that boundary and viewing identity and the SELF in relation, rather than coherent, separate, and opposed, permits an analogous view of identification in the reading process. Just as the SELF is fluid, dynamic, and formed in relation, so is identification a process involving a dialogue between the SELF and the "otherness" of writers, texts, literary characters, and interpretive communities.

Such a dialogic model of reading can serve not only students of Afro-American literature, but literary studies more widely. Appropriating the insights of a recent essay, let me suggest that "dialogic reading would not generally reduce others to consistent dialectical counterparts. . . . Nor would it minimize others as rhetorical opponents by attempting to discredit them." We must understand that our "self-worlds" can and do impinge on one another, that our meanings and motives are not always present to us, and that "the diversity of critical and theoretical voices is not an issue to be settled or a problem to be resolved but . . . a conversation to be constructed and entered."[34] Such a model is especially urgent when we consider that the work of black women writers overflows the boundaries of a narrowly defined "black community" into the circuit of discourses surrounding it. In other words, writings by black women are surrounded by what we might call "boundary" texts. These include, as Hortense Spillers has observed, "the various mechanisms of institutional and media life, including conferences, the lecture platform, the television talk show."[35]

If we would approach that "unified" black community splintered, many argue, by black women writers' imaginative daring, the boundaries of our "self-worlds" and the rigid identity themes and fantasies holding them up must be crossed. After all, as *Sula* playfully suggests, our conceptions of who we are never embrace *all* that we are. Venturing, then, one answer to the first epigraph: "What shall we call our 'self'?"—we shall call our*selves* by many names. Our metaphors of SELF cannot rest in stasis, but must glory in and overflow into everything that belongs to us.

1988

In his response in Afro-American Literary Study in the 1990s, *Michael Awkward suggested that "Boundaries" offered "potentially injurious consequences for the future of Afro-American feminist criticism," its dangers lying mainly in what he perceived to be my rejection of "race and culture as necessary guides in the analysis of black literary texts." I would suggest, for starters, that, rather than rejecting "race and culture," which Awkward conflates and uses interchangeably, I attempted to challenge an epistemology of race that operates mainly at the expense of repressing one gender, evident in the historical view that the "racial self" is paradigmatically and essentially male.*

Awkward's appeal to "race and culture," important though it is, treats each as self-evident and self-explanatory, as the end rather than the beginning of a discussion. Such a discussion would, of necessity, proceed from the concession that our ideas of race and culture—black style—are intrinsically incomplete and thus, far from assuming any final and unassailable explanatory power. But, more importantly, Awkward does little more than assert on the basis of a collection of isolated, inert examples that racial and cultural differences exist. He appropriates a faintly anthropological or fetishistic view of culture, reminiscent of what Frantz Fanon described as early as 1959 in his address to the Second Congress of Black Artists and Writers in Rome.

> *The culture that the intellectual leans toward is often no more than a stock of particularisms. He wishes to attach himself to the people; but instead he only catches hold of their outer garments.*[36]

The particularisms in Awkward's response here are black musical and sermonic traditions that promote the much cited and idealized participatory model "call and response," a term that he deems more appropriate than "dialogism." In Awkward's reckoning, the former preserves the "funkiness" of "blackness" while the latter throws it away.

In advancing this argument, Awkward succumbs to the very intellectual tendency I sought to question: the attempt to mold and compress the sweep of African American cultural expressions and production into the shape and image of a particular "ideal" that quickly becomes the one "true identity" to be maintained at all costs and secured from "outside" interference and influence. In his response, that "outside" influence is poststructuralism.

In Awkward's view, my critical stance in "Boundaries" signals a shift from a previous grounding in the text of "blackness" to an "energetically poststructuralist flight." And thus, to answer his appeals to "race," "culture," "wholeness," "community" by arguing that these categories are all constructs, tropes, writing about writing that bears the stamp and betrays the vanity of human wishes, is to seem to engage in the very commonplaces and axioms of "poststructuralist flight" of which he accuses me.

But perhaps his criticism might first be met at its most vulnerable point: the boundaries he constructs for recent critical history and the position of poststructuralism within them. Poststructuralism, in his response, operates much like "race" and "culture" as a self-evident unity, although what

Raymond Williams says of modernism could, with slight adaptation, apply as well to poststructuralism: it is the "most frustratingly unspecific, unperiodizing of all the major art-historical 'isms' or concepts . . ."[37] *We could argue, then, that poststructuralism, understood as a late-twentieth-century "discipline," or critical "practice," is by no means containable within these specific boundaries. Further, the marks by which we identify "it" can be traced much further back in time. If we take only one category of concern to Awkward—race—something of the problematics of establishing boundaries and distinct critical identities emerges with crystal clarity.*

Although Awkward attributes my concerns with exploring racial self-difference to the influences of poststructuralism on my thinking, he could just as easily have attributed these concerns to early-twentieth-century precursors. In his essay "Miscegenation," for example, W. E. B. Du Bois asks, "What is race?" and answers that "A racial type is after all but an artificial concept." Or we could invoke Du Bois's response to Roland A. Barton, a high school student who wrote to him to express his concern that the word "Negro," used to designate a "racial" type, was a "white man's word to make us feel inferior." In his response to the young man, Du Bois cautioned him against "the all too common error of mistaking names for things." Du Bois continued,

Names are only conventional signs for identifying things. Things are the reality that counts. If a thing is despised, either because of ignorance or because it is despicable, you will not alter matters by changing its name. If men despise Negroes, they will not despise them less if Negroes are called "colored" or "Afro-Americans."

Du Bois concludes, "Your real work, my dear young man, does not lie with names."[38]

Similarly, Nella Larsen and other Harlem Renaissance writers effectively exposed the cultural construction of race in their novels of passing. As one character says in Passing, *"Everything can't be explained by some general biological phrase" (p. 186). Given these random examples, can we conclude that to speak of "races" as verbal fiats that gain their power precisely from habitual usage and repetition of unanimous assent, is to engage in a "poststructuralist flight?"*

The point of invoking these examples about race is not to engage in intellectual one-upmanship or what Anthony Appiah terms "alternative genealogizing," for in this game, as Appiah astutely notes, we "end up always in the same place; the achievement is to have invented a different past." Make no mistake, then, my aim is decidedly not to have invented a different past for poststructuralism and to color it black, but rather to underscore something of the possibilities, but more the limitations, of this way of thinking.

Awkward wants to preserve the very idea of impermeable boundaries, although these boundaries keep colliding into each other with each turn of the critical and historical wheel. And while I am in sympathy with his question, does "Afro-American adoption of the type of interactive, dialogical relationships with other critical schools . . . require the critical erasure of the significance of racial and cultural differences in discussions of black texts?" I am much less certain than he of just how these "differences" translate into "discussions of black texts" beyond assertions that this or that reference, trope, technique, or theme is "black" in origin and essence. Put another way, what do we gain by arguing that the metaphor of flying that structures Song of Solomon *"belongs" more to an African than to a Greek mythological tradition? This all smacks of what Anthony Appiah and others call "nativism," a reference to impulses among certain intellectuals to prescribe for postcolonial African literatures "their own" critical theories and methods. He asks, "What exactly—in the postcolonial context—is the content of the nativist's injunction to read literature by means of a theory drawn from the text's own cultural or intellectual inheritance?" and points to the limitations of this injunction: "It ignores the multiplicity of the heritage of the modern African writer."[39]*

Anyone who has read Toni Morrison and Alice Walker has indeed discovered the dense web of reference and allusion, both direct and indirect, to a wide-ranging literary and cultural "heritage." Here, Barbara Johnson's response to Henry Louis Gates's "Canon-Formation, Literary History, and the Afro-American Tradition" is also pertinent:

> *The terms "black" and "white" often imply a relation of mutual exclusion. This binary model is based on two fallacies: the fallacy of positing the existence of pure, unified, and separate traditions, and the fallacy of spatialization. It is as though cultural differences were simply modeled after the spatial or geographical differences that often give rise to them, as if there could really remain such a thing as cultural apartheid, once cultures enter into dialogue, or conflict. . . . But spatial models are simply not adequate for cultural and linguistic phenomena. Cultures are not containable within boundaries.*

Johnson acknowledges, and I agree, that while new models are needed to describe the "signifying black difference," such models would inevitably acknowledge the "ineradicable trace of Western culture within Afro-American culture (and vice versa)."[40] There just is no more logical way.

But that said, we have not yet exhausted the full implications of Awkward's pressing and important concerns about whether "the commendable desire for critical dialogue . . . necessitate[s] that we bracket cultural difference" (p. 77). To simply say that a variety of intellectual traditions can be incorporated in "discussions of black texts" does not answer that institutional dimension that Awkward leaves aside in his critique. His desire to see that expressions of "cultural difference" found critical positions on African American literature can be interpreted both as a legitimate intellectual concern and as an underlying anxiety, which I share, about the institutionalization of poststructuralism in contemporary academic life and the effects of its hegemony on so-called marginal literatures. It is to this dimension that I turn in the final two chapters.

7

Reading Family Matters[1]

They were a family somehow and he was not the
head of it.
                                    —Toni Morrison, *Beloved*

The wish is father to the thought.
                                                —Proverb

It is not late-breaking news that literary criticism is another form of story-telling, of mythmaking. Nor is it news that literary texts take shape in the minds of readers and critics who form disparate interpretive communities. These communities are held together by shared assumptions, values, and desires that influence, if not determine, *what* they see when they read and *how* they receive and represent what they read. Or, to borrow from Mary Louise Pratt, reading and reception are "socially and ideologically deter-mined process[es]."[2] I would like to use these commonplace insights as departure points in a brief meditation on one interpretive community—primarily male—and its reading and reception of a group of contemporary black female writers—those published since the 1970s. More specifically, I would like to focus on the controversial and adhesive charge surrounding their work: that it portrays black males in an "unflinchingly candid and often negative manner" as "thieves, sadists, rapists, and ne-er-do-wells."[3]

Let me review and expand upon the observations from the last chapter. First, this debate has been waged primarily in the popular, white, East Coast literary media—*The New York Times Book Review, The New York Review of Books, New York Times Magazine*—though it has also spread to academic journals and scholarly collections. Second, for all its intensity, the debate has centered primarily on a very small sample of writers: Toni Morrison, Gayl Jones, Ntozake Shange, and, most frequently, Alice Walker. Finally, but perhaps most importantly, it has tended to polarize (though not neatly) along gender lines. With few exceptions, female readers see an implicit affirmation of *black women*, while males see a programmatic assault on black men, though I grant that these two responses are not mutually exclusive.[4]

Why focus on a debate that seems to have outlived its interest and usefulness? Why focus on a controversy that has in no way affected the reputations of the writers in question? Why spend time picking apart straw men whose arguments are so easily discredited? Why? Because for all their questionable arguments, from the perspective of readers more informed, these are men whose judgments help influence the masses of readers largely untutored in Afro-American literature, who take their cues of what and how to read from *The New York Times Book Review, The New York Review of Books,* and other organs of the literary establishment. As Richard Ohmann notes, *The New York Times Book Review* has "several times the audience of any other literary periodical" in the United States, a circulation that grants it a powerful and prestigious role in mediating the terms by which the writers and writings it selects will be received and understood. Further, periodicals such as *The New York Times Book Review* work with their counterparts—the college classroom and academic journal—and together they become, Ohmann adds, "the final arbiters of literary merit and even of survival."[5]

The route Ohmann traces from prestigious literary journal to academic journal to college classroom to literary survival is surely not so direct, but it is useful nonetheless for mapping some of the salient points and problems of this debate. Finally, to borrow from Cathy Davidson, there is an "unequal distribution of story time" in this debate.[6] Mainly, we see men telling *their* stories about the writings of black women but seldom a counter-response from a woman. While I do not presume to resolve the tensions on either side, I think that the debate over contemporary writings by black women might profit from my attempt to uncover and suggest something of what is fundamentally at issue.

Lest what follows be read as the critical companion of the alleged fictional attack on black men, let me rush to point out that here follows no composite portrait of "*the* black male reader." Because all readers experience and express complex and often contradictory positions, it is naive to suggest that any readership, male or female, can be so simply abstracted. It is possible and necessary, however, even despite dangers and limitations of a different sort, to historicize readers, to refer, after Paul Smith, "to specific modes of production, to definite societies at historically specific moments and conjunctures."[7] That is my modest attempt here.

I will leave aside for the moment speculations about why the most influential literary publications tend mainly to employ black men to review and comment on the literature of black women, as well as speculations about whose interests are really served in this debate. While these are certainly interesting questions, I am more interested here in what this debate illuminates about the inflections of gendered ideologies in the reading process.[8] As Maureen Quilligan rightly argues, "To pose questions about the gender of the reader is to pose questions that open the texts' relations to the political arrangements of their audiences."[9] The relation between this specific group of readers and the texts they review might be seen as the product of certain political arrangements. One could argue, for example, that the shifting power relations between black men and women in the literary sphere informs and partly explains the terms of this controversy, terms defined mainly by black men.

If this debate is but part of the design of a larger pattern, it is useful to trace it, if only telescopically. Actually, this is the second round of a debate sparked in 1976 by the blockbuster success of Ntozake Shange's choreopoem *for colored girls who have considered suicide when the rainbow is enuf.* It spread with the publication of Michele Wallace's *Black Macho and the Myth of the Superwoman* (1980).[10] These two works were the subject of widespread and acrimonious debate from many sectors of the black community. Vernon Jarret of the *Chicago Defender* likened *for colored girls* to the pro–Ku Klux Klan film *Birth of a Nation* and dismissed it as "a degrading treatment of the black male" and "a mockery of the black family." Perhaps the most controversial statement about Shange and Wallace, however, was an article by Robert Staples, "The Myth of Black Macho: A Response to Angry Black Feminists," published in *The Black Scholar* in March/April 1979. Identified significantly as "the noted *sociologist* on black sex roles," Staples reflects in his essay a tendency in the current debate (as in most discussions of Afro-American literature) to read literature in terms that are overwhelmingly sociological.[11]

Staples argues that Shange and Wallace were rewarded for their "diatribes again black men," charging *for colored girls* with whetting black women's "collective appetite for black male blood." He attributes their rage, which "happily married women" lack, to "pent up frustrations which need release." And he sympathizes with the black male need for power in the only two institutions left to black control: the church and the family.

During the 1960s, Staples continues, "there was a general consensus—among men and women—that black men would hold the leadership positions in the movement." Because "black women had held up their men far too long, it was time for the men to take charge." But as those like Shange and Wallace came under the powerful sway of the white feminist movement, he continues, they unleashed the anger black women had always borne silently. For releasing this anger, he concludes, they were promoted and rewarded by the white media.[12]

À la Freud, I categorize this story that Staples tells as a family romance, defined by Janet Beizer as the "attempt to rewrite origins, to replace the unsatisfactory fragments of a . . . past by a totalizing fiction" that recuperates loss and fulfills desire.[13] This family romance is de-romanticized in writings by the majority of black women. Text meets counter-text, and the conflict might be described, to borrow from Christine Froula, as the confrontation between the "daughter's story and the father's law." Froula argues compellingly that "the relations of literary daughters and fathers resemble . . . the model . . . describ[ing] the family situation of incest victims: a dominating, authoritarian father; an absent, ill, or complicitous mother; and a daughter who [is] prohibited by her father from speaking about abuse."[14]

Not surprisingly, it is for narrating, for representing male abuses within "the family," that contemporary black women are most roundly criticized in the family plots that follow. Though this narrative of the family romance inserted itself most aggressively in the discourse of the 1960s, this story of the Black Family cum Black Community headed by the Black Male who does battle with an oppressive White world continues to be told, though in ever more subtle variations. In Staples's version, as in the other essays discussed here, the rupture in the unified community, the haven against white racism, is the white woman offering the fruit of feminist knowledge.[15]

While his story has a subtlety that Staples's lacks, David Bradley's enlists the same rhetoric of family to argue that "Alice Walker has a high level of enmity toward black men." In "Telling the Black Woman's Story," published in the *New York Times Magazine* in January 1984, Bradley sets out to explain this enmity through pop psychobiography, tracing Walker's antagonism toward black men to a childhood accident when her brother shot her with a BB gun. "After that accident," Bradley explains, "she felt her family had failed her," specifically her father.[16]

Philip Royster goes Bradley one better to argue, in an obvious riff on her famous essay, that Walker "may be in search of not so much our mothers' gardens as our fathers' protecting arms." Royster reads all of her fiction as an example of Walker's desire "to be the darling of older men and her bitterness toward younger ones." He compares her work to Morrison's, in which "if a woman learns to be a daughter, then she will be able to be a wife to a black man and a mother to black children and a nurturer and preserver of black people."[17] Just which work by Morrison he has in mind here, I am not sure, since so much of Morrison's work features what Susan Willis calls "three-women households" that do not permit "male domination to be the determining principle for living and working relationships of the group."[18] The epigraph from *Beloved* alludes to another of these three-women households: "They were a family somehow and he was not the head of it."

Apart from their attempt to psychoanalyze Walker, using the language of family, the essays by Bradley and Royster reach a common conclusion and judgment: Walker's involvement with feminism has placed her outside the family of the larger black "community." In Bradley's essay there are repeated references to Gloria Steinem, feminism, and *Ms.* magazine, a world that he likens to a "steam-driven meat grinder, and [Walker] the tenderest of meat."[19]

Royster would like to see her escape the meat grinder, would like to welcome Walker back to what he calls "the extended family, the unity of the tribe," but on one condition: she, along with other black women, "may have to feel a greater loyalty toward black men . . . than toward women throughout the world."[20]

Mel Watkins offers another variety of a domestic story transplanted in critical soil. His much-discussed "Sexism, Racism, and Black Women Writers" continues to fuel the charge that black women writers "have chosen black men as a target" of attack. In so doing, they "have set themselves outside the tradition that is nearly as old as black American literature itself." They have broken an "unspoken but almost universally accepted covenant among black writers . . . to present positive images of blacks."[21]

In Watkins's version of the family romance, Afro-American literary history is written in a way that emphasizes family unity. Here we have a family of *writers* who were unified until contemporary black women decided, in Watkins's words, that "sexism is more oppressive than racism." In his abridged new literary history, the ancestral keepers of the tradition are William Wells Brown, W. E. B. Du Bois, James Weldon Johnson, and Richard Wright, all of whom shared a commitment to "establishing humane, positive images of blacks." Though a negative character, according to Watkins, even Bigger Thomas "is presented within a context," absent in black women's writings, that "elucidated the social or psychological circumstances that motivate" Bigger.[22] True enough. How else could the reader of any gender absorb the narration of Bigger's enjoyment of the "agony" he inflicts on his girlfriend, Bessie? He enjoys "seeing and feeling the worth of himself in her bewildered desperation." And after he bludgeons her to death with a brick and throws her body down the airshaft, it occurs to him that he has done a "dumb thing"—"throwing her away with all that money in her pocket."[23]

I cite this passage not to take the cheap route of tit for tat, but to suggest something about the critical double standard that glosses over the representation of violence, rape, and battering in Richard Wright's work and installs him in a "family portrait" of black writers but highlights that representation in *The Bluest Eye, The Third Life of Grange Copeland,* and *The Color Purple,* to justify "disinheritance." Watkins's literary history conforms strikingly to what Marilyn Butler describes in her essay "Against Tradition: The Case for a Particularized Historical Method." Butler argues forcefully that

> traditions are features of all regularized practices in all societies, for they
> are a basic tool of selecting and ordering the past in order to validate
> activities and people in the present. The literary critic calls on tradition
> when he draws up a genealogy or family tree of writers. . . . Transmission
> down the line is usually described as easy and harmonious, though there is
> often a gap, which tends to occur near to the present day.[24]

The gap in Watkins's family tree of writers is created by the contemporary black *feminist* writers who are the subject of his essay.

Watkins's rhetoric of boundaries, parameters, of public speech about private matters figures as well in Darryl Pinckney's essay "Black Victims, Black Villains," which appeared in the January 29, 1987 issue of *The New York Review of Books.* Following its appearance, I was led to conclude that Pinckney's essay was the winter season's family narrative, and Watkins's the summer season's, in this open season on contemporary black women writers in the establishment literary media.

Pinckney attempts a joint review of Walker's *The Color Purple,* Spielberg's film adaptation, and Ishmael Reed's novel *Reckless Eyeballing.* Why it was published in the first place is unclear, since *The Color Purple* had already been reviewed in *The New York Review of Books,* along with Ishmael Reed's novel *The Terrible Twos.*[25] Pinckney repeats this media match featuring Reed and Walker but with a new twist on the family plot. This time it is the black male locked outside the family fold, and, borrowing from Morrison's *The Bluest Eye,* "his own kin had done it."

The first part of the three-part essay reads *The Color Purple,* book and film, as stories of excessive violence that present black women as the helpless victims of brutal black men. Part two briefly reviews *Reckless Eyeballing,* after a disproportionately long preface anatomizing the deterioration of the Civil Rights Movement and the simultaneous rise of U.S. feminism. This shift "had a strong effect on Afro-American literature," Pinckney argues. "Black women writers seemed to find their voices and audiences" while "black men seemed to lose theirs." One such loser is Ishmael Reed, a thinly disguised Ian Ball in *Reckless Eyeballing.* Ball, a black playwright, has been "sex-listed" for not writing according to the feminist line and may well be the Flower Phantom who shaves the heads of black women whom he believes to be "collaborating with the enemies of black men."[26] Pinckney calls this subplot "a little nasty" and rushes to quote a long passage from the novel describing such a collaboration.

In part three Pinckney returns to *The Color Purple* and the Walker/Spielberg connection and links the work with other "highly insular stories" told by Hurston, Morrison, and Gayl Jones in which the white world has disappeared and with it the reason for the "struggling black families" whose stories these novels tell. The ideology of this organization should not go unnoticed, for it cleverly and subtly replicates Pinckney's argument. His review of Reed has been compressed and eclipsed, veritably sandwiched between Walker and Spielberg. The victims and villains of part one trade places in part two, as black males become the victims of a partnership between Alice Walker and Steven Spielberg, a black woman and a white man. Their power to eliminate the publishing options of the black male is made pointedly and metaphorically clear by part three, in which Reed has been erased altogether. An old folk expression reasserts itself here—"the freest people on earth are a black woman and a white man"—to explain the vagaries of the literary marketplace.[27]

Haki Madhubuti's reading of the U.S. publishing industry centers not on how and why it has excluded black men, but rather on how it has neglected some black women. In two essays on Sonia Sanchez and Lucile Clifton, Madhubuti explains their critical neglect in terms of "the exchange nature of the game played daily in the publishing world; the only business more ruthless and corrupted is Congress." Clifton is neglected because she "does not live in New York, may not have 'connections' with reviewers nor possess Madison Avenue visibility."[28] Likewise, Sanchez "does not have the national celebrity that her work and seriousness demand" because "she does not compromise her values, her art, or her people for fame or gold."[29]

In these two essays Madhubuti relies on archetypal distinctions between "good" and "bad" women, accordingly reserving condemnations for some (Alice Walker, Toni Morrison, and Ntozake Shange) and commendations for others (Lucile Clifton, Sonia Sanchez, Mari Evans, and, Gwendolyn Brooks). And one does not have to search for the *real* basis for the distinctions: attitudes about family. He praises Sonia Sanchez and Lucile Clifton for being "cultural workers" who refuse to "become literary and physical prostitutes" in order to "make it." He takes care to note that for Sanchez, writing poetry is combined with "raising ... her children, maintaining a home, [and] working fourteen-hour days." Her poetry, he continues, "highlights Black women as mothers, sisters, lovers, wives, workers, and warriors" committed to the "Black family and the Black woman's role in building a better world." "In a real fight," he concludes, Sanchez is "the type of black woman you would want at your side."[30]

In his essay on Clifton, the references to family proliferate. Madhubuti begins by describing Clifton as a "full-time wife, overtime mother, part-time street activist and writer of small treasures" whose focus is "the children, the family." He even speculates that she suffers neglect because "the major body of her work is directed toward children." He commends Clifton for her "unusually significant and sensitive" treatment of black male characters, ascribing it to "her relationship with her father, brothers, husband, and sons. Generally, positive relationships produce positive results." In his closing passages, Madhubuti tellingly quotes Clifton's poem "to a dark moses," demonstrating unambiguously the ideological basis of his critique: "you are the one I am lit for / come with your rod that twists and is a serpent / I am the bush / I am burning / I am not consumed." Not surprisingly, Madhubuti concludes, "I am excited about [Clifton's] work because she reflects me; she tells my story."[31] With this gesture Madhubuti unwittingly reveals a central tendency and irony in this debate. In the name of the black family and the survival of the larger black community, there is a thinly disguised desire for personal, individual gratification and reflection.

What is the legible subtext of these men's readings of black women writers? Let me make a direct and certainly predictable claim: this debate over black women writers' portrayal of black males is not principally about *this* issue (if it is at all). Rather, what lies behind this smokescreen is an unacknowledged jostling for space in the literary marketplace (certainly apparent in the essays by Haki Madhubuti mentioned above) that brings to mind Hawthorne's famous complaint about the "damn'd mob of scribbling women" of the 1850s. Furthermore, to enlist Judith Fetterley's remarks from a different context, this debate is a lament for "the sense of power derived from the experience of perceiving one's self as central, as subject, as literally because literarily the point of view from which the world is seen." This community of readers brings to the reading of black women's texts a complex of powerful assumptions, not the least of which is "the equation of textuality with masculine subjectivity and masculine point of view."[32] This equation has operated historically in discourses about blackness. Calvin Hernton does well to note that

> historically, the battle line of racial struggle in the U.S. has been drawn exclusively as a struggle between the men of the races. Everything having to do with race has been defined and counter-defined by the men as a question of whether black people were or were not a race of Men. The central concept and the universal metaphor around which all aspects of the racial situation revolve is "Manhood."[33]

It should not go unnoticed that critics leading the debate have lumped all black women writers together and have focused on one tiny aspect— the image of black men—of their immensely complex and diverse project, despite the fact that if we can claim a center for these texts, it is located in the complexities of black female subjectivity and experience. In other words, though black women writers have made *black women* the subjects of their own family stories, these male readers/critics are attempting to usurp that place for themselves and place themselves at the center of critical inquiry.

The desire of these black male readers to see themselves reflected favorably back to themselves is aggressively unfulfilled in the work of contemporary black women's literature. And the ideas and ideals of masculinity and femininity upheld by the nuclear family deeply entangled in this desire are actively opposed in black women's literature. This emphatic desire for the family's recuperation and the father's restitution to his "rightful" place within it, surges ironically at the very moment that this vision and version of family seem forever out of reach. In other words, as the fabric of the nuclear family progressively frays, the desire to be enfolded in it gathers force. Of course this ancient, urgent longing for the family's healing hold is not intrinsically masculine, nor does it always mask a naked will to power.

While this "regressive longing for the stem family of their nostalgic imagination"[34] must be seen as part of a much wider cultural trend, the frequency with which it has appeared in a variety of recent work by black men is suggestive. To choose a few random examples: In his moving autobiography *Brothers and Keepers,* John Wideman implies that the power of the family as a social unit could secure foundations badly shaken by the criminal activities of a brother. On the front jacket of the first edition is a jailed man in shadow, but on the back is a portrait of Wideman's family harmoniously gathered in front of the house: mother *and* father, children and grandchildren lined up in neat and orderly rows, faces smiling at each other, their bodies erect and composed. The family becomes the framing rhetoric and logic of Houston Baker's suggestive monograph *Modernism and the Harlem Renaissance*. Baker writes below a gallery of family photographs, beginning with a picture of his wife's father, "the family signature is always a renewing renaissancism that ensures generation, generations."[35]

Finally, in *The Truly Disadvantaged: The Inner City, the Underclass, and Public Policy*, William Julius Wilson, a black sociologist, lays the problem of an ineradicable underclass to inter-generational, female-headed households. His solution, as Adolph Reed astutely notes, is not to appeal for "pay equity, universal day care and other initiatives to buttress women's capacities for living independently in the world," but rather to increase the pool of black "marriageable" men.[36]

Wilson also narrates a family romance with a sociological twist. He nostalgically recalls the time when "lower-class, working-class, and middle-class black families all lived more or less in the same communities . . . sent their children to the same schools, availed themselves of the same recreational facilities, and shopped at the same stores."[37] So powerful is the desire to recuperate the family and a safe and uncomplicated black community that Wilson ignores, according to Reed, that the "glue" holding these earlier communities together "was not so much nuclear, 'intact' families as the imperatives of racial segregation." Reed continues pointedly that "the new concern with the black family—like the old concern with the black family . . . is . . . a moralistic ideology that . . . enforce[s] patriarchal institutions by appealing to a past that may have been largely mythical . . . and one that was certainly predicated on the subordination of women."[38]

This narrative of a fantasy family is unfulfilled in the majority of writings by contemporary black women. Much of their work exposes black women's subordination within the nuclear family, rethinks and reconfigures its structures, and places utterance outside the father's preserve and control. But while this work refuses to offer comforting and idealized fantasies of family life, it understands their origins and the needs they fill. To cite just one example, in her first novel, *The Third Life of Grange Copeland*, Alice Walker captures poignantly the origins of Brownfield's daydream family in his childhood observations of his father's numbing life as a sharecropper. As Brownfield waits with his father for the truck to come, he sees "his father's face [freeze] into an unnaturally bland mask. . . . It was as if his father became a stone or robot . . . an object, a cipher." And when the white Mr. Shipley appears, Brownfield is

> filled with terror of this man who could, by his presence alone, turn his father into something that might as well have been a pebble or a post or a piece of dirt, except for the sharp bitter odor of something whose source was forcibly contained in flesh.

Brownfield's only way to cope with this dehumanization is to retreat to a daydream that comforts him throughout his childhood:

> He saw himself grown-up, twenty-one or so, arriving home at sunset in the snow. . . . He pulled up to his house, a stately mansion with cherry-red brick chimneys . . . in a chauffeur-driven car. . . . Brownfield's wife and children . . . a girl and a boy—waited anxiously for him just inside the door. . . . They jumped all over him, showering him with kisses. While he told his wife of the big deals he'd pushed through that day, she fixed him a mint julep.[39]

The novel articulates an understanding, then, of this desire for the father's presence in the sanctity of the home, but it frustrates that desire and exposes this domestic space as the privileged site of women's exploitation.[40] It is telling, for example, that in Brownfield's idyllic fantasy, his wife and the cook are "constantly interchanged so that his wife was first black and glistening from cooking and then white and powdery to his touch."[41]

In the view of these reviews and essays, the possibilities for "wholeness" within the black family have been fractured by black women's consumption of the fruit of feminist knowledge, but more by their affiliations with white women. Even signs of embattled reconciliation between them after long estrangement and distrust have made the black male a stranger in his own home, an outcast in his own family.

The scene in *Reckless Eyeballing* in which Becky French, a white woman, and Treemonisha Smarts, a black woman, decide the fate of Ball's play, *No Good Man,* captures the cross-racial reconciliation that demands the black male's sacrifice. As the two women exchange stares, Ball thinks

> of them in the same households all over the Americas while the men were away on long trips to the international centers of the cotton or sugar markets. The secrets they exchanged in the night when there were no men around, during the Civil War in America when the men were in the battlefield and the women were in the house. Black and white, sisters and

half-sisters. Mistresses and wives. There was something going on here that made him, a man, an outsider, a spectator, like someone who'd stumbled into a country where people talked in sign language and he didn't know the signs.[42]

Quoting this passage in his review, Pinckney describes it as "a paranoid update" on a conspiratorial theme, and with that I can agree, but the passage suggests much more that bears directly on issues of gender and reading.

The male readers of this debate, whose gazes are fixed on themselves, seem to have entered a fictional territory marked by unreadable signs. Pinckney refers to this territory as the kitchen. He remembers when "Black women's concerns had belonged to what was considered the *private,* rather than the public, as if the kitchen range could not adequately represent the struggle. But it turned out that the concerns of the kitchen were big enough to encompass the lore of struggle and survival."[43]

Pinckney's distinction between public and private space is a distinction repeatedly deconstructed in the writings of the black women under review, for they understand the operations of power within intimate domains, operations captured in that now-familiar axiom, "the personal is political." But more to the point, Pinckney's metaphor of the kitchen calls to mind Susan Glaspell's short story "A Jury of Her Peers.' Feminist critics have read this story of a different form of family violence as a model of the workings of gender in the reading process. As the men of the story search for clues that will suggest a motive for Minnie's murder of her husband, they bypass the inside of the house and search its surroundings. They dismiss what one of them terms "the insignificance of kitchen things" and are consequently unable to "interpret this farm wife's world." While the story does not "exclude the male as reader," it attempts to educate him "to become a better reader."[44]

In terms of our debate, that process of re-education begins with questioning and adjusting the categories and constructs, the values and assumptions that we bring to bear *when* reading that have almost always been formed *before* reading. Put another way, that process begins with questioning what Fredric Jameson calls "the always-already-read," the "sedimented layers of previous *interpretations.*"[45] Alice Walker's story "Source," from her collection *You Can't Keep a Good Woman Down,* offers a different model of reading, one that reinforces the strategic possibilities of Toni Morrison's *Sula.*[46]

Choosing "Source" as a model seems especially appropriate because, of all the black women writers under critique in this debate, Walker has been the object of the most savage, sustained, and partisan attack (primarily for *The Color Purple*) and the lightning rod for these reviewers' hostility to feminism. It is notably ironic, then, that well before that controversial novel was published, Walker had, perhaps in an uncanny moment of prescient anticipation, staged in "Source" many general concerns and assumptions—both literary and cultural—at work in this debate.

The title announces the story's concern with origins, beginnings, with questions of male subjectivity and its relation to language, authorship, authority, and representation. Repeated references to Mt. McKinley function as figures of masculine potency and transcendence. In its parallel plot lines—one involving reading matters, the other family matters—the story stages competing words and conflicting discourses framed as a secular myth of origins. Further, it engages and complicates the salient and interlocking assumptions inherent in this controversy. For example, the story confronts head-on the twin beliefs inherent in these reviews: the belief in the text as *reflection* rather than *production* of self and world; the belief in a pre-given, positive masculine identity. In the process, like *Sula,* it poses questions about the nature of identification and recognition in the reading process.

> Source: from Latin *surgere*
> to raise, rise
> the point of origin
> a generative force or stimulus
> genealogical lineage

A veritable reference work, "Source" alludes to a number of books, song titles, films, and historical figures, including "Eleanor Rigby," *Steppenwolf, Imitation of Life, The Autobiography of an Ex-Colored Man, Confessions of Nat Turner, Birth of a Nation,* and *Louisa Picquet, the Octoroon: A Tale of Southern Slave Life.* These titles are suggestive and instructive, for they cast into bold relief the status of the story as *story,* as text. But more importantly, most of these titles comment on the constructed (not found) and contingent nature of identity and subjectivity. These allusions establish and announce the narrative's self-conscious insistence on its own *fictionality,* its own textuality, in a way that compares to Shari Benstock's reading of footnotes in the literary text. I agree with her that footnotes (and here I would substitute Alice Walker's various allusions to artistic works) "belong to a fictional universe, stem from a creative act ... and direct themselves toward the fiction and never toward an external construct, even when they cite 'real' works in the world outside the particular fiction."[47]

The "real" works of Walker's story, the sources behind her "Source," instruct the reader about the disguises of identity, about identity as disguise. From the opening allusion to "Eleanor Rigby" (who keeps her face in a jar by the door) to *The Autobiography of an Ex-Colored Man* to *Steppenwolf* to *Louisa Picquet, the Octoroon,* the underlying issue is the same: identity is textually constructed, not pre-given or found. The "real" persons function similarly: "once 'inside' the fiction, both fictional characters and real personages exist at the same fictive level."[48]

While Walker liberally sprinkles references to historical personages throughout her fiction, she seems fully sensitive to both their fictive status in her work *and* their "fictive" status in the world. She compounds the story's many ironies and self-complications by suggesting that such *actual* historical figures may even have *made* up their identities. The reference to Kathleen Cleaver is a case in point. Although readers familiar with the Black Panther party recognize her as one of its leaders, the narrative stresses that this identity is assumed, is made, is produced by the contingencies of time and place.

Anastasia's memory of her first meeting with Kathleen Cleaver "before *she* was Kathleen Cleaver" is suggestive. Male-identified, like Anastasia, Cleaver "sat in a corner all evening without saying a word. . . . Men did all the talking" (p. 153). However, after the men are dead or jailed, Cleaver is forced to change, a change that figures in her dress: in "boots and sunglasses and black clothes" she "poses for photographers [while] holding a gun" (p. 153).

This dynamic, ever-changing, historically and spatially situated nature of identity is counterposed to the static conception of identity embodied in Source, the title character, the only stationary figure in the text. While all moves around him, Source sits on a bed and receives those who come to hear his static message: "the universe is unchangeable" (p. 153). His name evokes the "original," "pre-given," positive racial self, historically and paradigmatically male. It is this conception of self that is demanded by reviewers. Although the story's title leads the reader to expect a story about this guru/teacher/father figure, Source is not the work's center of reference. Rather, the nominal "center" is relocated to the margins of the text. His presence is deferred until the narrative action is well under way. And even then, his appearance is brief and clearly subordinated to the narrative's dramatization of the reunion between Irene and Anastasia.

The narrative of this reunion brings to a head conflicting discourses about family and identity, discourses that the story figures through its controlling metaphor of teaching. It juxtaposes Source's method—requiring passive and unquestioning acceptance and transcription of his authority—to Irene's—requiring that her students "take an active part in their own instruction" (p. 142).

These conflicting methodologies come to rest in Anastasia, who must negotiate between them and, in effect, between Irene and Source. As flower child and Source's mistress, Anastasia finds unacceptable Irene's critique and rejection of Source's authority. In a section that dramatizes the family's site as production and construction of the daughter's identity, Anastasia defends Source to a suspicious and judgmental Irene. Always painfully confused about her racial identity (she looks white but is considered black), Anastasia has spent much of her life drifting, changing identities as she changes "personal fashion" (p. 143). After several such changes—"Southern Innocent," "New York Super Vamp," "Kathleen Cleaver type"—she meets Source, who hastens her along to her next change to flower child. Significantly, Source describes their first meeting by remembering that Anastasia looked like Kathleen Cleaver, her "hair like an angry, wild animal bush." He tames her, substituting her "militancy" for calm, and renames her Tranquillity.

Further, he helps her accept that "[she] is nothing," that "nobody's anything." More importantly, Source arranges the reunion between Anastasia and her family—arranges, more precisely, her reunion with her father, who "now wrote of God's love, God's grace, God's assured forgiveness, and of his own happiness that his daughter, always at heart 'a good girl,' had at last embarked on the path of obedience . . . [which] alone led to peace everlasting in the new and coming system of the world" (p. 148). It is this "new and coming system" that Irene's questioning presence threatens. She sits with "a clenched fist resting on the letters from Anastasia's father" (p. 148) and poses a challenge to the universal negatives of Source's teaching: "Nobody's anything." "You can't change anything." Ensuring the continued circulation of his words, Source has his daughter write them down.

Reading this "new and coming system" accurately as an age-old sanction for the daughter's seduction and submission, Irene is invited to leave. Irene's lifework is teaching students to respect and inscribe "their own personal histories and their own experience" (p. 142), not to reinscribe themselves in another's "universal truths." Structured into Irene's method of teaching "Advanced Reading and Writing" is a provision for students to write their own books, which effectively contravenes the assumption that "bearing a father's word," as Source's daughter does, is "women's only acceptable role with respect to language."[49]

Source's daughter is literally and literarily bearing his word, as she is pregnant with his child. Here Margaret Homans's observations about women who "act as amanuenses . . . usually for men," are pertinent. "Like the mother of the Word, the woman who carries language from one place or state of being to another does not herself originate or even touch it, and she gets nothing for her labor, which she performs for others."[50] In addition, Irene's students are required to shift any identity constructs that lock them into a single reading personality or type.

"Source" incorporates various categories of readers and scenes of instruction. And while each characterizes a woman reader, the implications are more broadly applicable. Fania represents one category. Like many of the men sustaining this debate, Fania is a "resisting reader," to borrow from Judith Fetterley, refusing both to learn to read anything that hurts (p. 145) or in which she fails to recognize herself. While the narrative clearly sympathizes with Fania's reading strategies, it challenges her to move beyond her resistance to explore her "undeveloped comprehension of [self and] world" (p. 153). For Fania, that expansion begins with the slave narratives of black women. "A stout, walnut-colored woman," Fania identifies with the narrative of *Louisa Picquet, the Octoroon,* though she does not *recognize* Picquet as identical with herself.

While Irene succeeds in teaching Fania a way to read that effectively displaces the recognizable and the familiar as privileged conventions of reading, she is in like need of instruction. And, in an interesting narrative twist, as readers witness her instruction, they are taught themselves. The narrative sets the reader up for the familiar and "recognizable" story of a deprived but socially committed black woman and an indulged, confused, and irresponsible mulatto with a "lack of commitment to anything . . . useful" (p. 166). However, the story swerves from such banalities, for while Irene casts herself in the role of Anastasia's teacher, their roles reverse in the course of the narrative and teacher becomes learner and learner teacher. This reversal captures the very issues of constructed identities and idealized self-definition with which the story wrestles and that are most pertinent to the controversy about black women writers.

Though Irene is partly represented as an idealist with a knowledge of self that qualifies her to represent the race, she falls far short of that carefully constructed and controlled ideal. (Walker clearly intends a parallel with Nella Larsen's similarly deluded narrator Irene in *Passing,* the seeming foil to Clare.) Correlatively, Anastasia, who changes identities as she "changed fashion," helps Irene to "unmask her own confusion" about self and race.

The productive tension between Irene and Anastasia and the symbolic role reversals they undergo can only occur away from Source's watchful gaze and the influence of his teachings. Anastasia has bought these teachings uncritically, crediting them with reuniting her with her family. (Interestingly, while Anastasia accepts Source's teachings, which coincide with her father's words, she "never read the newsletter that Irene and her [students] published" [p. 142].) But Anastasia pays for the family reunion, arranged on Source's terms and turf, with her own psychic and physical health. Her recovery requires that she review Source's teachings and unmask their repressive aims.

While Source would teach that "the good of life is indifference" (suggesting undifferentiation, non-difference) and that "nobody's anything," Anastasia progressively distances herself from his rhetoric and his universalization of stasis. Arguing that "only a fascist would say nobody's anything," Anastasia changes Source's words and substitutes her own, emphatically: "Everybody's *some*thing. Some *body*." In rejecting Source's positivization of the negative, Anastasia begins the process of unnaming and the recognition of the arbitrary relation between the name and the thing that necessarily calls into question any confident claims about a positive black male identity. With "a permanent tremor under [her] eye," "constant colds, diarrhea, loose teeth and skin eruptions," Anastasia asks pointedly, "If I was so tranquil, why was this happening?" Implicitly renouncing the name that Source has given her—Tranquillity—she has learned, to paraphrase a passage from *Invisible Man*, that "to call a thing by name is [not] to make it so." Similarly, Source, despite his name, is not the absolute source, the self-present origin, the namer, the author whose authority is unchallengeable.

Much the same might be said about Alice Walker as the source, the author, the originator of "Source"—suggestions not lost on Walker. The multiple listing of textual sources in the story might be read as Walker's commentary on the process of authorship, suggesting a distance from received notions of a single author and the concept of single, self-identity that it implies. Although, with that said, one cannot then take Walker's own words as Truth, it is nonetheless pertinent and useful to note how Walker answers her critics beyond the story's walls. Not surprisingly, that response takes the form of a discussion of identity. In an essay titled "In the Closet of the Soul," she writes:

> crucial to our development . . . is an acceptance of our actual as opposed to our mythical selves. We are the mestizos of North America. We are black, yes, but we are "white," tan, and we are red. To attempt to function as only one, when you are really two or three, leads, I believe, to psychic illness. Regardless of who will or will not accept us, including

perhaps, our "established" self, we must be completely (to the extent it is possible) who we are.[51]

It is precisely this question about self-identity that is thematized in "Source." Like *Sula,* the narrative exploits, complicates and affirms a dynamic conception of identity that resists any notion of a single identity to be "positively" represented in fiction. More, both through its figuration of Anastasia's "identity changes," and through its unmasking of Irene's "self-saving vanity" (p. 141), the text reveals the workings of desire in the construction of identity. In this richly textured story, then, Shoshana Felman's words come directly to mind: "Indeed it is not so much the critic [reader/reviewer] who comprehends the text, as the text that comprehends the critic."[52] The narrative understands the critics who would charge Walker and her black female contemporaries with shattering the "established" image, the positive identity. More to the point, the text understands what their rhetoric of family reveals and conceals.

Whether or not one agrees that the text comprehends the critics of African American women novelists, it is certain that these reviewers have had a constraining influence on the writers they attack. Since this controversy began, certain black women writers have expressed fear and concern about how their depictions of black men would be received, and, more sobering, others might even be said to have adjusted their aesthetic vision because of the pressures of negative publicity. To take just one example, Gloria Naylor admits to being "self-conscious" about her first novel. "I bent over backwards," she says, "not to have a negative message come through about the men. . . . I worried about whether or not the problems that were being caused by the men in the women's lives would be interpreted as some bitter statement I had to make about black men."[53]

Similarly, in a 1987 interview, Ntozake Shange agreed with Brenda Lyons's perception that between the controversial *for colored girls* and her most recent novel, *Betsey Brown* (1985), there was "a movement away from radical feminist politics . . . toward what seems a return to family-centered values."[54] While there is, of course, no necessary causal connection between the controversy and Shange's aesthetic shift, it should not go unnoticed that Shange moves aesthetically toward representing the very value system espoused in these reviews. And while family- and female-centered writing need not be seen as incompatible, it is significant that Shange dedicates *Betsey Brown* to her family. And the back flap of the first edition features a photograph of her beaming down admiringly at her daughter. Completing the portrait is Ishmael Reed's lone blurb, which praises Shange for her "uncanny gift for immersing herself within the situations and points of view of so many different types of women." By delimiting her audience to women, he continues, "she has achieved an almost oracular status among her female readers." Although a "writer of many masks," he concludes, "the masks come off" with *Betsey Brown*.

I leave it to the reader to speculate about what Reed might mean by Shange's masks, but in characterizing her as a writer for *female* readers, his meaning is clear. His comments represent a shift, however feeble, to a more sanguine response to a black woman writer. But it is only a momentary shift, for his venom re-erupts in his *roman à clef, Reckless Eyeballing*. Ian Ball is a clear self-portrait whose story allegorizes Reed's now well-known and predictable perception that the work of talented black men is being eclipsed by the power bloc of black women writers midwifed and promoted by white feminists.

"Sex-listed" in a feminist publication suggestively titled *Lilith's Gang*, Ball goes on to experience a positive reversal of literary fortune. But the more interesting development is a parallel "reversal" for Treemonisha Smarts, a thinly disguised Ntozake Shange. At novel's end, drunk with what the narrative describes as the "skull and cross-bones" of literary success, Treemonisha has abandoned her successful career, moved to Yuba City, California, with a recovering drug addict and failed musician, renounced her involvement with voyeuristic white feminists, and resolved to "get fat, have babies, and write, write, write" (p. 130). (Reed's fantasy, no doubt.) In this scenario, writing for a woman is best not accompanied by the "skull and cross-bones" of literary success, although chasing that same success has been Ian Ball's driving ambition. We could say that with *Reckless Eyeballing*, Reed's "masks come off," revealing plainly, at least to this reader, that reading family matters.

But this controversy is clearly not reducible simply to conflictual interaction between the texts of contemporary black women and a group of resisting male readers. And, thus, its resolution is no simple matter of "adjusting" identity constructs and altering reading strategies at the finite level of the text, for, in the language of "Source," always "up there" is the Higher Power, the meta-structure, which has not only already textualized "identity," but has also already determined whether there will be "reading" at all.

The story is sharply alert to the political economy of reading and writing and it understands the inextricable relation between the source of funding and the source of words. In talking to Anastasia about how federal cuts ended the Advanced Reading and Writing course she was teaching to poor women in the rural South, Irene explains, "In the beginning there was no funding" and "the two women could not help grinning in recognition of the somehow *familiar* sound of this" (pp. 143–44, emphasis in text). But Irene, like Walker, defamiliarizes the familiar (familial) and secularizes the sacred origins of this creation myth. She understands the twin relation of church to state and underscores the power of their entwined control over these women's reading and writing.

Using references to Mt. McKinley, Walker allegorizes white male dominance over language and representation and illustrates how, by erasing difference, that power is institutionalized and maintained. The highest peak in North America, Mt. McKinley was renamed for president William McKinley in 1896, replacing the Indian name "Denali" (The Highest One). And while it is clear that Walker associates the "great elusive" Mt. McKinley with a power wielded mainly by white men, she knows that black men are also inescapably the agents of that hegemony in many respects. The narrative establishes an equivalent relation between Source's "bare feet," which he "cover[s] and uncover[s]" with a "white robe" (p. 150) and another mountain in Seattle mentioned, but unnamed, at story's end. Tourists pointing in the distance "thought they were finally seeing the great elusive [Mt. McKinley], a hundred miles away. They were not. It was yet another, nearer, mountain's very large feet . . ." (p. 167).

While these male gazes are fixed on black women's texts, in which they seek to find idealized reflections of themselves, they fail to see the mountain, the meta-structure that has the naming power and in whose name and interests that power is secured. It is this looming, distant structure orchestrating and dominating this literary battle royal, this already fixed match between black men and black women.[55] And one could argue that this fixed match reproduces an older meta-narrative written in the slave master's hand. In that narrative, as in this, the bodies/texts of black women have become the "battlefield on and over which men, black and white, [fight] to establish actual and symbolic political dominance and to demonstrate masculine" control.[56] This attempt to control both black women's written *bodies* and their *written* bodies[57] must be read and its service to the family plot interpreted, for that plot makes women permanent daughters content to transcribe their father's words.

1989

PART V

Hesitating between Tenses or
Allegories of History

There are other deeper forces at work, which
perhaps only imagination in its full processes,
can touch and reach and recognize and embody.
If we see this, we usually still hesitate
between tenses: between knowing in new ways
the structures of feeling that have directed
and now hold us, and finding in new ways the
shape of an alternative, a future that can be
genuinely imagined and hopefully lived.
                                    —*Raymond Williams*

History is "cannibalistic," and memory becomes
the closed arena of conflict between two
contradictory operations: forgetting, an
action directed against the past, and the
return of what was forgotten.
                                    —*Michel de Certeau*

8

Witnessing Slavery after
Freedom—*Dessa Rose*[1]

How could she bear witness to what she'd never lived?
—Gayl Jones, *Corregidora*

Can we identify a work of art if it does not bear the mark
of a genre?
—Jacques Derrida, "The Law of Genre"

The subject of black women's written *bodies* and their *written* bodies is
appropriately at the center of a flood of contemporary novels about slavery, lending validity to Ralph Ellison's remark that "the Negro American
consciousness is not a product of a will to historical forgetfulness."[2] While
the subject of slavery has become a kind of literary "free for all," such
has not always been the case. The emergence of what Bernard Bell terms
"neoslave narratives" and Henry Louis Gates, the "slave narrative
novel,"[3] is mainly a post-sixties phenomenon.[4] Margaret Walker's *Jubilee*
(1966) might be chosen arbitrarily as something of a catalyst, for since it
was published, novels about slavery have appeared at an unstoppable rate.[5]

Why the compulsion to repeat the massive story of slavery in the contemporary African American novel so long after the empirical "event"
itself? Is it simply because contemporary writers can "witness" slavery
from the "safe" vantage point of distance? What personal need, what
expressive function does re-presenting slavery in narrative serve the
twentieth-century black American writer? Is it to find in slavery sociologi-

cal insights into contemporary society? To see in slavery an analogy of present-day varieties of inequality, both social and symbolic? Is the retelling meant to attempt the impossible: to "get it right," to "set the record straight"? Perhaps all of the above in some combination.

Whatever the reason(s), I agree with Hortense Spillers that "every generation of systematic readers is compelled not only to reinvent slavery in its elaborate and peculiar institutional ways and means, but also in its prominent discursive features." As a phenomenon we can "know" only through discourse, Spillers continues, slavery "inscribes a repertoire of relationships of texts and among texts that is purely open to modes of improvisation and rearrangement."[6]

It is significant that, among the current generation of writers, African American *women* are at the forefront of reinventing slavery. Their efforts to improvise on and rearrange the complex reaches of its textual field have roots in both intellectual and mass cultural terrain: in revisionist historiographies of slavery and the marketing of slave narratives for contemporary academic consumption, at one end; and popularizations of slavery such as Alex Haley's immensely successful *Roots* (the first and second generations), at the other. At the heart of all these enterprises is a preoccupation with manhood and masculinity, a preoccupation illuminated graphically and not surprisingly in the slave narrative. It is well-known that the majority of published slave narratives were written by black men. According to John Blassingame, black women published less than 12 percent of extant slave narratives, for only rarely did escaped female slaves receive encouragement to tell their life stories.[7] In these neo-slave narratives, contemporary black women encourage themselves to insert their inventions into the store of warring texts, of conflicting representations and interpretations of chattel slavery.[8] Margaret Walker admits, for example, that her motivation for writing *Jubilee* was "to set the record straight where Black people are concerned in terms of the Civil War, of slavery, segregation and Reconstruction."[9] Like Walker, Sherley Anne Williams seems to suggest that history's lies can be corrected and its omissions restored. In the author's note to her novel *Dessa Rose,* she admits to "being outraged by a certain, critically acclaimed novel . . . that travestied the as-told-to memoir of slave revolt leader Nat Turner."[10] (Of course, she refers to William Styron's controversial novel *The Confessions of Nat Turner* [1967].)[11] Styron's "meditation on history"[12] is an example of what Williams, in her preface, considers the betrayal of blacks by the written word. Her outrage is understandable considering the repeated scene of blacks' erasure *from* the historical record and the nature of their representation *in* it. But while Williams's author's note explicitly critiques a novel that allegedly takes history lightly and misrepresents the "known facts" about a black hero—Nat Turner—it licenses itself to do much the same: invent and re-create history.

But while *Dessa Rose* and other contemporary fictionalizations of slavery by African American women improvise on many discursive features of slavery's signal texts, their most suggestive mark of improvisation is on perhaps the most prominent discursive feature of male slave narratives: the sexual victimization of women, a feature tied to the silencing of the feminine.[13] As Jennie Franchot observes, "the atrocities of slavery find their most powerful synecdoche in the silenced figure of the slave mother forced to endure rape, concubinage, and the theft of her children." This pattern is strikingly evident in Frederick Douglass's autobiographies, in which his "continued exposure of the black woman's suffering body is crucial to his lifelong mission of disclosing the sins of the white fathers."[14]

While these neo-slave narratives do expose such atrocities, they shift their stress away from the silenced victim, the object of sexual abuse. They announce their emphasis on female subjectivity, in the grammatical sense of the term, beginning with their titles, many of which take the form of proper names: *Sally Hemings, Corregidora, Beloved, Dessa Rose.*

In distinguishing her story from the web of slavery's most familiar textualizations, *Dessa Rose* takes care to note:

> Not all white mens acted animals towards us, understand, but enough of them did till this is what we always feared with them—and what our mens feared for us. I was spared this in bondage, but I had seen the way some white mens looked at me, big belly and all, when I was on that coffle.
> (p. 178)

And, in wanting to conceal the "history writ about her privates" (the scars of her flesh made word), she fails to satisfy the expectations of the reader as voyeur, the position in which so many male slave narratives cast the reader.[15] In reconfiguring this signal "law" of the slave narrative as genre—sexual victimization of slave women—all other imaginary relations shift accordingly: those between slave men and slave women and between slave woman and slave mistress. The latter relation is the genesis of the novel. While the conventional story of sexual victimization requires their estrangement and mutual antipathy, Williams imagines a different script. She takes two different documented stories—one involving a pregnant black woman who helped to lead a slave revolt in Kentucky, the other concerning a white woman in North Carolina, who reportedly gave sanctuary to runaway slaves. Thinking it "sad . . . that these two women never met" in *fact,* Williams brings them together in *fiction.*

Williams's decision to reconfigure a salient convention of the slave narrative as genre works reciprocally with the novel's running meditation on
the politics and problematics of language and representation. It does not
sidestep concerns about the network of sociohistorical realities and power
asymmetries that influence the manner and matter of representing slavery.
In other words, it does not back away from the power relations necessarily
involved in textualizing slavery. Who has been publically authorized or
self-authorized to tell the story? Under what circumstances? What has
been acceptably sayable about that story? How have black women figured
in it? Figured themselves in it?

The concerns that *Dessa Rose* foregrounds—the who, what, when, and
how of representation—are richly suggestive and resonate far beyond slavery and its discourses, past and present. We could even argue that the
novel is engaged as much with the "present" and its discourses, in heterogeneous and messy array, as it is with "reconventionalizing" the classic
slave narratives. In other words, the novel engages not only details from
inherited texts of slavery, but also raises questions about, comments upon,
agrees with, and explicitly challenges many issues at the forefront of contemporary critical discourse, thus granting to fiction the prerogatives of
commentary on the genre of criticism, and reasonably so. Sherley Anne
Williams is as much a literary critic as she is a novelist and poet, listing
to her credit a book-length study of what she calls "neo-black literature,"
as well as a number of articles.[16]

In its method of storytelling—staging multiple and often contradictory
versions of Dessa's enslavement and subsequent escape—the novel shares
in the now-commonplace critique of the trappings of narrative and the
semantics of "Truth." The novel confronts unabashedly the inescapably
ideological contingencies of all discourse, itself included, and yet it backs
away from any postmodern orthodoxy of undecidability. In other words,
while there might not be one "truth" about Dessa (or about slavery more
generally), there are "certainties" that the text stubbornly claims and vali-
dates and "certainties" that it tries to subvert.

> I know this darky, I tell you; I know her very well.
> —*Dessa Rose*

Just whose "word" can and should be taken in *Dessa Rose* is a question
the novel worries in its multiple versions of Dessa's life as a slave. A
continuous thread of quotation marks woven throughout the text calls
attention to words as words, evoking uncertainty and ambiguity. But then
again, this stylization of quotation marks can be said to quarantine mis-

namings and representations from the implicit textual authority of a counterdiscourse.

The first recorded version of Dessa's story comes from the aptly named Adam (namer) Nehemiah (chronicler) and is littered with words punctuated repetitively with quotation marks. Nehemiah's "authority" as an agent of white male law and rationality is aggressively undermined by the text. His section is a veritable parody of the "as-told-to" device of gathering empirical evidence and documenting events to construct historicist discourse. In his case, Nehemiah is supposedly collecting the facts about Dessa's unrepentant participation in a slave revolt in which many whites were killed. The "facts" that he collects, however, are "some kind of fantastical fiction" (p. 39) recreated in his hand.

The novel compounds the ironies and limitations inherent in Nehemiah's account, which is suspect from the start. It is retrospective, based on discrepant sources, and reconstructed from notes. First, though it purports to be *about* Dessa, a *particular* slave woman, Nehemiah's account actually essentializes Dessa and attempts to fit her into a recognizable proslavery text. His is a representation culled from an inherited store of racist myths about slaves and slavery. "He has been told [slaves] fell asleep much as a cow would in the midst of a satisfying chew" though "he had not observed this himself" (p. 36). And, throughout his chronicle (significantly titled "Darky," a generic, gender-neutral classification of slaves), Nehemiah admits to being unable to "remember [Dessa's] name" (p. 45). Failing to remember it, he performs a series of substitutions, also lifted from the standard vocabulary of the proslavery text: "darky," "fiend," "devil-woman," "treacherous nigger bitch," "virago," and "she-devil." Although Nehemiah takes notes on the names of slaves that Dessa refers to in her reveries, in his translation they are all reduced to "darky" (p. 39).

Nehemiah's colossal act of serial misnaming mistakes the name for the thing, or to borrow from Kimberly Benston, it "subsume[s] the complexities of human experience into a tractable sign while manifesting an essential inability to *see* (to grasp, to apprehend) the signified."[17] In telling Dessa's story, Nehemiah creates an abstraction and assigns it a place distant from himself, a distance structured in the novel's use of architectural space (place) and somatophobic imagery. Although Nehemiah conducts his first meeting with Dessa in the root cellar that is her jail, he decides that "being closeted with the darky within the small confines of the cellar was an unsettling experience" (p. 23) and so holds subsequent meetings outside where "he kept a careful distance between them. . . . He would lean forward long enough to wave her to a spot several feet from him, using the vinegar-soaked handkerchief . . . meant to protect him from her scent" (p. 56). These images of smell and verticality (he is *up* in the attic of Hughes's farmhouse; she is outside it and *down* in the root cellar)[18] signify the physical distance and sociopolitical inequality between Dessa and Nehemiah that go far to explain his empowerment, as well as his inability to see and to name her.

Hoping to ensure the continued circulation of these performative misnamings and descriptions, Nehemiah is at work on a book on the origins of uprisings among slaves. Commissioned by his publisher, Browning Norton, Nehemiah's projected book, *The Roots of Rebellion in the Slave Population and Some Means of Eradicating Them,* exposes his project as a form of slave trading (trading in words) and a tool in the technocratic machinery (he is the son of a mechanic) of social control. But this is no simple story of a black woman's total victimization by that machinery, for Nehemiah proves no match for Dessa.

The narrative symmetrically opposes Nehemiah's public discourse to Dessa's poignant expressions of personal loss and longing. For every question he wants answered with facts about the uprising—"Where were the renegades going?" "Who were the darkies that got away?" (p. 36)—Dessa answers with some memory of Kaine's confrontation with the slave system or by singing a song. Throughout their sessions, she cleverly misleads him and mocks what he represents. And in the studied circularity of her telling (leading Nehemiah back to the same point of previous sessions) and her skill at "turn[ing] his . . . questions back upon themselves," Dessa sabotages his enterprise. Her confessed enjoyment of "play[ing] on his words" sends him scrambling to write "quickly, abbreviating with a reckless abandon, scribbling almost as he sought to keep up with the flow of her words" (p. 60). Her refusal to "confess" anything to Nehemiah that would facilitate yet another misrepresentation is an act of resistance against the adverse power of literacy and codification. At novel's end Nehemiah's "book" is incomplete; it has literally fallen apart and is nothing more than loose pages "scatter[ed] about the floor," unreadable scribbling that even the sheriff (another agent of the father's law) cannot read. Further, Nehemiah's own name has been abbreviated; he is "Nemi" and has *become* the reduction he would create.

> The evidence of things not seen.
> —Heb. 11:1

That misnaming is generative is a point graphically illustrated in section two of *Dessa Rose.* In escaping from Nehemiah, Dessa seizes physical freedom, but she does not escape the text of slavery. She continues to be misnamed and performs her own misnaming. We might say that sections one and two juxtapose two consubstantial systems of representation—one is verbal, the other visual. Told largely from the point of view of Rufel, a white woman, this second section is structured on the language of the visual that she employs while remembering her own past and her own complicity in and victimization by the institution of slavery.

Whereas the first section is based on a series of oppositions—of orality and literacy, of public and private discourse, of a free white man and an enslaved black woman—the second problematizes "the whole business of choosing sides" (p. 78) and moves toward an ethic and an energy of cooperation. That ethic is most readily apparent in the links established between Dessa and Rufel, an escaped slave and a one-time slave mistress. Both are separated from their families, both are mourning personal losses, both are raising children, both live under a system that denies them full control over their bodies. But these commonalities are produced by radically different material circumstances and thus engender radically different effects.

While Rufel's section uses the problem of naming and representation to attempt to bridge the "schism in the sisterhood"[19] between black and white women, it neither simplifies that process nor attempts to merge their differences and make them the same. It makes a difference that one woman is white and the other is black. The process of transgressing their oppositions and antagonisms and the impregnable social boundaries that separate them begins with efforts to get out of the text of slavery that both misnames and missees.

As slave mistress in action, if not in fact, Rufel replicates and extends Nehemiah's practice of essentializing slaves and consigning them to places. Whereas his section is titled "Darky"—a gender-neutral nomination— Rufel's is titled "Wench"—a female-specific nomination, but one no closer to naming Dessa Rose. True to her trade as a caricaturist, Rufel has an exaggerated and distorted image of Dessa and the other escaped slaves harbored on her run-down plantation, forcing them to fit a different sacred text: the visual image of slaves produced and reproduced in nineteenth-century popular culture. Rufel associates Ada with "the stock cuts used to illustrate newspaper advertisements of slave sales and runaways: pants rolled up to the knees, bareheaded, a bundle attached to a stick slung over one shoulder, the round white eyes in the inky face" (p. 140). Coming close upon Nathan at the shoreline, "she turned to the darky aghast. . . . Never had she seen such blackness. She . . . expect[ed] to see the bulbous lips and bulging eyes of a burnt-cork minstrel" but saw instead "a pair of rather shadowy eyes and strongly defined features that were—handsome" (p. 125). Finally, as she remembers her faithful servant, Mammy, whose death she mourns, Rufel performs another familiar substitution, visualizing Mammy's "cream-colored bandanna," the traditional sign of the slave woman's servitude. She corrects that memory by recalling that "the silky-looking cloth on the darky's head bore little resemblance to the gaudy-colored swatch most darkies tied about their heads. This was a scarf, knotted in a rosette behind one ear" (p. 123). These passages suggest that, while Rufel seems able to adjust her vision of these slaves, she cannot right their names, not even Mammy, the name of the slave woman she professes to love.

Significantly, it is over Rufel's misnaming of Mammy that she and Dessa have their first major confrontation, and their mutual misnaming is a source of continual difficulty and mistrust between the two women. As Rufel fits Mammy into her largely idealized memories of her life as a Southern belle in Charleston, Dessa bursts out, "'Mammy' ain't nobody name, not they real one" (p. 119). Dessa forces Rufel to see that if she didn't know Mammy's name, she didn't know Mammy. Even the most basic details about Mammy are unknown to Rufel, who is left to wonder in hindsight: "Had Mammy minded when the family no longer called her name? . . . How old *had* Mammy been? . . . Had she any children?" (p. 129).

Though the confrontation between Rufel and Dessa over "Mammy" is painful to them both, it puts each in touch with the buried aspects of her past and initiates the process of intimacy and trust. That process is figured in the poetics of space and architecture. Whereas Nehemiah's section employs images of vertical space to underscore the *distance* between him and Dessa, Rufel's uses images of horizontal space to figure the possibility of *closeness* between the two women.

Rufel's Sutton's Glen is a down-at-the-heels plantation. Its "BIG HOUSE" consists of two large rooms and a lean-to kitchen. Significantly, it has no second floor. The slave "Quarters" consist of "one room with a dirt floor" (p. 165) with one side for women and one for men (p. 116). This spatial configuration is used to abrogate the hierarchies of place, the divisions in the social order that place Rufel on top and Dessa below. Brought to Sutton's Glen weak and delirious from childbirth, Dessa is taken to Rufel's bedroom and placed in her bed. While the bed (implying no necessary eroticization) becomes the symbolic site of mediation between these two women, working to mitigate their mutual suspicion and distrust, only mutual acts of imagination and self-projection can buttress the bridge.

The burden of initiation falls largely on Rufel, who maintains a place of privilege and power despite her own victimization by the slave system. For example, according to the laws and customs governing Southern race relations, Rufel's WORD is equivalent to truth. As Ada says, "White woman ain't got no excuse to be trifling when all it take is they word" (p. 176), a point made clearly evident when Dessa is temporarily recaptured. It is Rufel's word, as a Southern Lady, even in the form of a disguise, that helps to free Dessa for the last time, underscoring Rufel's power over Dessa's life, her body, her story.

While Rufel can shelter Dessa, she cannot believe that Dessa has been physically abused. Consistent with her penchant for the visual as well as her need for entertainment, Rufel wants to *hear* Dessa's story and *see* the visual "evidence," but Dessa, also suspicious, refuses to comply. The narrative that Rufel hears of Dessa's abuse is mediated, coming second-hand from Nathan. Rufel disbelieves the story because she sees no scars on Dessa's back. When Nathan explains that they are on her hips and thighs, Rufel asks, "How do you know?" Clearly, Rufel needs "to see them scars before she would buy the story" (p. 189). "How else was she to know the truth of what they said?" For Rufel "seeing is believing;" to see is to know, a point raising questions about the recent feminist discourse that associates "looking," or the "gaze," with the masculine, dissociating it from the particularity of race and social situation. Rufel's eye objectifies and stabilizes the slaves at Sutton's Glen, a practice linked to her *racial* privilege.[20] References to slaves averting their gazes and lowering their lashes in her presence figure throughout Rufel's narrative (pp. 134, 139, 143).

In order for any distance to be bridged between Rufel and Dessa, Rufel must suspend the notion that only visual, empirical evidence can verify the truth of Dessa's abuse. She must rely on her imagination, instead, the act not of objectifying, but of identifying with, of getting into another's place. As she listens to Nathan recount Dessa's story, Rufel "could almost feel the fire that must have lived in the wench's thighs," the "branding iron searing tender flesh" (p. 138). She expresses disgust at "that vicious trader," "to violate a body so" (p. 135). She asks sympathetically, "How did they bare such pain?" (p. 138), but, importantly, she uses "bare" (again suggesting the visual) not "bear."

Significantly, Rufel hears this story not from Dessa herself, but from Nathan. Dessa has avoided this public exposure as fiercely as she has hidden her bodily scars. To expose them is to expose the horrors of victimization, to participate symbolically in a slave auction—to be publically exhibited, displayed. Further, this "history writ about her privates" (p. 21) is a script written in the slave master's hand and bound up in his enslaving psychosexual myths and fantasies. Here, Dessa's body is *her* text and, owning it, she holds the rights to it. For Dessa, concealing the story from

Rufel is just that—a radical act of ownership over her own body/text in a system that successfully stripped slaves' control over their most intimate property. Because Dessa perceives Rufel's physical relationship with Nathan as theft of a possession,[21] it is no wonder that she wants to own her story. Additionally, to publicize this "history writ about her privates" is synonymous with baring a past too painful to bear.

> The future was a matter of keeping the past at bay.
> —Toni Morrison, *Beloved*

Dessa's refusal to confess the intimate details of her life to either Nehemiah or Rufel is both an act of resistance (she is the repository of her own story) and a means of containing her pain by forgetting the past. Her refusal to "confess" to Nehemiah and Rufel is understandable, but Dessa is no more able to speak about her past in the atmosphere of trust and caring that obtains among the escaped slaves at Rufel's Glen. "Even when the others spoke around the campfire, during the days of their freedom, about their trials under slavery, Dessa was silent. . . . That part of the past lay sealed in the scars between her thighs" (pp. 59–60). But, like so many African American novels, *Dessa Rose* links getting "beyond" slavery to remembering it, paradoxically burying it and bearing it, a process exemplified in the naming of Dessa's baby. Consistent with her desire to bury the past, Dessa rejects Nathan's suggestion to name the baby after Kaine, his father. "The baby's daddy, like that part of her life, was dead; she would not rake it up each time she called her son's name." And so she wants to name the baby for the men who rescued her from Nehemiah. Rufel (again, possessed of the power to "name") strikes a compromise, by suggesting a name that incorporates both tenses: "Desmond Kaine"—"Des" for Odessa, "mond" to represent the men . . . who were responsible for his free birth" (p. 148) and "Kaine" to represent the past.

The child is the evidence that forgetting the past cannot be willed so easily. "Even buried under years of silence [she] could not forget," but she chooses to undergo the process of remembering in the presence of other slaves. When she does decide to tell her story in her own voice, in the final section of the novel, she tells it first and mainly to an audience of black women—a dominant pattern in Afro-American women's fiction—which points to the delicate relationship between teller and listener, writer and audience, in the establishment of textual authority.

Although Dessa slowly develops trust for Rufel, it is and can only be a partial trust: "I'd catch myself about to tell . . . some little thing, like I would Carrie or Martha. . . . She did ask about that coffle and scaping out that celler. I told her some things, how they chained us, the way the peoples sang in the morning at the farm. But I wouldn't talk about Kaine, about the loss of my peoples. . . . So we didn't talk too much that was personal" (p. 216). It should be noted here that Dessa does not share confidences with Rufel, only details of a collective, historical record, details in the public domain, if you will.

This is the difficult and precarious balance that contemporary novels about slavery must strike—that between the public record and private memory, between what Bakhtin calls "authoritative discourse" ("privileged language that . . . permits no play with its framing context [Sacred Writ, for example]") and "internally persuasive discourse . . . which is more akin to retelling a text in one's own words."[22] Bakhtin's distinction coordinates with the polarity between Nehemiah's discourse and Dessa's. The novel plots the progressive movement away from Nehemiah's *written* "authoritative discourse" within which Dessa is framed (with all of the multiple valences of that term), and the emergence of Dessa's own story, *spoken,* without Nehemiah's mediation, in her own words and with her own inflections. To borrow from William Andrews, Dessa tells a "free story."[23]

Let me rush to insert here that I do not mean to suggest (nor, does the novel, I believe) that because Dessa must *speak* her text rather than *write* it, it is therefore *ipso facto* "freer" and without mediation—that because Dessa is illiterate, she is necessarily always self-present and thus has a higher claim to truth. Dessa's story is mediated largely by the operations of memory, but the novel suggests that, by virtue of her social and material circumstances, her version of her story must be seen as more reliable than Nehemiah's could ever be.

Moreover, in Dessa's section, the initial, sharply drawn distinction between orality and literacy is complicated by recontextualization. Removed from the site of enslavement and oppression, the notion of "writing" is expanded and joined with speech.[24] That complication is structured in Dessa's acquisition and use of the language of literacy, apparent in her repeated use of writing metaphors. Thinking back on her life with Kaine, Dessa expresses gladness that Kaine "wasn't Master, wasn't boss," adding "these wasn't peoples *in my book*" (p. 184, emphasis added). Similarly, when she comes upon Nathan and Rufel making love, she fixes on the stark contrast between his blackness and the surrounding whiteness— "white sheets, white pillows, white bosom." "He wasn't nothing but a *mark* on them." From there, she generalizes about black/white relations: "That's what we was in white folks eyes, nothing but marks to be used, wiped out" (p. 171). Though illiterate, Dessa understands the functional quality of language. She notices that, in organizing the flimflam scheme,

Harker, also illiterate, "made up some marks that wasn't writing but he used it like that" (p. 195). Finally free to wander about town during one of the stops on the flimflam trail, Dessa indulges her fascination with the printer's shop: "I couldn't see that printing machine often enough to suit me," she says (p. 215). And in a final gesture that valuates the written word, Dessa wants her story recorded (p. 236), but importantly, she invests herself with the power and authority to validate it, for she has her son "say it back" (p. 236) after he has written it.

> Blow up the law, break up the "truth" with laughter.
> —Hélène Cixous, "The Laugh of the Medusa"

In the text that Dessa authorizes her son to tell, she particularizes her experiences within more familiar generic conventions of slavery. "I was spared much that others suffered," she says (specifically, sexual abuse and sales on the auction block) (p. 176). More, unlike the familiar story of slavery, especially that told in antebellum slave narratives, the inflection of laughter dominates Dessa's text, and, I must add, it is not the laughter fabricated in plantation myths of the happy darky strumming on the old banjo. It is, rather, the laughter implied in Cixous's "The Laugh of the Medusa"—"law-breaking" laughter, "truth-breaking laughter," or what Henri Bergson describes in *Laughter:* "everything that comes under the heading of 'topsyturvydom.'" According to Bergson, comedy frequently sets before us a character ensnared in his own trap: "the villain who is the victim of his own villainy, or the cheat cheated." In every case, he concludes, "the root idea involves an inversion of the roles, and a situation which recoils on the head of its author."[25]

In Dessa's story, which is largely the account of a well-oiled scam, she and her comrades turn the "authoritative" text of slavery back on itself. They use all the recognizable signs of that text but strip them of their meaning and power. These escaped slaves contrive to repeatedly sell themselves back into slavery only to escape again. They exploit Southern law and custom and faithfully enact the narrow roles it assigns slaves and women. Dessa plays the "Mammy"; Rufel, the "Mistress"; and Nathan, her "Nigger driver." Allowing for the ever-present threat of discovery, they plan, if captured, for Dessa and the other slaves to "act dumb and scared," while Rufel is "to act high-handed and helpless" (p. 194). In other words, they re-enter a familiar script and enact the roles it assigns, roles misread and misrecognized as is classically demonstrated when Dessa is indeed recaptured by Nehemiah. He drags her to the jail and alleges that she is an escaped slave matching the description on a reward poster: "Dark complexed. Spare built. Shows the whites of her eyes" (p. 222). When the sheriff responds that the description "sound[s] like about twenty negroes [he] knows of personally" (p. 222), Nehemiah orders Dessa to show her scars. From here Dessa has Southern gentility and patriarchy on her side. Both Nehemiah and the sheriff stand up when Rufel enters the room and inveighs against scandalous people who "prey on defenseless womens" (p. 226). Batting her eyes, she suggests that Nehemiah has simply mistaken Dessa for someone else, which gives Dessa confidence that the sheriff "couldn't take [his] word against the word of a respectable white lady" (p. 225), especially not in a dispute over something *down there*. "Cept for them scars, it was the word of a crazy white man against a respectable white lady" (p. 226).

In this system, Nehemiah's recourse is to *ask* Rufel if she would lie for Dessa. He cannot *accuse* her of lying, because a "white man ain't posed to call no white lady a lie" (p. 227). The slave woman summoned to check Dessa's scars likewise denies that she has any. Ironically, then, the "evidence" the law uses to support its judgment to free Dessa comes not from Nehemiah, but from two women. More importantly, Dessa, who learned early on that "a nigger can't talk before the laws, not against no white man" (p. 49) and who admitted at one time that she had "no idea what a 'court' was" (p. 55), stands before the sheriff, the servant of the law, and Nehemiah, one of its arch-defenders, and pleads her case. These women, all three victimized by Southern patriarchy and its racial and sexual politics, find a power within that system by turning it back on itself, by turning its assumptions about blacks and women topsy-turvy.

And, except for that narrow escape, they have fun in the process, calling up "the comical things happened on the [flimflam] trail" (p. 216). As Dessa says, "We laughed so we wouldn't cry; we was seeing ourselfs as we had been and seeing the thing that had made us. Only way we could defend ourselves was by making it into some hair-raising story or a joke" (p. 208). She continues, "I told myself this was good, that it showed slavery didn't have no hold on us no more" (p. 213).

Am I suggesting something as outlandish (to say nothing of morally repugnant) as that Dessa's story would have us see that slavery was an institution to be laughed at, laughed about, laughed over? Clearly not. This is no book of "laughter and forgetting," to borrow from Milan Kundera, no dramatization of the thesis that slavery was not really "so bad" after all. It clearly was, and the historical record on that score is well known. For nearly four centuries, millions of human beings were kidnapped, some willingly sold into bondage by their own kin, and transported across the ocean to provide the labor power that made the

misnamed "Peculiar Institution." But these all-too-well-known horrific details were not the whole story, as historians such as John Blassingame,
Eugene Genovese, Herbert Gutman, and Deborah Gray White have done
well to establish. Contemporary Afro-American writers who tell a story
of slavery are increasingly aiming for the same thing: to reposition the
stress points of that story with a heavy accent on particular acts of agency
and resistance within an oppressive and degrading system. In a conversation with Charlayne Hunter-Gault following the publication of *Beloved,*
Toni Morrison explains that slavery was "so intricate, so immense and so
long, and so unprecedented," that it can take the writer over. She adds,
"we know what that story is. And it is predictable." The writer must,
then, focus not on the institution but on the people, which puts the "authority back into the hands of the slave."[26]

To repeat, Dessa Rose is the final authority on her story, controlling her
own text. But controlling a text of slavery, or any other text for that
matter, especially a written one, is no guarantee of freedom. Triumph over
language does not translate directly into triumph over social and material
circumstances and the differential power relations they create. The novel
establishes this point most clearly after Dessa has escaped Nehemiah for
the final time. Dessa and Rufel walk about the town of Arcopolis (an
anagram of Acropolis?), with all the associations of logocentrism and law
(polis), and yet what has developed between these two women is a threat
to both the word and the law. They have threatened this system by challenging, if not escaping, its terms. They free themselves from the mutual
antagonism and distrust, the name-calling that assigns each a confining
place and role. As they walk along, Dessa, now accustomed to calling Rufel
"Mis'ess," addresses her as such. Rufel answers, "I ain't your mistress. My
name Ruth." In a reciprocal gesture that reclaims her own "proper name,"
Dessa answers, "My name Dessa, Dessa Rose. Ain't no O to it" (p. 232).
Here, Dessa Rose claims naming, acting, and subjective agency for a black
woman. But it is significant that this naming and agency still operate within
a network of power inequality. While "free" of Nehemiah, and thus, ostensibly, a "subject," she is not free of others who exercise the power over
her that renders her a "subject" in a different sense.[27]

Dessa wants to hug Rufel at this point but hugs Rufel's daughter instead.
Throughout the novel their children have functioned both to mediate and
mollify the differences between them and to symbolize the possibilities of
a new order.[28] Returning to the opening questions about the who, what,
and why of "telling" slavery, we can say that *Dessa Rose,* and other
contemporary novels of slavery, witnesses slavery after freedom in order
to engrave that past on the memory of the present, but more importantly,

on future generations. My decision here to interpret and tell the story of *Dessa Rose* is analogous to one reason why contemporary Afro-American women writers are telling slavery: to remember the story to keep it alive and to seize some control over its remembering.

1988

9

Transferences

Black Feminist Thinking:
The "Practice" of "Theory"[1]

The old patterns, no matter how cleverly rearranged to imitate progress, still condemn us to cosmetically altered repetitions of the same old exchanges.
—Audre Lorde, "Age, Race, Class, and Sex"[2]

To exist historically is to perceive the events one lives through as part of a story later to be told.
—Arthur C. Danto, *Narration and Knowledge*[3]

That remembering is political and inextricably bound to culturally contested issues is now granted as freely as is the understanding that "*why* we remember and *what* we remember, the motive and the content, are inseparable."[4] In this final chapter, I want to consider the implications of memory and remembering in the construction of "historical knowledge" in general and of "critical theory" more specifically.

To speak of "historical knowledge" at all is to stage or enter a vigorous debate between those who see "history" and "knowledge" as ontological givens and those who don't. I identify with those who don't, with those who recognize that, despite its basis in the concrete certainties of "then" and "there," complete with recognizable names and familiar faces, history is a fantastical and slippery concept, a making, a construction.[5] I side with those who see history, to invoke the current *lingua franca,* as a "contested terrain" that often functions to repress and contain the conflicts and power asymmetries that mark the sociopolitical field.

That contemporary students of culture and its institutions have by and large willingly adjusted their assumptions and altered their practices to fit these axioms is a salutary development. But I share Renato Rosaldo's fear that in our zeal to establish historical contingency, to show that *everything* is constructed, human beings tend to "lose their specific gravity, their weight, and their density, and begin to float." We would do well to heed Rosaldo's warning against the dangers of declaring historical knowledge constructed and simply ending the discussion there, for we must show in nuanced historical perspective, however difficult that is, "how it was constructed, by whom, and with what consequences."[6]

Here, I want to take some liberties with time and construe the present moment as the future's past in order to determine what "historical knowledge" of "literary theory" we are constructing at this moment and with what consequences to what specific bodies. In other words, how are we telling the history or story of recent theoretical developments? Who are the principals in that story? What are the strategies of its emplotment? How does it reconstitute timeworn structures and strategies of dominance? Produce imagined divisions of scholarly labor that recode familiar hierarchical relations? I ask these questions because I share with many others a keen interest in how race and gender figure into our scholarly pursuits, drives, and desires. If we want an example of how "literary theory" gets historicized and of how social categories get woven into intellectual narrations, we need look no further than the representation of writings by African American women in contemporary academia. The period since 1977 provides a convenient point of access.

I agree with Hortense Spillers that "in a very real sense, black American women are invisible to various public discourses, and the state of invisibility for them has its precedent in an analogy on any patriarchal symbolic mode that we might wish to name."[7] And while some have tried to restore them to discursive sight, their efforts have been often compromised by the compulsions of historical legacy and the imperatives of contemporary social design. Such compulsions and imperatives are especially evident in debates of the past several years[8] about the supposed opposition between "theory" and "practice" (sometimes appearing as "theory" and "politics").[9] These debates illuminate how often the divisions and cleavages of scholarly labor exist in masked relation to the divisions and cleavages of social life.[10] More specifically, the theory/practice opposition is often racialized and gendered, especially in discussion of black feminist thinking, which, with precious few exceptions, gets constructed as "practice" or "politics," the negative obverse of "theory." While some black women have indeed helped to encourage this perception by viewing their writing as an enclosed and unified domain, fending off foreign intellectual invasions, they are neither the origins nor the primary agents of the theory/practice division that underwrites a familiar sociocultural contract.[11]

To raise questions about the social inflections of scholarly discourse is to confront the complex and steadily shifting contexts in which we position ourselves as intellectuals and in which we are positioned in turn. This situation leads, perhaps inescapably, to what Valerie Smith rightly terms the "split affinities" that render "inapplicable to the lives of black women any 'single-axis' theory about racism or sexism" and point to the difficulties of assuming any fixed critical position or pledging permanent allegiance to any one-dimensional idea of identity.[12]

What follows is not a singular narrative, but rather miscellaneous examples—call them "case studies"—about black feminist thinking that crop up in a variety of critical discussions. While I want to critique the treatment of "black feminist thinking" and "theory" as false unities, for purposes of easy reference I must refer to both in the singular, even as I am reminded that Hazel Carby's statements about black feminist criticism also apply to "theory," which must also be seen as a "locus of contradictions," a "sign that should be interrogated."[13] And although I select examples from a variety of critical denominations, I do so not to universalize or indict any whole, but rather to indicate the pervasiveness of the theory/practice division that has assumed a structural relevance and significance that can no longer be ignored.[14]

Uncovering the Truth: Coloring "Feminist Theory"

As we know, in the emplotment or narrativization of any history, much depends on familiar vocabularies of reference—on the circulation of names, proper names, and some names are more proper than others.[15] I want to talk briefly about the circulation of one name—Sojourner Truth—and the "knowledge" that name helps to construct about black feminist thinking within the general parameters of feminist discourse.[16]

In the opening chapter of her study *Am I That Name? Feminism and the Category of "Women" in History,* Denise Riley begins with a reference to Sojourner Truth and her famous and much-quoted question—"Ain't I a Woman?"—posed before the 1851 Women's Rights Convention in Akron, Ohio. Riley supposes that, in the current historical moment, Sojourner "might well—except for the catastrophic loss of grace in wording—issue another plea: 'Ain't I a Fluctuating Identity?'" The temptation here is simply to find the humor in Riley's rewriting and move on, except that to do so is to miss the sociocultural assumptions that attach to it, assumptions that escape the boundaries of Truth's time to project themselves boldly in our own.

Riley's move to appropriate Sojourner Truth introduces a subtle racial marker that distinguishes between Truth's original words and Riley's displacement. A familiar move in contemporary literary-critical discussion, Riley's "modernization" functions allegorically to make a common, if subtle, insinuation about black feminist thinking in general: It needs a new language. That language should serve a theory, preferably a poststructuralist theory, signaled in this context by the term *fluctuating identity*.[17]

To trace the move from Sojourner Truth's "Ain't I a Woman" to Riley's "Ain't I a Fluctuating Identity" is to plot, in effect, two crucial stages in a historical narrative of academic feminism's coming of age. Following this evolutionary logic, academic feminist discourse can be said to have "grown out of" an attachment to what Riley terms that "blatant[ly] disgrace[ful] and transparently suspicious" category—"Woman." That category happens to be personified by Sojourner's rhetorical and declarative question. Riley concedes that Sojourner represents one move in a necessary "double move" of feminist theory that recognizes that "both a concentration on and a refusal of the identity of 'woman' are essential to feminism."[18]

Constance Penley makes essentially the same point in *The Future of an Illusion*. Whereas in Riley's study Sojourner marks the point of departure, in Penley's she marks the point of closure. In the last two pages of the final chapter, she walks on to take a bow with Jacques Lacan. His "notorious bravura"—"the woman does not exist"—is counterposed to Sojourner Truth's "Ain't I a Woman?" Echoing Riley, Penley explains this counterposition as "two ideas or strategies ... vitally important to feminism," though they might appear completely at odds. Penley classifies the one strategy—represented by Lacan, Althusser, and Derrida—as "epistemological" and "metaphysical"; the other—represented by Sojourner Truth—is "political." That Truth's declarative question—"Ain't I a Woman"—might be read as "political" *and* "epistemelogical" simultaneously seems not to have occurred to Penley, partly because she manipulates both these categories, consciously or not, to conform to an already polarized and preconceived understanding.[19]

Is it purely accidental that, in these two essays, Sojourner Truth comes to represent the politics but not the poetics that feminism needs? Is hers a purely neutral exemplarity? Agreeing with Gayatri Spivack that "it is at those borders of discourse where metaphor and example seem arbitrarily *chosen* that ideology breaks through,"[20] I would argue that Sojourner is far from an arbitrary example. Possible intentions notwithstanding, Sojourner Truth as a metonym for "black woman" is useful in this context both to a singular idea of academic feminism in general and, in particular, to ongoing controversies within that discourse over the often uneasy relations between theory and politics.

The belief that feminism and whiteness form a homogeneous unity has long persisted, along with the equally persistent directive to feminist theorists to "account" for the experiences of women of color in their discourses. The unexamined assumption that white feminist discourse bears a special responsibility to women of color helps to maintain the perception that feminism equates with whiteness and relates maternalistically to women of color.

Such assumptions are implied in the recently published *Feminist Theory in Practice and Process*. In "Naming the Politics of Theory," one section of the introduction, the editors challenge "feminist theory . . . to recognize the myriad forms of black women's race, gender, and class politics and to envision theories that encompass these lived realities and concrete practices."[21] Elizabeth Spelman's observation, from another context, is useful here: "It is not white middle-class women who are different from other women, but all other women who are different from them."[22]

That difference has become magnified and has assumed an even greater urgency since academic feminism, like all discursive communities on the contemporary scene, has accepted the constructive challenge to take its processes into self-conscious account; that is, since it has accepted the challenge to "theorize" about the work it does and the claims it makes. The strain to fulfill both requirements—to "theorize," on the one hand, and to recognize material "differences," on the other, has created a tension within academic feminist discourse (read *white*). That tension is often formulated as a contrast, if not a contest, between "theory" and "practice/ politics," respectively.

I must rush to add that race (here, read *black*) and gender (here, read *female*) are not the only stigmatized markers on the practice/politics side of the border, for they trade places in a fluid system in which differences of nationality, sexuality, and class are interchangeable.[23] The now-quiescent French/American feminist theory debate—illustrated most controversially in Toril Moi's *Sexual/Textual Politics*—provides one example of what I mean. Moi clumps Anglo-American, black, and lesbian women on the practice/politics/criticism side of the border; French women, on the theory side. After blasting the claims of Anglo-American feminist criticism, Moi then turns to answer those who "might wonder why [she has] said nothing about black or lesbian (or black lesbian) feminist criticism in America. . . . The answer is simple: this book purports to deal with the theoretical aspects of feminist criticism. So far, lesbian and/or black feminist criticism have presented exactly the same *methodological* and *theoretical* problems as the rest of Anglo-American feminist criticism" (emphasis in text). Moi adds, "This is not to say that black and lesbian criticism have no . . . importance," but that importance is not to be "found at the level of *theory* . . . but the level of *politics*" (emphasis added).[24]

In the context of these critical developments, the use of "Sojourner Truth" projects myriad meanings needed to perform the work of distinction and differentiation in the culture of academe. To begin with, as a metonym for "black woman," the name can be read as a mark of racial difference and distinction within "feminist theory," which points up its internal conflicts and ambivalence over the relative merits and value of "political" discourse. That marks of racial difference can be hidden in itineraries represented as "purely" (and thus neutrally?) epistemological, is evident in the following summary by Jane Flax:

> Feminist theorists have tried to maintain two different epistemological positions. The first is that the mind, the self, and knowledge are socially constituted, and what we can know depends on our social practices and contexts. The second is that feminist theorists can uncover truths about the whole as it "really is." Those who support the second position reject many postmodern ideas and must depend upon certain assumptions about truth and the knowing subject.[25]

The assumptions about Sojourner Truth examined so far—both explicit and implied—cast her categorically in that second position, despite the fact that the short text of the "Ain't I a Woman?" speech is a compressed but powerful analysis and critique of the social practices within the context of slavery that depend on biases of class and race to construct an idea of universal or True Womanhood. She challenged that dominant knowledge, offering and authorizing her experiences under slavery as proof of its underlying illogicality.

The truth that Truth knows, then, is not reducible to a mere statement turned slogan that acts as theory's *Other,* or theory's shadow side. The politics contained within *that* epistemology, within that way of knowing Truth, must be interrogated and the foundations on which it rests laid bare. Those foundations are sharply exposed when we remember the moment in Truth's career perhaps most frequently remarked: the degrading demand to bare her breasts.

After delivering a speech in Silver Lake, Indiana, in 1851, one Dr. T. W. Strain alleged that she was a man. To prove that she wasn't, Truth bared her breasts.[26] The scene captures graphically Truth's fixity in the body and thus her distance from the "proper" white feminists enlisted to "verify" her sex. Her recuperation in these modern contexts forges a symbolic connection with that prior history, a conjunctive relationship to that past. It is precisely this earlier scene of verification that is being symbolically reenacted today. The demand in this present context is not to bare the breasts to verify black womanhood, but to bare the evidence that proves positively the qualifications of black feminist discourse as "theory."

But the selection of Sojourner Truth as metonym raises still other problems that connect to the relation between the symbolic and the social, the relation between the present and the past. The fact that Sojourner Truth was illiterate and that the words by which we know her were transcribed by stenographic reporters or admiring white friends has only begun to be interrogated with any complexity. Recent work by Nell Irvin Painter has begun to engage the nexus of paradoxes, ironies, and contradictions of these transcriptions and to inquire into why, until recently, Sojourner Truth, a "naive rather than an educated persona, seems to have better facilitated black women's entry into American memory" than any of her educated black female contemporaries. Painter's point is obviously not that only lettered or tutored black woman should have facilitated that memory, but that Sojourner Truth as figure keeps alive the "disparities of power and distinctions between European and Euro-Americans and natives, domestic and foreign."[27]

As a sign to a rematerializing critical discourse of its "sins of omission" around race, the utterance of "Sojourner Truth" or any other metonym for black women seems to perform for some an absolution of critical guilt; but the utterance is all. "Sojourner Truth"—or any other metonym for black women—is a name of which no more need be said. Truth's experiences beyond popularized clichés are not fully addressed.[28] She is useful simply as a name to drop in an era with at least nominal pretensions to interrogating race and the difference it makes in critical discussion.

But the repetition of Sojourner Truth's name makes no *real* difference. In dominant discourses it is a symbolic gesture masking the face of power and its operations in the present academic context. As a figure in remove, summoned from the seemingly safe and comfortable distance of a historical past, "Sojourner Truth" can thus act symbolically to absorb, defuse, and deflect a variety of conflicts and anxieties over race in present academic contexts. However, "Sojourner Truth" stirs up far more controversy than it settles, preventing any easy resolution of feminism's conflicts. Locked within that name is the timeless and unchanging knowledge (the very definition of "truth") of race and gender embedded in Western philosophy that now finds it way, like the return of the repressed, into the organization of knowledge in contemporary academe.

The repeated invocation of "Ain't I a Woman?"—detached from historical context—neither captures its immediacy for Truth's time nor reactivates it for our own. Put another way, the repeated invocation of "Sojourner Truth" functions not to document a moment in a developing discourse but to freeze that moment in time. Such a chronopolitics operates not so much as history but as an interruption of history, at least as black women might figure in it, a phenomenon recalling Hegel's description of Africa as outside the "real theatre of History" and of "no historical part of the World." "It has no movement or development to exhibit. . . . What we properly understand by Africa is the Unhistorical, Undeveloped Spirit, still involved in the conditions of mere nature, and which has to be presented . . . on the threshold of the World's history."[29]

The proposition that black feminist discourse is poised on the threshold of theory's history has predictable consequences. Not least, this view helps to reconstitute the structures and strategies of dominance, even in work that strives zealously in an opposite and oppositional direction.

Gendering African American Theory

We can observe such strategies of dominance in *Gender and Theory,* a recent anthology edited by Linda Kauffman. Kauffman tries studiously to prevent a reproduction of the simplistic divisions and antagonisms between black and white, male and female, "theory" and "politics." She explains in her introduction that while the title—*Gender and Theory*—posits a couple, the essays are arranged to permit men to respond to the essays by women and vice versa. That "structure is designed . . . to draw attention to such dichotomies in order to displace them by dissymmetry and dissonance."[30] Despite that goal, these very oppositions appear.

In fact, we could argue that if theory is often to practice/politics what Europe is to America, what white is to black, what straight is to gay, in Kauffman's anthology, theory is to practice what black male is to black female. This reductive accounting represents black women as categorically resistant to theory.

"Race" in Kauffman's anthology is constructed once again as synonymous with "blackness." Barbara Christian's "The Race for Theory" and Michael Awkward's response, "Appropriative Gestures: Theory and Afro-American Literary Criticism," are placed at the very end of the volume and thus apart from the preceding pairs of essays, none of which interrogates the racial inflections of "gender and theory." The racial opposition coordinates with oppositions of gender and genre, making theory male and practice female.

The question Kauffman poses in her introduction—"In what ways are Afro-American theory and Afro-American feminism complementary, and in what ways are they antagonistic?"—gets answered in the two concluding essays: "Afro-American theory" is gendered male and Afro-American feminism is gendered female, and they function effectively as structural antagonists. Such a seemingly innocent juxtaposition has already quickly decided its conclusion: Michael Awkward's response to Barbara Christian calls for a "theory" to her "practice."

One of the strengths of Awkward's response to Christian lies in its implicit recognition that poststructuralist theory cannot be homogenized, nor can it stand synecdochically for all theory. Although it is clear that he thinks Christian has missed the theoretical mark, he asserts that Barbara Smith's "Toward a Black Feminist Criticism" was "essentially a theoretical statement" "if not [a] poststructuralist discussion of critical practice and textual production." Smith's essay, he goes on to say, "theorizes despite its lack of a clearly informed awareness of deconstruction, reader-response theory, [and] semiotics."

Here, Awkward's vocabulary—"if not" and "lack of"—essentially negates whatever value he initially assigned Smith's essay, which is structured as the negative of the positive—an undifferentiated poststructuralism acting as the sole frame of reference. Making an uncritical link between black women as "writers" and black women as "critics" that holds the latter responsible for the survival of the former, Awkward offers a cautionary note: "If this field [black women's literature] is to continue to make inroads into the canon, if it is to gain the respect it doubtlessly deserves as an ideologically rich literary tradition, within an increasingly theoretical academy, it will require that its critics continue to move beyond description and master the discourse of contemporary theory."[31]

If, as Awkward suggests, "black women's literature still does not assume the prominent place in courses and criticism" that it merits, I would ask whether that marginality can be explained exclusively by a lack of theorizing on the part of black women or rather whether that marginalization is often structured into the very theories that Awkward wants black women to master. Again, my point should not be read as a simplistic rejection of "theory," even as it is narrowly associated, in Awkward's essay, with poststructuralist projects, but as a call for a more searching examination of the processes and procedures of marginalizing any historically subjugated knowledge.

Awkward's essay does more than close Kauffman's volume; it performs a kind of closure, or functions as a kind of "final word," that extends far beyond the boundaries of the collection *Gender and Theory*. He leaves intact the clichéd and unstudied distinctions between theory and practice represented by Paul de Man and Barbara Christian, respectively. It is paradoxical and ironic that an essay that privileges poststructuralist theory and extols de Man relies on an uncritical construction of theory as an autonomous entity with semantic stability and immanent properties that separate it from practice. It is all the more ironic that such a dichotomy should dominate in an essay that valorizes a body of theory identified most popularly with blurring such inherited and unmediated oppositions. But the dichotomies of Awkward's essay mark a difference and issue a set of limits—social limits—that extend beyond the academic realm. In identifying with Paul de Man, Awkward consolidates his own critical authority against Barbara Christian's, making theory a province shared between men.[32]

That theory is a province shared between men is nowhere more evident than in the wasteful *New Literary History* exchange between Joyce Joyce, Henry Louis Gates, and Houston Baker, which brought to the boiling point one of the most controversial shifts in the history of African American literary study: the "race" debate.[33] While this shift produced a schism among scholars in African American literary study, that schism has been oversimplified and exaggerated and construed, all too often, as a gender war over the uses and abuses of "theory" for African American literary study, a war with black men on the side of "theory" and black women against it.

Joyce Ann Joyce largely aided that perception with her much-discussed and critiqued essay "The Black Canon: Reconstructing Black American Literary Criticism." Recuperating the salient principles of the Black Aesthetic movement, Joyce argued for the responsibility of the black writer to his or her audience, for that writer's absolute and sovereign authority, for the use of the black literary text in fostering "Black pride and the dissolution of 'double consciousness,'" and the inappropriateness of "white" critical theories to analyses of black literature. In their responses to Joyce's essay, both Henry Louis Gates and Houston Baker were warranted in questioning these aspects of her argument, but they were less so in dismissing as naive and anachronistic her questions about "the historical interrelationship between literature, class, values, and the literary canon" (p. 336).[34] Gates and Baker choose to evade these questions in order to focus on Joyce's stubborn resistance to reading "race" as a pure signifier or arbitrary function of language. Joyce will not concede to her opponents in this debate that the complexities and irrationalities of social life in the United States are reducible to language games. And, even if they are, she comes just short of arguing, race still functions as a "transcendent signified" in the world.

Although he positions himself opposite Joyce in the *New Literary History* exchange, Houston Baker makes this same point eloquently in his essay "Caliban's Triple Play," a critical response to "Race, Writing and Difference," the special issue that Gates edited for *Critical Inquiry*.[35] Baker notes persuasively the power and resilience of "racial enunciative statements" that assert themselves painfully at the level of felt and lived experience. His compelling arguments in this essay indicate a clear reluctance to hypertextualize race, a stance that would seem to connect him with Joyce, but such a connection must be sacrificed in order to forge and secure a greater bond between Gates and Baker, one that transcends and papers over their critical differences. The rhetoric of erotics that tinges Gates's response to Joyce clearly indicates that much more is at issue and at stake than Joyce's alleged unexamined resistance to theory.

Gates's decision to use Tina Turner's pop hit "What's Love Got to Do with It," which Joyce rightly if reactively perceives as glorifying the objectification of women, clearly sexualizes this exchange:

> It is an act of love of the tradition—by which I mean *our* tradition—to bring to bear upon it honesty, insight, and skepticism, as well as praise, enthusiasm, and dedication; all values fundamental to the blues and to signifying, those two canonical black discourses in which *Houston and I* locate the black critical difference. It is merely a mode of critical masturbation to praise a black text simply because it is . . . "black."
> (Gates, p. 347, emphasis added)

In identifying *the* "two canonical black discourses," associated in their critical articulations with himself and Baker, Gates prepares the way for Baker to further consolidate a growing chain of male theoretical authority distinct from the dragrope of "black women critics," who constitute a "new black conservatism." Although Baker argues that his critique is "directed against specific conservatisms, misjudgments, and errors," rather than "toward a group," it so happens that "black women" are linked to a widespread, if unspecified, group that shows "essential animosity toward recent modes of critical and theoretical discussion." It is black women who fail to seize the abundant opportunities for the kinds of "theoretical daring and critical inventiveness" that mark the age and set the agenda for a transformative politics.[36] In Baker's view, that daring and inventiveness are seen mainly in the work of Derrida, Althusser, Lacan, and Baudrillard.

Curiously, in Baker's reasoning, all positions and/or questions not readily assimilable to their projects are conservative and atheoretical. More curious is the fact that the agenda for a transformative politics must repress gender, for those questions asked by the "conservative" black women, whom Baker chastises and corrects, are questions about the relations between gender and artistic production, questions that a good many people might regard as interventions in clear service of a transformative politics. Further, those in that service might challenge Baker to consider the various ways feminists have found his agents of change—Derrida, Althusser, Lacan, and Baudrillard—both useful to and limited for feminist projects. Indeed, to borrow Baker's words, if not his meaning, "the towers of an old *mastery* are reconstituted" in any implied suggestion that feminist critique works against, rather than in harmony with, other varieties of transformative politics and discursive priorities.

Notes toward a Counter History

Where might we go from here? I would start with the forthright assertion that the challenge of any discourse identifying itself as black feminist is not necessarily or most immediately to vindicate itself as theory. Its challenge is to resist the theory/practice dichotomy, which is too broad, abbreviated, and compromised by hedging definitions to capture the range and diversity of contemporary critical projects, including the range and diversity of the contributions of black women to that discourse. A far more valuable and necessary project would proceed from the commonplace assumption that no consideration of *any* intellectual project is complete without an understanding of the process of that project's formation. And thus any responsible accounting of the work of black women in literary studies would have to provide a history of its emergence and consider that emergence first on its own terms.

Of course, part of the historical accounting of recent critical production is under way, but unfortunately it leaves questions of the relations between race and critical discourse largely unexplored. A counter history, a more urgent history, would bring "theory" and "practice" into a productive tension that would force a re-evaluation of each side. But that history could not be written without considering the determining, should I say the over-determining, influences of institutional life out of which all critical utterances emerge.

It follows, then, that we would have to submit to careful scrutiny the past two decades, which witnessed the uncanny convergence and confluence of significant historical moments, all contributing to the present shape and contours of literary studies. These are: the emergence of a second renaissance of black women writing to public acclaim; a demographic shift that brought the first generation of black intellectuals into the halls of predominantly white, male, and elitist institutions; the institutionalization and decline of African American studies and women's studies; and the rising command in the U.S. academy of poststructuralism, regarded as a synonym for theory.

Our historical narrative would have to dramatize the process by which deconstruction came to stand synecdochically for poststructuralist theory, its dominion extending from the pages of arcane journals of critical theory, to the pages of such privileged arbiters of culture as the *New York Times Magazine* and *The New York Review of Books,* to the less-illustrious pages of *Time* and *Newsweek*.[37] The analysis would have to explore how deconstruction became associated as much with an ideological position as a revitalizing and energetic intellectual project at roughly the same time that a few black women, following Barbara Smith's challenge, began to articulate a position identified as black feminist criticism. Smith focused on recuperating the writings of black women for critical examination and establishing reading strategies attentive to the intersections of gender, race, and class in their work.[38]

If we were to isolate the salient terms of black feminist criticism and poststructuralist theory for this historical narrative, they might run as follows:

(1) While black feminist criticism was asserting the significance of black women's experience, poststructuralism was dismantling the authority of experience.

(2) While black feminist criticism was calling for nonhostile interpretations of black women's writings, poststructuralism was calling interpretation into question.

(3) While black feminist criticism required that these interpretations be grounded in historical context, deconstruction denied history any authoritative value or truth claims and read context as just another text.

(4) While the black woman as author was central to black feminist writers' efforts to construct a canon of new as well as unknown black women writers, poststructuralism had already rendered such efforts naive by asking, post-Foucault, "What Is an Author?" (1969) and trumpeting post-Barthes, "The Death of the Author" (1968).

(5) While black feminist critics and African Americanists more gener-

ally were involved in recuperating a canon of writers and outlining the features of a literary tradition, a critical vocabulary emerged to question the very idea of canons and traditions.

But the salient terms of these admittedly tendentious synopses would also have to reveal some useful correspondences. Both black feminist criticism and deconstruction perceived the regulation and exclusion of the marginal as essential to maintaining hegemonic structures. Both described the structural and hierarchical relations between the margins and the center. Our narrative might then pause to ponder how these two reading strategies came to be perceived as antithetical, how their specific *units* of critical interest came to be polarized and assigned an order of intellectual value that drew on a racist and sexist schema with heavy implications and investments in the sociopolitical arrangements of our time.

Choosing Sides

It is important that this shorthand history not be read to mean that poststructuralist theories and their practitioners constitute a reaction formation against the emergent non-canonical literatures, and thus black feminist thinking would do well without them. No, my aim is not to demonize poststructuralist theories or to see them as having invented the present hierarchies that pervade critical inquiry. The hierarchical arrangements of knowledge within which black feminist thinking is marginalized extend far beyond and are well anterior to these theories. Such arrangements are part and parcel of what has already been written about black intellectuals, male and female alike, part and parcel of a general and historical devaluation of black intellectual activity in whatever form it takes.[39]

What viable position can then be taken in this context? We might begin to assert a provisional conclusion: When the writings of black women and other critics of color are excluded from the category of theory, it must be partly because theory has been reduced to a very particular practice. Since that reduction has been widely accepted, a great many ways of talking about literature have been excluded and a variety of discursive moves and strategies disqualified, in Terry Eagleton's words, as "invalid, illicit, non-critical."

The value of Eagleton's discussion of literary theory lies mainly in its understanding of how critical discourse is institutionalized. In that process, the power arrogated to some to police language, to decide that "certain statements must be excluded because they do not conform to what is acceptably sayable"[40] cannot be denied. The critical language of black women is represented, with few exceptions, as outside the bounds of the acceptably sayable and is heard primarily as an illicit and non-critical variety of critical discourse defined in opposition to theory. Its definition and identity continue to be constructed in contemporary critical discourses, all of which must be recognized, distinguished, and divided from each other in the academy's hierarchical system of classifying and organizing knowledge. To be sure, the discourses that exist at any given historical juncture compete with each other for dominance and meaning, compete with each other for status as knowledge, but we must be constantly on guard for what Biodun Jeyifo is right to term a *misrecognition* of theory, although this misrecognition has "achieved the status of that naturalization and transparency to which all ideologies aspire and which only the most hegemonic achieve."[41]

Given this *misrecognition* of theory and the privileged status it enjoys, even in moments of embattlement, it is readily understandable why some black feminists and other women of color in the academy would argue for the rightful *recognition* of their work as "theory." bell hooks offers only one example.[42] In evaluating the position of black women in theory, hooks goes directly to the necessary site of any such evaluation: the micropolitics of the corporate university. In analyzing the production of feminist theory, she perceives "only one type of theory is seen as valuable" in the academy—"that which is Eurocentric, linguistically convoluted, and rooted in Western white male sexist and racially biased philosophical frameworks" and rightly observes that, because this is the only "type of theory . . . seen as valuable," other varieties get overlooked.

Given hooks's astute understanding of the ways in which the parameters of "theory" have been constructed institutionally so as to eliminate the writings of black women, her observation that "little feminist theory is being written by black women and other women of color" (p. 38) runs oddly counter to her otherwise forceful critique. For her assessment is accurate only if "theory" is very narrowly conceived to fit the very definition she decries. Moreover, her lament for the paucity of theory by black women seems dependent on a false distinction between "theory" and "creative writing."[43]

In describing the pedagogical imperatives of the feminist classroom, hooks observes that in the economy of the average feminist syllabus, the "imaginative works [of black women] serve purposes that should be addressed by feminist theory," a tendency that does "disservice to black women writers and all women writers." However useful novels and confessional writings are in the larger projects of feminist theory, hooks adds "they cannot and do not take the place of theory" (p. 38).

hooks's fears that the tendency in classes on feminist theory to identify "writing by working-class ... and women of color as 'experiential' while the writings of white women represent 'theory'" reinforces racism and elitism. Because of a long history that has constructed analytical thinking as the exclusive preserve of whites, hooks's concerns are fully understandable.[44] Although she is right to argue that "it does not serve the interests of feminist movement for feminist scholars to support this unnecessary and dangerous separation" between (theoretical) writing and writing that focuses on the experiential, her critique works only if she preserves that very distinction, ironically valorizing "theory" in the process.

While I would not presume to speak for or issue directives to "women of color," which would, in any case, assume a false and coherent totality, I openly share my growing skepticism about the tactical advantages of this position. I am far more interested, for the moment, in joining the growing number of critics—many of them "Third World"—who have begun to ask the difficult questions about the material conditions of institutional life and have begun to view theory, in its narrow *usages* (rather than in any intrinsic properties to be assigned to it), as an ideological category associated with the politically dominant. It is important that such a statement *not* be read as a resistance to "theory," but an insistence that we inquire into why that category is so reductively defined, and especially why its common definitions exclude so many marginalized groups within the academy. Such is Barbara Christian's point in "The Race for Theory," although in their rush to contain her inquiry, critics missed that aspect of her critique.

The question that Christian raises about the theory/practice distinction and the racial assumptions that it encodes is echoed in the writings of a growing number of students of minority and postcolonial discourses. For example, Rey Chow addressed the problem of "the asymmetrical structure between the 'West' as dominating subject and the 'non-West' or 'Third World' as the oppressed 'other'." She goes on to say, "contrary to the absolute difference that is often claimed *for* the 'Third World' ... the work of a twentieth-century Chinese intellectual foretells much that is happening in the contemporary 'Western' theoretical scene."[45] Chow's observations go far beyond and far deeper than a plea for a liberal, pluralist position here, beyond a plea for "equal time." Neither she nor the growing number of Third World intellectuals who have begun to interrogate the uses to which "theory" is being increasingly put are so naive as to suggest that the power of its gravitational field in academic discourse can be so simply and reactively resisted. Most of us know that the debate over the uses and abuses of theory, formulated as such, followed by a growing demand to choose sides, is a sterile and boring debate that diverts us from the more difficult pursuit of understanding how theory has been constructed as an exclusively Western phenomenon.

The view that theory cannot exist outside that narrow orbit is especially apparent in what Edward Said refers to as a "maddening new critical shorthand" that "makes us no less susceptible to the dangers of received authority from canonical works and authors than we ever were. We make lackluster references to Nietzsche, Freud, Lacan as if the name alone carried enough value to override any objection or to settle any quarrel."[46] Said's list of names requires its constructed others to embody the most popular terms of critical opprobrium. I am concerned to note that often these are the names of black American women who become fetishized, to quote Valerie Smith, and "employed, if not sacrificed, to humanize their white [and male] superordinates, to teach them something about the content of their own subject positions."[47] And nowhere is this more apparent than in a recent exchange with Jane Gallop, Marianne Hirsch, and Nancy K. Miller in *Conflicts in Feminism*, edited by Marianne Hirsch and Evelyn Fox Keller.

Rememories

> This was not a story to pass on.
> —*Beloved*

In that exchange, Gallop describes the process of her coming to write the history-in-progress of feminist criticism through a reading of 1970s anthologies, a reading that would offer a more balanced version of the now largely disparaged seventies feminist criticism than recent years have seen. A part of the process of this project involved Gallop's own conversion to the idea of race. Asked by Hirsch how inclusive her history would be and whether she planned to include anthologies that foregrounded race, Gallop answered, and I quote in detail, perhaps in unseemly detail:

I'm doing Pryse and Spillers's *Conjuring*. Race only posed itself as an urgent issue to me in the last couple of years. Obviously there has been a larger shift in the valent feminist discourses in which I participated. I didn't feel the necessity of discussing race until I had moved myself out of a French poststructural orbit and began talking about American feminist literary criticism. . . .

I was telling this guy in Syracuse that I thought in writing *Reading Lacan* I had worked through my transference both onto Lacan and onto things French in general. And he asked, "So who do you transfer onto now?" My first thought was to say, "no one." And then one of the things I thought of was a non-encounter with Deborah McDowell. I read work from my book last February at the University of Virginia. I had hoped Deborah McDowell would come to my talk: She was there, she was the one person in the audience that I was really hoping to please. Somebody in the audience asked me if I was writing about a black anthology. I answered no and tried to justify it, but my justification rang false in my ears. Some weeks later a friend of mine showed me a letter from McDowell which mentioned my talk and said that I was just doing the same old thing, citing that I was not talking about any books edited by black women. I obsessed over McDowell's comment until I decided to add a chapter on Pryse and Spillers's *Conjuring*. I had already vowed not to add any more chapters out of fear that I would never finish the book. As powerful as my fear of not finishing is, it was not as strong as my wish for McDowell's approval. *For McDowell, whom I do not know, read black feminist critic.* I realize that the set of feelings that I used to have about French men I now have about African American women. Those are the people I feel inadequate in relation to and try to please in my writing. It strikes me that this is not just idiosyncratic. This shift, for me, passed through a short stage when I felt like what I was saying was OK. The way McDowell has come to occupy the place of Lacan in my psyche does seem to correspond to the way that emphasis on race has replaced for me something like French vs. American feminism. (Emphasis added.)[48]

It is important to note that Gallop sees her whole project as a "struggle over whose version of history is to be told to the next generation" (p. 362). She continues, "Mainly I am saying that feminist criticism has not been well enough understood. I am writing a history of something that is too known in the sense that it is familiar, but that we don't really perceive anymore because we have our set notions and categories for what is going on."

Gallop's reference to our "set notions and categories" is far more suggestive and incisive than perhaps even she intends. And the philosophy of history that her reference encodes encourages me to assert my own, by way of looking back in time and simultaneously returning to Sojourner Truth.

In 1863 Harriet Beecher Stowe published "Sojourner Truth: The Libyan Sibyl" in *Atlantic Monthly*. It begins:

Many years ago, the few readers of radical Abolitionist papers must often have seen the singular name of Sojourner Truth, announced as a frequent speaker at Anti-Slavery meetings, and as travelling on a sort of self-appointed agency through the country. *I had myself often remarked the name, but never met the individual.* On one occasion, when our house was filled with company, several eminent clergymen being our guests, notice was brought up to me that Sojourner Truth was below, and requested an interview. Knowing nothing of her but her singular name, I went down, prepared to make the interview short, as the pressure of many other engagements demanded. (Emphasis added.)

Stowe's "I had myself often remarked the name, but never met the individual" has a striking ring or at least a structural similarity to Gallop's "For McDowell, whom I do not know, read black feminist critic." Having risked the dangers of a typological philosophy of history, let me suggest that in these two narratives, removed from each other by a century and a quarter, past and present become spectral adjacencies. While there are obvious risks in forging such a comparison, I do so out of understanding that intellectual inquiry is necessarily influenced and constrained by cultural traditions and social circumstances.

We might argue, then, that through the power of involuntary memory, the past is *transferred* to the present. While I obviously intend this play on words here, it is not idle play, for I want to capture that aspect of the transference that connotes a piece of repetition; the repetition is a transference of the forgotten past onto aspects of current situations. I want, moreover, to stress the rhetorical continuities between Stowe and Gallop in their own right as the legacy of a tradition of prefabricating blackness.

Both Stowe and Gallop commit what Ralph Ellison terms the "crime of reducing the humanity of others to that of a mere convenience, a counter in a banal game which involves no apparent risk to ourselves."[49] In "The Libyan Sibyl," Sojourner Truth is the counter to Stowe's conversion narrative, which assimilates Truth's complex life story to the civilizing rhetoric of Protestant evangelicism. In "Conflicts in Feminism," Deborah McDowell is the counter to an academic feminism now submitting to what Gallop calls the pressure of race.

But let me rush to insert here that my goal is neither to expose weaknesses in Jane Gallop's thinking nor to suggest that they are peculiar to her. In fact, in giving pause to her conversion narrative, I merely want to situate her within a general history. And Gallop would surely understand that, for as she prepares the reader for the delicate negotiations she must perform in the anthology study *Around 1981: Academic Feminist Literary Theory,* she takes care to note that

> We are [all] stuck inasmuch as we speak from within history . . . . [We] can only know from within history, with at best partial ideological awareness, and in specific relation to institutionalized discourses and *group interests.* (Emphasis added.)[50]

As Gallop recounts the process of her own conversion or coming to race, she reveals again much more than she realizes. She confesses: "I can't discount being attacked in the name of Marxism or historicism or racial difference, things that I recognize as serious political, as opposed to what I think of as high theoretical" (*Conflicts,* p. 352). Racial difference figures in her confession as a proper name, my name.

The assignment so far of black women to the "serious political" as opposed to the "high theoretical" is an oversimplified taxonomic distinction based primarily on the convenience of the privileged few, and thus it is perhaps fitting that Gallop's truncated account of her intellectual development turns on references to class mobility:

Around 1981, [I] experienced more anxiety about not being sophisticated enough whereas now my anxiety is about being bad, about having a white, middle-class outlook . . . . The anxiety about being a slob is an anxiety about not being high class enough, anxiety about being too low, whereas the other is anxiety about being too high. If you are looking up towards Derrida, Paris, sophistication, you feel like you're too low and you're anxious about not having something that comes from a higher class . . . . Now the situation is the opposite. (*Conflicts,* p. 353)

Race, in this context, equals lower class equals black feminist, a multiplication of equations that helps to construct an identity, a subjectivity for black feminist thinking among the general critical discourses of our time. Although black feminist criticism can be marked at one point on an as yet unfinished trajectory, it is consigned to the status of the permanent underclass. In that sense, the identity of black feminist criticism has so far been anything but fluctuating. It has been solidly fixed to a reference schemata and a racial stigmata in a history we've read before.

NOTES

Preface

1. Although "New Directions for Black Feminist Criticism" is included here, it was not intended as a part of the original project.

2. The dissertation actually focused on writers of the Harlem Renaissance. See "Women on Women: The Black Woman Writer of the Harlem Renaissance" (Ph.D. diss., Purdue University, 1979).

3. In "The Skewed Path: Essaying as Unmethodical Method" in Alexander Butrym, ed., *Essays on the Essay: Redefining the Genre* (Athens: University of Georgia Press, 1989), R. Lane Kauffman makes an interesting observation in this connection in suggesting that "the crisis of contemporary thought may be described in terms of this dilemma . . . the historical conflict between fragmentary and totalizing modes of thought—between essay and system." He continues, "On the one hand, in an era of totalitarianism, the inherent tendency of systems to closure and their operational role in what has been called the 'political economy of Truth' continue to make the system suspect as an epistemological and discursive norm. On the other hand, the fragmentary-essayistic mode championed by some critics harmonizes with the accelerating compartmentalization of knowledge in academic institutions and in society at large. . . . The responses to this dilemma in the works of the French poststructuralists Jacques Derrida, Jean-François Lyotard, Roland Barthes, and Michel Foucault constitute the most significant developments in contemporary Continental essayism. These thinkers, no less than the Frankfurt School critical theorists, have felt the magnetic pull of philosophical systems—whether phenomenological, structuralist, Marxist, or psychoanalytical" (p. 232).

4. Such experiences might be likened to "getting religion," as we described "conversion" during my childhood in Alabama. For a discussion of the religious rhetoric in contemporary critical discourse, see Edward Said, "Religious Criticism," in his *The World, the Text, and the Critic* (Cambridge: Harvard University Press, 1983). Said sees a "manifestly religious aestheticism" in contemporary criticism that descends from the New Criticism. He argues, "Once an intellectual, the modern critic has become a cleric in the worst sense of the word. How their discourse can once again collectively become a truly secular enterprise is . . . the most serious question critics can be asking one another" (p. 292). I disagree with Said that criticism has uniformly "refused to see its affiliations with the political world it serves" (p. 292), but, as I will suggest, sometimes its political affiliations stop at the borders of the printed page.

5. Nancy Miller, "Getting Personal: Autobiography as Cultural Criticism," in her *Getting Personal: Feminist Occasions and Other Autobiographical Acts* (New York: Routledge, 1991), pp. xi, 24.

6. For one account of this history see Cheryl Wall's introduction to her edited volume *Changing Our Own Words: Essays on Criticism, Theory, and Writing by Black Women* (New Brunswick: Rutgers University Press, 1989).

7. During the Harlem Renaissance Jessie Fauset, Nella Larsen, and Zora Neale Hurston published ten novels among them, a proliferation unrivaled until the 1970s, during which time a steady stream of novels by black American women was published and continues unabated to this day.

8. E. Franklin Frazier, *Black Bourgeoisie* (New York: Collier, 1957; rpt. 1975), pp. 193, 194.

9. Wilson J. Moses, "The Lost World of the New Negro, 1985–1919," *Black American Literature Forum* 21 (Spring/Summer 1987): 65.

1. New Directions for Black Feminist Criticism

1. Louise Bernikow, *The World Split Open: Four Centuries of Women Poets in England and America, 1552–1950* (New York: Vintage, 1974), p. 3.

2. William Morgan, "Feminism and Literary Study: A Reply to Annette Kolodny," *Critical Inquiry* 2 (Summer 1976).

3. The year 1970 was the beginning of the Modern Language Association's Commission on the Status of Women, which sponsored convention panels and workshops that were feminist in approach.

4. Stated by Barbara Desmarais and quoted in Annis Pratt, "The New Feminist Criticisms: Exploring the History of the New Place," in *Beyond Intellectual Sexism: A New Woman, a New Reality,* ed. Joan I. Roberts (New York: McKay, 1976), p. 176.

5. Patricia Meyer Spacks, *The Female Imagination* (New York: Avon, 1972), p. 5. Ellen Moers, *Literary Women: The Great Writers* (Garden City, New York: Anchor, 1977), is another example of what Alice Walker terms "white female chauvinism."

6. Alice Walker, "One Child of One's Own—An Essay on Creativity," *Ms.*, (August 1979): 50.

7. Robert Stepto, *From Behind the Veil: A Study of Afro-American Narrative* (Urbana: University of Illinois Press, 1979), p. x. Other sexist critical works include Donald B. Gibson, ed. *Five Black Writers* (New York: New York University Press, 1970), a collection of essays on Wright, Ellison, Baldwin, Hughes, and Leroi Jones; and Jean Wagner's *Black Poets of the United States: From Paul Laurence Dunbar to Langston Hughes,* trans. Kenneth Douglas (Urbana: University of Illinois Press, 1973).

8. Stepto, p. 166.

9. David Littlejohn, *Black on White: A Critical Survey of Writing by American Negroes* (New York: Viking, 1966), pp. 48–49.

10. Ellman's concept of "phallic criticism" is discussed in a chapter of the same name in her *Thinking about Women* (New York: Harcourt Brace Jovanovich, 1968), pp. 28–54.

11. Introduction to Robert Hemenway, *Zora Neale Hurston: A Literary Biography* (Urbana: University of Illinois Press, 1967), p. xiv. Although Walker makes this observation specifically about Hurston, it is one that can apply to a number of black women writers.

12. Barbara Smith, "Toward a Black Feminist Criticism," in *All The Women Are White, All the Blacks Are Men, but Some of Us Are Brave* (Old Westbury, N.Y.: Feminist Press, 1982), p. 159. Reprinted from *Conditions: Two* 1 (October 1977).

Subsequent references are to the Feminist Press version and will be indicated by page numbers in parentheses.

13. See Evelyn Hammonds, "Toward a Black Feminist Aesthetic," *Sojourner* (October 1980), for a discussion of the limitations on black feminist critics. She correctly points out that black feminist critics "have no newspapers, no mass-marketed magazines or journals that are explicitly oriented toward the involvement of women of color in the feminist movement" (p. 7).

14. Dorin Schumacher, "Subjectivities: A Theory of the Critical Process," in *Feminist Literary Criticism: Explorations in Theory,* ed. Josephine Donovan (Lexington: University Press of Kentucky, 1975), p. 34.

15. Annette Kolodny, "Critical Response: The Feminist as Literary Critic," *Critical Inquiry* 2 (Summer 1978): 824–25. See also Cheris Kramerae, Barrie Thorne, and Nancy Henley, "Perspectives on Language and Communication," *Signs* 3 (Summer 1978); and Nelly Furman, "The Study of Women and Language: Comment on Vol. 3, No. 3," *Signs* 4 (Autumn 1978).

16. Stephen Henderson, *Understanding the New Black Poetry: Black Speech and Black Music as Poetic References* (New York: Morrow, 1973), pp. 31–46.

17. Some attempts have been made to define or at least discuss lesbianism. See Adrienne Rich's two essays, "It Is the Lesbian in Us . . ." and "The Meaning of Our Love for Woman Is What We Have," in her *On Lies, Secrets, and Silence* (New York: Norton, 1979), pp. 199–202 and 223–30, respectively. See also Bertha Harris's "Notes toward Defining the Nature of Lesbian Literature," *Heresies* 1 (Fall 1977); and Blanche Cook's "'Women Alone Stir My Imagination': Lesbianism and the Cultural Tradition," *Signs* 4 (Summer 1979); 728–39. Also, at least one bibliography of black lesbian writers has been compiled. See Ann Allen Schockley's "The Black Lesbian in American Literature: An Overview," *Conditions: Five* 2 (Autumn 1979): 133–42.

18. Annette Kolodny, "Some Notes on Defining a 'Feminist Literary Criticism,'" *Critical Inquiry* 2 (Autumn 1975): 90.

19. Lillian Robinson, "Working Women Writing," in *Sex, Class, and Culture* (Bloomington: Indiana University Press, 1978), p. 226.

20. Robinson, "The Critical Task," in *Sex, Class, and Culture,* p. 52.

21. I am borrowing here from Kolodny, who makes similar statements in "Some Notes Defining a 'Feminist Literary Criticism,'" p. 75.

22. See Andrea Benton Rushing, "Images of Black Women in Afro-American Poetry," in *The Afro-American Woman: Struggles and Images,* ed. Sharon Harley and Rosalyn Terborg-Penn (Port Washington, N.Y.: Kennikat, 1978), pp. 74–84. She argues that few of the stereotypic traits that Mary Ellman describes in *Thinking about Women* "seem appropriate to Afro-American images of black women." See also her "Images of Black Women in Modern African Poetry: An Overview," in *Sturdy Black Bridges: Visions of Black Women in Literature* (New York: Anchor/Doubleday, 1979), pp. 18–24. Rushing argues similarly that Mary Ann Ferguson's categories of women (the submissive wife, the mother angel or "mom," the woman on a pedestal, for example) cannot be applied to black women characters whose cultural imperatives are different from white women's.

23. *The Messenger* 9 (April 1927): 109.

24. *The Messenger* 5 (July 1923): 757.

25. Tillie Olsen, *Silences* (New York: Delacorte, 1978), p. 257.

26. Kolodny, "Some Notes," p. 89.

27. Lillian Robinson, "Dwelling in Decencies: Radical Criticism and the Feminist Perspectives," in *Feminist Criticism,* ed. Cheryl Brown and Karen Alsex (New Jersey: Scarecrow Press, 1978), p. 34.

28. For a discussion of Toni Morrison's frustrated female artists, see Renita Weems, "Artists without Art Form: A Look at One Black Woman's World of Unrevered Black Women," *Conditions: Five* 2 (Autumn 1979): 48–58. See also Alice Walker's classic essay "In Search of Our Mother's Gardens," *Ms.* (May 1974), for a discussion of black women's creativity in general.

29. Toni Morrison, *The Bluest Eye* (New York: Pocket Books/Simon and Schuster, 1970), pp. 88–89.

30. Toni Morrison, *Sula* (New York: Bantam, 1980), p. 106.

31. Kolodny, "Some Notes," p. 86.

32. In an NEH Summer Seminar at Yale University, Summer 1980, Carolyn Naylor of Santa Clara University suggested this to me.

33. For a discussion of this idea, see Michael G. Cooke, "The Descent into the Underworld and Modern Black Fiction," *Iowa Review* 5 (Fall 1974): 72–90.

34. Mary Helen Washington, *Midnight Birds* (Garden City, N.Y.: Anchor/Doubleday, 1980), p. 43.

35. Washington, *Midnight Birds,* p. xvii.

36. See Saundra Towns, "The Black Woman as Whore: Genesis of the Myth," *The Black Position* 3 (1974): 39–59; and Sylvia Keady, "Richard Wright's Women Characters and Inequality," *Black American Literature Forum* 10 (1976): 124–28, for example.

37. Spillers, "The Politics of Intimacy: A Discussion," in *Sturdy Black Bridges,* p. 88.

38. Wole Soyinka, *Myth, Literature and the African World* (London: Cambridge University Press, 1976), p. 61.

39. Jane Gallop, "The Problem of Definition," *Genre* 20 (Summer 1987): 121.

40. Valerie Smith, "Black Feminist Theory and the Representation of the 'Other,'" in Cheryl Wall, ed., *Changing Our Own Words: Essays on Criticism, Theory, and Writing by Black Women* (New Brunswick: Rutgers University Press, 1990), p. 39.

41. Cheryl A. Wall, "Taking Positions and Changing Words," in *Changing Our Own Words* (New Brunswick: Rutgers University Press, 1989), p. 2.

42. bell hooks, "Ain't I a Woman: looking back," in *Talking Back: thinking feminist, thinking black* (Boston: South End Press, 1989), pp. 149–50.

43. The rhetoric of sisterhood is not unique to early articulations of black feminist criticism. In a suggestive essay, Helena Michie notes this tendency to "reclaim the family and to reproduce it in altered form. The figural response to patriarchy is 'sisterhood' invoked as its challenge." See "Not One of the Family" in Marleen S. Barr and Richard Feldstein, eds., *Discontented Discourses: Feminism Textual Intervention Psychoanalysis* (Urbana: University of Illinois Press, 1989), p. 15.

44. In a treatment of the contingencies of sexual identity and its formations, Jeffrey Weeks makes analogous observations about the force of affective affiliations. He suggests that, while "categorizations and self-categorizations"—both essential to identity formation—may "control, restrict, and inhibit," they can simultaneously provide "comfort, security, and assuredness." See *Sexuality and Its Discontents* (London: Routledge, 1985), p. 189. In a recent set of discussions of race, Anthony Appiah has expressed reservations about the discourse of racial solidarity. He argues that the

metaphors of kinship that attempt to assimilate "'race feeling' to 'family feeling'" are "usually expressed through the language of intrinsic racism." See "Racisms" in *Anatomy of Racism* (Minneapolis: University of Minnesota Press, 1990), p. 11. However useful Appiah's position is in complicating our understanding of how racial metaphors function, it glides too quickly over the fact that "intrinsic" racism is almost always a defensive position taken in response to disempowerment. Seldom is it taken offensively.

45. Hazel Carby, "'Women's Era': Rethinking Black Feminist Theory," in *Reconstructing Womanhood* (New York: Oxford University Press, 1987), p. 15.

46. Patricia Williams, *The Alchemy of Race and Rights* (Cambridge: Harvard University Press, 1991), p. 119.

47. bell hooks, "feminist theory: a radical agenda" in *Talking Back: thinking feminist thinking black* (Boston: South End Press, 1989), p. 36.

48. Cornel West, "Minority Discourse and the Pitfalls of Canon-Formation," *Yale Journal of Criticism* (Fall 1988): 197.

49. Carol Iannone, "Literature by Quota," *Commentary* 91 (March 1991): 50–53.

50. Hortense Spillers, "A Hateful Passion, a Lost Love," *Feminist Studies* 9 (1983): 295.

2. Race of Saints

1. Written in 1987, this essay introduced the edition of Emma Dunham Kelley's novel *Four Girls at Cottage City*, one volume in the Schomburg Library of Nineteenth-Century Black Women Writers.

2. Nina Baym, *Woman's Fiction* (Ithaca: Cornell University Press, 1978).

3. William Andrews, *Sisters of the Spirit: Three Black Women's Autobiographies of the Nineteenth Century* (Bloomington: Indiana University Press, 1986), pp. 10–11.

4. Carole Smith-Rosenberg, "The Female World of Love and Ritual," *Signs* 1 (Autumn 1975): 1–29.

5. See "Stowe's Dream of the Mother-Savior: *Uncle Tom's Cabin* and American Women Writers Before the 1920s," in *New Essays on Uncle Tom's Cabin*, ed. Eric J. Sundquist (Cambridge: Cambridge University Press, 1986), pp. 155–95.

6. Frances E. W. Harper, "Women's Political Future," in Bert James Loewenberg and Ruth Bogin, eds., *Black Women in Nineteenth-Century American Life* (University Park: Pennsylvania State University Press, 1976), pp. 244–45.

7. Here and elsewhere in the narrative, male ministers are shown to be ineffectual. In a discussion about the church's opposition to the "evils" of theatergoing, Erfort pulls from his breast pocket a pamphlet titled "The Common Sense View of the Theatre." Justifying theater-going by tracing it to its religious origins, the author of the pamphlet then places the blame for empty church pews not on the existence of theaters, but on the ineffectiveness of ministers.

8. Lori Kelley, *The Life and Works of Elizabeth Stuart Phelps, Victorian Feminist Writer* (Troy, New York: Whitson, 1983).

3. "The Changing Same"

1. I borrow the title and its underlying premise from Leroi Jones (a.k.a. Amiri Baraka), "The Changing Same (R & B and New Black Music)" in *The Black Aesthetic*,

ed. Addison Gayle, Jr. (New York: Anchor/Doubleday, 1971), pp. 112–25. In the essay, Jones traces the continuities in the black musical tradition, which has its roots in African religion and spirit worship, he argues. He submits that, even as it has changed, in both vocal and instrumental forms, black music has remained the same, continuing patterns and impulses that originated in Africa and were transplanted and "Christianized" in America—shouts, hollers, call and response (lead and chorus), for example. Analogously, we can observe continuities in black women's fiction from the nineteenth century forward, even as the tradition changes.

2. This essay is a version of a lecture presented at the Mary Ingraham Bunting Institute Colloquium Series, Radcliffe College, March 1984.

3. Frances E. W. Harper, *Iola Leroy or Shadows Uplifted* (1892; rpt. New York: AMS, 1971), p. 257. Subsequent references are to the 1971 edition and will be indicated by page numbers in parentheses in the text.

4. Alice Walker, *The Color Purple* (New York: Washington Square, 1982), p. 181. Subsequent references are to this edition and will be indicated by page numbers in parentheses in the text.

5. Throughout the discussion I will refer to the black female literary tradition in the novel, but the reference is restricted to Afro-American women novelists.

6. Although these two texts best exemplify my concerns here, I might also have chosen Harriet Wilson's 1859 novel *Our Nig,* Emma Dunham Kelley's 1892 novel *Megda,* or Pauline Hopkins's 1900 novel *Contending Forces* to represent the public paradigm as seen in the nineteenth-century novelists. To represent the private paradigm characteristic almost exclusively of late-twentieth-century, black women novelists, I might have chosen either Gwendolyn Brooks's *Maude Martha* (1953), Toni Morrison's *Sula* (1976), Gayl Jones's *Corregidora* (1975) or *Eva's Man* (1976), Toni Cade Bambara's *The Salt Eaters* (1980), Ntozake Shange's *Sassafras, Cypress, & Indigo* (1982), or Gloria Naylor's *The Women of Brewster Place* (1983).

7. Susan Lanser, *The Narrative Act* (Princeton: Princeton University Press, 1981), pp. 137–38. Although Lanser refers specifically to point of view in narrative, her use of "public" and "private" can be applied more broadly to other narrative structures, modes, and genres.

8. Throughout the following discussion, my use of "public" and "private" will ring familiar to students of Afro-American literature who will notice the similarity between the terms I use and other dichotomies used to describe Afro-American literature. For example, in his essay "The Literature of the Negro in the United States," included in his collection *White Man, Listen,* Richard Wright distinguishes between what he calls the "Narcissistic Level" and "The Forms of Things Unknown." The former is characterized by formal, self-conscious, and imitative writing, indicting racist attitudes and institutions. The latter is spontaneous, expressive writing deriving from black folk forms. In *The Negro Novel in America* (New Haven: Yale University Press, 1958), Robert Bone sees the same stylistic patterns in the Afro-American novel that Wright described in his essay. Bone simply renames the categories assimilationism/integrationism and Negro nationalism. I have chosen "public" and "private" instead in an attempt at greater terminological simplicity than Wright employs and in an attempt to avoid the value judgments and political overtones of Bone's distinctions. Finally, unlike either Wright's or Bone's terms, public and private are more flexible as descriptive paradigms, their implications and resonances more suggestive for the questions about narrative voice and literary audience that this discussion raises. I should

hasten to add that, like any literary taxonomy, mine cannot be strictly applied to every novel written by an Afro-American woman. That would grossly oversimplify a very rich and complex tradition. Further, there is overlap between the public and private modes, sometimes within a single text as evidenced in *The Color Purple*. I intend these terms merely as convenient points of entry into individual texts rather than as substitutions for the subtle distinctions that those texts require.

9. In the case of *The Color Purple*, the public/private distinction requires a finer and more precise definition that includes gender as well as cultural specificities. As I will discuss later, for example, in tone, texture, gesture, and strategy, the narrative strongly implies a female addressee. Deciding that "God must be sleep" or "glorying in being deef," Celie begins to address her letters to her sister, Nettie. Likewise, Celie and not Mr. ——— is the intended recipient of Nettie's letters.

10. Peter Rabinowitz, "'What's Hecuba to Us?' The Audience's Experience of Literary Borrowing," in Susan Suleiman and Inge Crosman, eds., *The Reader in the Text: Essays on Audience and Interpretation* (Princeton: Princeton University Press, 1980), p. 243; Wolfgang Iser, *The Implied Reader* (Baltimore: Johns Hopkins, 1974); Jane P. Tompkins, ed., *Reader-Response Criticism* (Baltimore: Johns Hopkins, 1980); and Walter J. Ong, "The Writer's Audience is Always a Fiction," *PMLA* 90 (1975), pp. 9–21.

11. Frederic Jameson, *The Political Unconscious: Narrative as a Socially Symbolic Act* (Ithaca, N.Y.: Cornell University Press, 1981), p. 153.

12. Jonathan Culler, *Structuralist Poetics* (Ithaca, N.Y.: Cornell University Press, 1975), p. 230.

13. Mary Helen Washington notes correctly that "one of the main preoccupations of the black woman writer has been the black woman herself." See *Black-Eyed Susans* (New York: Anchor/Doubleday, 1975), p. x. This preoccupation with fashioning a self is not peculiar to black women writers. As Henry Gates notes accurately, "the single most pervasive and consistent assumption of all black writing since the eighteenth century has been that there exists an unassailable, integral, black self . . . whole . . . knowable, retrievable [and] recuperable." See "Frederick Douglass and the Language of the Self," *The Yale Review* 70 (1981): 604.

14. Attempting to chart these variations by examining two texts from different periods might seem a curious strategy, but as students of literary history have begun to observe, juxtaposing works from diverse periods can reveal as much if not more about historical continuities and discontinuities than can a strict chronological narrative. See Herbert Lindenberger, "Toward a New History in Literary Study," *Profession 84*, pp. 16–22.

15. During the nineteenth century, black women formed a network of clubs throughout the country in which politically minded black women were committed to racial uplift (or Negro improvement). The clubs were largely unaffiliated until they convened in Boston in 1895 for their first national conference and became the National Association of Colored Women (NACW) in 1896. Predating both the NAACP and the Urban League, the NACW was the first national black organization with a commitment to racial struggles. For a detailed description of the activities of the organization, see "Black Feminism versus Peasant Values" in Wilson J. Moses, *The Golden Age of Black Nationalism* (Hamden, Conn.: Archon, 1978), 103–31; and Paula Giddings, *When and Where I Enter: The Impact of Black Women on Race and Sex in America* (New York: Morrow, 1984), 95–117.

16. See Paula Giddings, *When and Where I Enter;* and Elizabeth Davis, *Lifting as They Climb: The National Association of Colored Women* (n.p.: National Association of Colored Women, 1933).

17. Founded and edited by Mrs. Ruffin, a social activist, *The Woman's Era* was the first magazine in the United States to be owned, published, and managed by black women exclusively.

18. Quoted in Moses, *The Golden Age,* p. 115.

19. Though Harriet Wilson's recently discovered novel *Our Nig* (1859) predates these novels influenced by the efforts of the club movement, the emphasis on the priceless gem of virginity is still strong. See the edition of the novel edited and with an introduction by Henry Louis Gates, Jr., (New York: Vintage, 1983).

20. Since readers are undoubtedly familiar with them, I need not rehearse these stereotypes nor offer explanations for the cultural functions they have served throughout history. Paule Marshall has identified the two extremes of these clichéd images as the "nigger wench" and the mammy. See "The Negro Woman in American Literature," *Freedomways* 6 (1966): 20.

21. For a discussion of "the cult of true womanhood," see Barbara Welter's article of the same name in *American Quarterly* 18 (1966): 151–74. For a discussion of the "cult of domesticity," see Aileen Kraditor, *Up from the Pedestal* (Chicago: Quadrangle, 1968). Nancy Cott combines the two concepts in her treatment of "women's sphere" in New England in *The Bonds of Womanhood* (New Haven: Yale University Press, 1977). According to Cott, the "cult of true womanhood" was a Northern bourgeois tradition that "prescribed a role of utility, not leisure, decoration, or helplessness for women." The image of the lady, on the other hand, was Southern and "belonged more directly to the historical tradition immortalizing the [idle] aristocratic lady." Though they began as separate, indigenous traditions, the "Southern tradition influences Northern conceptions of women's roles more than vice versa," adds Cott, which explains why "by mid-[nineteenth] century Northern rhetoric on women's roles sounded increasingly like Southern" (p. 11). Harper seems to have combined elements of both the Northern and Southern traditions in her portrait of Iola Leroy.

22. Barbara Christian, *Black Women Novelists: The Development of a Tradition* (Westport, Conn.: Greenwood, 1980), p. 22.

23. See "If the Present Looks Like the Past, What Does the Future Look Like?" in *In Search of Our Mother's Gardens* (New York: Harcourt Brace Jovanovich, 1983), p. 301.

24. I am grateful to Elizabeth Ammons for suggesting that the glorification of motherhood as woman's heroic work was "modern" at the turn of the century. It was part of the attempt to elevate women's traditional work into a modern, disciplined, even scientific calling. It is possible, then, to see Iola Leroy as a part of that movement. Significantly, she lectures on and teaches the objectives of the "domestic science" movement, which attempted to make women's work a highly developed skill, a step up and forward, not backward. See her essay "Stowe's Dream of the Mother-Savior: *Uncle Tom's Cabin* and American Women Writers before the 1920's" in Eric Sundquist, ed., *Five New Essays on Uncle Tom's Cabin* (London: Cambridge University Press, 1986), pp. 155–95.

25. John Wideman, "Defining the Black Voice in Fiction," *Black American Literature Forum* 11 (1977): 81.

26. Arlene Elder, *The 'Hindered Hand': Cultural Implications of Early African-American Fiction* (Westport, Conn.: Greenwood, 1978), p. 16.

27. Allow a few examples to suffice. Iola, like Stowe's Cassy, does not discover she is a slave until her white father dies and she is then sold into slavery. Before she is remanded to slavery, however, Iola ardently defends the institution to a black school-mate, arguing the classic plantation line: slaves are content with their lot. Her friend responds, "I do not think that slave mother who took her four children, crossed the Ohio River on the ice, killed one of the children, and attempted the lives of the other two, was a contented slave" (p. 98). Although in this speech Harper has made slight modifications in Stowe's plot, the reminiscences of Eliza's famous trek across the ice to escape slave hunters and Cassy's administration of laudanum to her child are both strong. (Incidentally, Harper's poem "Eliza Harris" dramatizes Eliza's escape.) Finally, the death of Iola's young sister, Grace, is modeled directly on the death of Stowe's Little Eva. "Swiftly the tidings went through the house that Gracie was dying. The servants gathered around her with tearful eyes, as she bade them all good-bye. When she had finished and Mammy had lowered the pillow, an unwonted radiance lit up her eye and an expression of ineffable gladness overspread her face, as she murmured: 'It is beautiful, so beautiful!'" (p. 108).

28. Elder, *The 'Hindered Hand,'* p. xiv.

29. Although my aim here is not to trace the linear development of character in black women's fiction, it is useful to provide at least a sketch of the tradition between Harper and Walker. Harper's legacy continues in some particulars in the novels of Jessie Fauset and Nella Larsen in the 1920s and '30s, which focus on middle-class, upwardly mobile heroines. The heroines' motivations shift, however, from a concern for racial uplift and corporate mission to a frequently destructive obsession with material security and social status. (See Fauset's four novels, *There Is Confusion* (1924), *Plum Bun* (1929), *The Chinaberry Tree* (1931), and *Comedy, American Style* (1933); and Larsen's *Quicksand* (1928) and *Passing* (1929). Zora Neale Hurston can be regarded as a transitional figure between the nineteenth-century tradition, represented by Harper and continued by Fauset and Larsen, and the contemporary tradition, represented by Alice Walker and her black female contemporaries. They shift away from the public conception of character and art to one more private, more culturally self-contained, one seemingly indifferent to public example and approval. The best example of this shift is the novel *Their Eyes Were Watching God.*

30. Walker, *In Search of Our Mother's Gardens,* p. 49.

31. Among the black female novelists to depict the "ordinary" black heroine are Ann Petry in *The Street* (1948), Gwendolyn Brooks in *Maude Martha* (1953), and Sarah E. Wright in *This Child's Gonna Live* (1969).

32. Before the 1970s there are noticeably few lesbian relationships in black women's fiction. Nella Larsen flirts with the possibility of such a relationship in her novel *Passing* (1929). Other such relationships in black women's novels include those in Gloria Naylor's *The Women of Brewster Place* (1982), Ntozake Shange's *Sassafras, Cypress, and Indigo* (1982), Ann Allen Shockley's *Loving Her* (1974) and *Say Jesus and Come to Me* (1982), and Rosa Guy's *Ruby* (1976).

33. It is useful to note that, in creating Celie, Alice Walker has not only revised nineteenth-century prototypes, but also previous characters of her own creation. For example, the title character of Walker's second novel, *Meridian* (New York: Simon and Schuster, 1976), is depicted in images that resemble these early heroines. She is

mythical, spiritual, described in Christ-like imagery, and sacrifices all personal gain for a larger social good.

34. The following conversation between Shug, Tobias, and Celie reinforces the point:

> "All womens not alike Tobias [Shug] say.
> Believe it or not. Oh, I believe it, he say.
> Just can't prove it to the world."
> First time I think about world, [says Celie].
> What the world got to do with anything, I think. (61)

35. As Alice Walker reminds us, "The majority of black women who tried to express themselves by writing and who tried to make a living doing so, died in obscurity and poverty usually before their time. . . . Phillis Wheatley died, along with her three children, of malnutrition, in a cheap boardinghouse where she worked as a drudge. Nella Larsen died in almost complete obscurity after turning her back on her writing in order to become a practical nurse, an occupation that would at least buy food . . . and a place to sleep. And Zora Neale Hurston . . . died in poverty in the swamps of Florida, where she was again working as a housemaid," and was buried in an unmarked grave. See "A Talk: Convocation 1972," in *In Search of Our Mother's Gardens*, p. 35.

36. It is reminiscent, for example, of Janie in Zora Neale Hurston's *Their Eyes Were Watching God* (1937), a novel that Walker freely admits has influenced her own work. Before Janie gains her full voice, she describes being split in two. For a discussion of how metaphors of self-division function in *Their Eyes*, see Barbara Johnson, "Metaphor, Metonymy and Voice in *Their Eyes Were Watching God*" in Henry Louis Gates, Jr., ed., *Black Literature and Literary Theory* (New York: Methuen, 1984), pp. 205–219.

37. See Susan Lanser, *The Narrative Act;* Mary Louise Pratt, "'Poetic Language' Fallacy" and "Natural Narrative: What Is 'Ordinary Language' Really Like?" in her *Toward a Speech Act Theory of Literary Discourse* (Bloomington: Indiana University Press, 1977); and Stanley Fish, "How Ordinary Is Ordinary Language?" *New Literary History* 5 (1973): 41–54.

38. See John Wideman's "Defining the Black Voice in Fiction" for a discussion of such legitimating filters in Afro-American literature.

39. The same is implied in Hurston's *Their Eyes Were Watching God*. The authority that Janie's story has is due to her intimate and receptive audience, again a woman, her friend Pheoby. They have been "kissin friends" for twenty years, and when Pheoby comes to hear Janie's epic story, she enters by the "intimate gate."

40. Walker, "Saving the Life That Is Your Own" in *In Search*, pp. 3–14.

41. "Do You Know This Woman?" *Ms.* 10 (June 1982): 35–37, 89–94.

42. Bloom, *Anxiety of Influence* (New York: Oxford University Press, 1973); and *A Map of Misreading* (New York: Oxford University Press, 1975). In her excellent essay "A Hateful Passion, a Lost Love" *Feminist Studies* 9 (1983): 293–323, Hortense Spillers makes a similar point about the nature of literary influence among black women writers.

43. Although Kristeva does not use the term "intertextuality" in conjunction with discussions of influence, it is possible to use the concept in such discussions without violating the integrity of Kristeva's original definition. In formulating her definition, Kristeva borrows from Mikhail Bakhtin's "conception of the 'literary word' as an

intersection of textual surfaces . . . as a dialogue among several writings. . . . Any text is constructed as a mosaic of quotations; any text is the absorption and transformation of another." See "The Bounded Text" and "Word, Dialogue, and Novel" in Julia Kristeva, *Desire in Language: A Semiotic Approach to Literature and Art,* trans. Thomas Gora, Alice Jardine, and Leon S. Roudiez, ed. Leon Roudiez (New York: Columbia University Press, 1980), pp. 64 and following.

44. Both Robert Stepto (*From Behind the Veil* [Urbana: University of Illinois Press, 1979]) and Henry Louis Gates ("The 'Blackness of Blackness': A Critique of the Sign and the Signifying Monkey," *Critical Inquiry* 9 [1983]: 685–723) have provided excellent adaptations of the theory of intertextuality in their readings of certain Afro-American texts. While they go far toward defining the Afro-American narrative tradition, neither examines, in any thoroughgoing way, the place of Afro-American female writers in the tradition as they define it.

45. See "The 'Blackness of Blackness,'" pp. 696–97.

46. Shange, *nappy edges* (New York: St. Martin's, 1978), pp. 4-5, 11.

47. See Jane Tompkins's *Sensational Designs* for a discussion of the political work nineteenth-century fiction was "designed" to do.

48. Houston Baker, *The Journey Back* (Chicago: University of Chicago Press, 1980), p. 109.

49. Hoyt Fuller, "Towards a Black Aesthetic," in *The Black Aesthetic,* ed. Addison Gayle, Jr. See other essays on the subject in that collection.

50. For a discussion of the popularity of *The Color Purple,* see Trudier Harris, "On *The Color Purple,* Stereotypes, and Silence," *Black American Literature Forum* 18 (Winter 1984): 155–61. The film adaptation of the novel has been the subject of intense and heated debate. Much of the criticism has been waged by black men who see the novel and the film as alike in their degrading depiction of black men.

51. Hortense Spillers, "Cross-Currents, Discontinuities: Black Women's Fiction," in Marjorie Pryse and Hortense Spillers, eds., *Conjuring: Black Women, Fiction, and Literary Tradition* (Bloomington: Indiana University Press, 1985), p. 251.

52. Molly Hite, introduction to Emma Dunham Kelley, *Megda* (1891; rpt. New York: Oxford University Press, 1988), p. xxix.

53. Hortense Spillers, introduction to Mrs. A. E. Johnson, *Clarence and Corinne; or God's Way* (1890; rpt. New York: Oxford University Press, 1988), p. xxxiii.

54. Henry Louis Gates, "In Her Own Write," foreword to Schomburg Library of Nineteenth-Century Black Women Writers (New York: Oxford University Press, 1988).

55. Susan Sontag, "'Thinking Against Oneself': Reflections on Cioran" in *Styles of Radical Will* (New York: Farrar, Straus and Giroux, 1969), p. 75.

56. Here, Molly Hite's discussion of the novel is useful. She links *The Color Purple* to such late Shakespearean romances as *The Winter's Tale* in its depiction of a "pastoral community . . . that implicitly restores a submerged Edenic ideal of harmony between individual human beings and humanity and the natural order." See "Romance, Marginality, Matrilineage: Alice Walker's *The Color Purple* and Zora Neale Hurston's *Their Eyes Were Watching God,*" *Novel* 22 (Spring 1989): 261. In her introduction to the Schomburg edition of Emma Dunham Kelley's *Megda,* Hite observes that same quietism and stability in Emma Dunham Kelley's novels. She argues that "the society that *[Megda]* represents" is stable and that "exhortations to quietism recur periodically,

reinforcing the implication that personal salvation is the only thing at issue in this Christian *bildungsroman*," p. xxvii.

57. Hazel V. Carby, introduction to *Iola Leroy* (Boston: Beacon, 1987), p. xxii.

58. Wilson J. Moses, *The Golden Age of Black Nationalism* (Connecticut: Archon, 1978), pp. 122–31.

59. For a discussion of the racial construction of sexuality, see John D'Emilio and Estelle Freedman, *Intimate Matters: A History of Sexuality in America* (New York: Harper and Row, 1988).

60. Elizabeth Ammons, *Conflicting Stories: American Women Writers at the Turn into the Twentieth Century* (New York: Oxford University Press, 1991), pp. 31, 30.

61. Claudia Tate, "Allegories of Black Female Desire; or, Rereading Nineteenth-Century Sentimental Narratives of Black Female Authority," in Cheryl Wall, ed., *Changing Our Own Words: Essays on Criticism, Theory, and Writing by Black Women* (New Brunswick: Rutgers University Press, 1989), pp. 103, 126.

62. Jonathan Culler, *Framing the Sign: Criticism and Its Institutions* (Norman: University of Oklahoma Press, 1988), p. xiv.

63. Dominick LaCapra, *Soundings in Critical Theory* (Ithaca: Cornell University Press, 1989), p. 207.

4. On Face

1. W. E. B. Du Bois and Alain Locke, "The Younger Literary Movement," *The Crisis* 27 (February 1924): 161–62.

2. Alain Locke, "Both Sides of the Color Line" *Survey* (June 1929), pp. 325–36.

3. Locke, "The Saving Grace of Realism," *Opportunity* (January, 1934): 9. After she read the review, Fauset wrote Locke a letter in which she described his writings as "stuffed with a pedantry which fails to conceal their poverty of thought." She accused him of "play[ing] [it] safe with the grand white folks" and of being a "subscriber to that purely Negroid school whose motto is 'whatever is white is right.'" She asked him to send her an example of her "mid-Victorian style" and expressed her hopes that he would not review more of her work. Fauset to Alain Locke, January 9, 1933, Moorland-Spingarn Collection, Howard University.

At the time Locke wrote this review, Fauset had been writing for ten years, during which time she had also served as literary editor of *The Crisis,* publishing, some for the first time, the most prominent figures of the Harlem movement—Claude McKay, Jean Toomer, Anne Spencer, and arguably the most famous, Langston Hughes. It was Fauset who accepted Hughes's most anthologized poem, "The Negro Speaks of Rivers." After accepting additional poems by Hughes for *The Crisis,* Fauset wrote him a letter generous in its praises of his work: "You assuredly have the true poetic touch, the divine afflatus, which will someday carry you far." Quoted in Arnold Rampersad, *The Life of Langston Hughes* (New York: Oxford University Press, 1986), p. 70.

4. Claude McKay, *A Long Way from Home* (New York: Harcourt Brace and World, 1937), pp. 112–13. Without suggesting that writers who review each other's work must conform to a code of reciprocal "back scratching," it is nonetheless interesting to note that Fauset was far more fair and measured in her assessments of her contemporaries' work than they were of hers. For example, she commended Claude McKay's *Harlem Shadows* for its "deep emotionalism" and for his "perception of what is fundamentally important to mankind everywhere," (*The Crisis,* May 1922).

In a letter to Arthur Spingarn, she enclosed a poem by Jean Toomer, praising it for its "marked proof of an art and of a contribution to literature which will be distinctly Negroid and without propaganda," (Jessie Fauset to Arthur Spingarn, January 20, 1923, Beinecke Library, Yale).

5. Robert Hemenway, headnote to William Stanley Braithwaite, "The Novels of Jessie Fauset," in Robert Hemenway, ed., *The Black Novelist* (Columbus, Ohio: Charles Merrill, 1970), p. 46.

6. Robert Bone, *The Negro Novel in America* (1958; rpt. New Haven: Yale University Press, 1972), pp. 97, 101.

7. Hazel Carby, *Reconstructing Womanhood* (New York: Oxford University Press, 1987), p. 167.

8. Barbara Christian, *Black Women Novelists: The Development of a Tradition* (Westport, Conn.: Greenwood, 1980), p. 43.

9. Mary Dearborn, *Pocahontas's Daughters: Gender and Ethnicity in American Culture* (New York: Oxford University Press, 1986), p. 51.

10. Karen Sanchez-Eppler, "Bodily Bonds: The Intersecting Rhetorics of Feminism and Abolition," *Representations* 24 (Fall 1988): 41.

11. Works such as Lothrop Stoddard's *The Rising Tide of Color,* Madison Grant's *The Passing of the Great Race,* Clinton Burr's *American Race Heritage,* and Alfred Wiggam's *The Fruit of the Family Tree* all attempted to define race as a strictly biological matter. It is conceivable that Fauset's first novel, *There Is Confusion,* is in dialogue with *The Fruit of the Family Tree.* The novel dramatizes questions of racial and genealogical "purity" and "descent," seeing them as the basis of inequities in socioeconomic and "political" inheritance. Although the novel dramatizes distinctions of birth and heritage that affect the lives of all its characters, the text centers on how these distinctions figure in the genealogy of Peter Bye. Bye is a product of the racial intermixture during slavery that so entangled black and white bloodlines as to make racial distinctions fictive but powerful constructions of culture, encoding and maintaining unequal relations of class, property, and privilege.

12. The novel of passing is a genre that has preoccupied African American writers throughout their literary history. *Plum Bun* is part of a roster that includes pre-Harlem Renaissance novels such as William Wells Brown's *Clotel* (1853), Charles Chesnutts's *The House behind the Cedars* (1900), and James Weldon Johnson's *The Autobiography of an Ex-Colored Man* (1912). Fauset returned to the genre again and again, beginning with her early short stories, "Emmy" and "The Sleeper Wakes," published in *The Crisis,* and ending with her last novel, *Comedy, American Style* (1933). Other novels of passing published during Fauset's era include Walter White's *Flight* (1926) and Nella Larsen's *Passing* (1929).

13. Ian MacInnes, "Closure and the Fiction of Female Development," unpublished essay.

14. "The Sleeper Wakes" was published in three installments in *The Crisis,* 20 (August 1920): 168–72; (September 1920): 226–29; and (October 1920): 267–74.

15. According to Marcia Lieberman, in fairy tales and romance, "marriage is associated with getting rich"; thus "the reward basis" they inscribe is "overwhelmingly mercenary." See "'Some Day My Prince Will Come': Female Acculturation through the Fairy Tale," *College English* 34 (1972): 386.

16. Arguably the most powerful dramatization of the power of dominant cultural

fantasies on the imaginations of emerging black women is Toni Morrison's *The Bluest Eye* (New York: Simon and Schuster, 1970).

17. It is interesting to consider this passage in light of controversies over intermarriage that emerged with renewed vigor in the teens and twenties. During part of the time that Fauset was literary editor of *The Crisis* and he was the editor, W. E. B. Du Bois wrote a group of editorials in support of intermarriage. He argued that "to prohibit such intermarriage would be publicly to acknowledge that black blood is a physical taint," but the greatest reason for opposing laws against intermarriage was that they would "leave the colored girl absolutely helpless before the lust of white men. It reduces colored women in the eyes of the law to the status of dogs." He concluded that all laws against intermarriage must be killed "not because [black men] are anxious to marry white men's sisters, but because we are determined that white men should leave our sisters alone," ("Intermarriage," *The Crisis* 5 [1913]). In a later editorial, Du Bois argued that efforts to prevent intermarriage "encourage[d] prostitution and degrade[d] women of Negro descent." He astutely noted the hypocrisy and contradictions in the fact that while interracial marriage was illegal in Mississippi, 122,000 acknowledged mulattoes existed in the state. Such a situation, he continued, refused "to black girls any adequate protection against white brutes or gentlemen," ("Intermarriage," *The Crisis* 29 (1925). Finally, in "Miscegenation," written in January, 1935, Du Bois returned with added vigor and bitter denunciation to the subject: "the bitterest protest and deepest resentment in the matter of inter-breeding has arisen from the fact that the same white race which today resents race mixture in theory has been chiefly responsible for the systematic misuse and degradation of darker women the world over, and has literally fathered millions of half-castes in Asia, Africa, and America." The essay, commissioned by Dr. Victor Robinson for an Encyclopedia Sexualix, was never published. See "Miscegenation," in Herbert Aptheker, ed., *Against Racism: Unpublished Essays, Papers, Addresses, 1887–1961* (Amherst: University of Massachusetts Press, 1985), p. 95.

18. The free love movement, which began in the 1870s, was common among Greenwich Village intellectuals in the 1920s. They opposed legal and clerical marriage, which, in their estimation, stifled love. See Linda Gordon, *Woman's Body, Woman's Right* (New York: Penguin, 1974).

19. Nancy Hartsock, *Money, Sex and Power: Toward a Feminist Historical Materialism* (New York: Longman, 1983), p. 155.

20. See for example Joseph A. Boone, "Modernist Maneuverings in the Marriage Plot: Breaking Ideologies of Gender and Genre in James's *The Golden Bowl*," *PMLA* 101 (May 1986): 374–88; and Lennard J. Davis, *Resisting Novels: Ideology and Fiction* (New York: Methuen, 1987).

21. I am indebted to one of my students, Susan Lanham, for this point, and to another, Carole Allen, for her observations that in Fauset's last novel, *Comedy, American Style,* there is a constant erosion of the romantically constructed ideal of a household comprised of Mother, Father, and Children who live happily ever after, for at the novel's end, the protagonist, Olivia Carey, is alone on a park bench in Paris.

22. D. A. Miller, *The Novel and the Police* (Berkeley: University of California, 1988), p. 106.

23. Nathan Huggins, *Harlem Renaissance* (New York: Oxford University Press, 1971), p. 128.

24. Langston Hughes, *The Big Sea* (New York: Hill and Wang, 1940), pp. 316, 325.

25. Mrs. Mason also served as Zora Neale Hurston's patron. For a discussion of their complicated relationship, see Robert E. Hemenway, *Zora Neale Hurston: A Literary Biography* (Urbana: University of Illinois Press, 1977). Hurston would later write that "publishers and producers are cool to the idea" of literature "about the higher emotions and love of upper-class Negroes and the minorities in general. . . . It is assumed that all non–Anglo-Saxons are uncomplicated stereotypes." See "What Publishers Won't Print," rpt. in Alice Walker, ed., *I Love Myself When I Am Laughing,* (Old Westbury: Feminist Press, 1979), pp. 169–73.

26. Fauset, "The Negro in Art: How Shall He Be Portrayed," *The Crisis* 32 (June 1926): 72.

27. Du Bois, *Voices of a Black Nation: Political Journalism in the Harlem Renaissance,* ed. Theodore Vincent (San Francisco: Ramparts, 1973), pp. 352–60.

28. "The Negro in Art: How Shall He Be Portrayed," *The Crisis* 32 (June 1926): 72.

29. Fauset admitted combing the popular magazines of the time for ideas for plotting her novels.

5. The "Nameless . . . Shameful Impulse"

1. A version of this chapter introduced the edition of *Quicksand and Passing,* published by Rutgers University in 1986 in its American Women Writers series.

2. Nella Larsen, *Quicksand and Passing* (1928; rpt. New Brunswick: Rutgers University Press, 1986), pp. 94–95. Subsequent references will be indicated by page numbers in parentheses.

3. See, for example, Hiroko Sato, "Under the Harlem Shadows: A Study of Jessie Fauset and Nella Larsen," in Arna Bontemps, ed., *The Harlem Renaissance Remembered* (New York: Dodd Mead, 1972), pp. 63–89; Robert Bone, *The Negro Novel in America* (1958; rpt. New Haven: Yale University Press, 1972); David Littlejohn, *Black on White: A Critical Survey of Writing by American Negroes* (New York: Viking, 1966; Addison Gayle, *The Way of the New World* (New York: Anchor/Doubleday, 1976).

4. In "The Aesthetics of Race and Gender in Nella Larsen's *Quicksand,*" in *PMLA* 105 (January 1990), Ann E. Hostetler asserts that "Larsen goes far beyond Fauset in both stylistic experimentation and the daring self-examination of her protagonist" (p. 36). See also Hiroko Sato, "Under the Harlem Shadows: A Study of Jessie Fauset and Nella Larsen," in *The Harlem Renaissance Remembered,* p. 84; and Amritjit Singh, *The Novels of the Harlem Renaissance* (University Park and London: Pennsylvania State University Press, 1976).

5. Jessie Fauset, *There Is Confusion* (1924; rpt. New York: AMS, 1974), p. 292.

6. Zora Neale Hurston, "The Gilded Six Bits," in *Spunk: The Selected Short Stories of Zora Neale Hurston* (Berkeley: Turtle Island Foundation, 1985), pp. 54–68.

7. Zora Neale Hurston, *Seraph on the Suwanee* (1948; rpt. New York: AMS, 1974), pp. 310, 311.

8. For a discussion of black women blues singers see Michele Russell, "Slave Codes and Liner Notes," in Gloria Hull, Patricia Bell-Scott, and Barbara Smith, eds., *But Some of Us Are Brave* (Old Westbury: Feminist Press, 1982), pp. 129–40.

9. *The Messenger* 9 (September 1927): 150.

10. *The Negro Woman's World* 2 (February, March, April, 1936). *Negro Woman's World,* published by a group of civic-minded women of Washington, D.C., was designed as a magazine for and about black women, perhaps the first of its kind in the

United States. The first copy of the magazine was published October 1934 at a cost of ten cents per copy. The magazine survived, despite the Depression, through February 1936, attracting attention throughout many states. It contained articles on controversial subjects, nonfiction, serialized fiction, beauty hints, poetry, advice to the lovelorn, etc.

11. Carole S. Vance, "Pleasure and Danger: Toward a Politics of Sexuality," in Carole S. Vance, ed., *Pleasure and Danger: Exploring Female Sexuality* (Boston: Routledge and Kegan Paul, 1984), p. 1. For an excellent discussion of black women's sexuality in Vance's anthology see Hortense Spillers, "Interstices: A Small Drama of Words," pp. 73–100. See also Rennie Simson, "The Afro-American Female: The Historical Context of the Construction of Sexual Identity," and Barbara Omolade, "Hearts of Darkness," both in Ann Snitow, ed., *Powers of Desire: The Politics of Sexuality* (New York: Monthly Review, 1983).

12. Carl Van Vechten, *Nigger Heaven* (New York: Knopf, 1926), pp. 222–23.

13. For a discussion of the psychic duality in Larsen's heroines, see Addison Gayle, *The Way of the New World* (New York: Anchor/Doubleday), p. 139.

14. See for example, Hugh Gloster, *Negro Voices in American Fiction* (New York: Russell and Russell, 1948) and Saunders Redding, *To Make a Poet Black* (Chapel Hill: University of North Carolina Press, 1945).

15. Naxos is, no doubt, a composite of Larsen's experiences at Tuskegee Institute in Alabama and Fisk University in Tennessee. In her novel *Meridian* (1976), which owes much to *Quicksand,* Alice Walker titles her Southern black college "Saxon," criticizing—as does Larsen her fictional college—its attempt to erase all racial distinctiveness and to encourage conformity to an Anglo-Saxon "norm."

16. The effort to regulate the relation between color and clothing for black women was common in Larsen's day. One of the more amusing examples can be found, again, in *The Negro Woman's World.* In "Your Coloring and Your Clothing" one Amelia H. Higgins, "Art Instructor," advised her readers that "complexion as well as personality is influenced by one's choice of clothing . . . the brunette, either brown or black haired, can wear a wide range of colors because her coloring is not easily subdued." After offering recommendations to the "olive-skinned girl" and the "brown-skinned debutante," she advises the "very dark woman" to wear "soft rose colors, warm tans, wine color and black. She should avoid the high shades unless her personality is positively all-conquering," *Negro Woman's World* 1 (December 1934): 11. In "Christmas Day Diary 1934," a companion piece in the same issue, Ms. Higgins provided a "sketch of a wardrobe suggested for one of the types." Interestingly, she chooses the "Little Olive 'Deb.'" For a breakfast dance, she recommends "the aquamarine crepe dress showing a dominant vertical line broken by a short horizontal one terminating into kick pleats from the knees to the hem line. The blouse of egg shell moire with its neckline broken by a chic knife-pleated collar having a similar finish with inverted cuffs at the wrist. The blue felt hat, off-face model, matches the kid gloves and the medium heeled ties. The coat of Hudson seal with squirrel collar completes the attire for the breakfast dance." The September 1934 issue of the magazine included fashion notes by Sadie Hall, fashion editor of *The New York Amsterdam News,* complete with updates from Paris (military trend, "the results of the Italio-Ethiopian combat," she suggests) and tips for creating through makeup the "Oriental secret, which the Hollywood stars are using."

17. While the Naxos community would define Helga as a sexual nonentity, the

Danish society would define her in sexual terms exclusively, again suggested in imagery of color and clothing. Thinking that Helga's clothing is that of a "prim American maiden," her aunt wants her bedecked in "flaunting flashy things" (p. 69): colors of "indigo, orange, green, vermilion . . . dresses of velvet and chiffon" (p. 74). When Helga is first introduced to Danish society, her aunt forces her to wear a green velvet dress "cut down" to "practically nothing but a skirt" (p. 70). Larsen's use of clothing symbolism is a pattern in black women's fiction often associated with the sensual, the sexual. See, for example, Toni Morrison's *The Bluest Eye* and Alice Walker's *The Color Purple*. For further description of the iconography of clothing, see Deborah E. McDowell, "New Directions for Black Feminist Criticism," *Black American Literature Forum* 14 (Winter 1980): 153–59. For a related discussion, see Susan Willis, "Black Women Writers: Taking a Critical Perspective," in Gayle Greene and Coppelia Kahn, *Making a Difference: Feminist Literary Criticism* (London and New York: Methuen, 1985), p. 229.

18. The imagery used to describe Helga's search for employment interestingly foreshadows and parallels that used to describe her rationale for marrying the Rev. Green. "Nobody wanted her services. At least not the kind that she offered. A few men . . . offered her money, but the price of the money was too dear." This passage significantly anticipates and echoes Helga's thoughts prior to her marriage when she describes marriage as the "price she must pay" for sex, subtly suggesting a relationship between marriage and prostitution.

19. The description of Helga's conversion closely resembles Arthur Huff Fauset's description of a typical service at United House of Prayer for All People, a cult founded by Bishop Charles Emmanuel Grace, a.k.a. "Daddy Grace," in the 1920s. See *Black Gods of the Metropolis: Negro Religious Cults in the Urban North* (Philadelphia: University of Pennsylvania Press, 1944).

20. While many novels show marriage as a dead end, especially for women, two strong examples from the 1920s come to mind: Ellen Glasgow's *Barren Ground* (1925) and Emma Summer Kelley's *Weeds*. For a discussion of novels of marriage by women, see Annis Pratt, *Archetypal Patterns in Women's Fiction* (Bloomington: Indiana University Press, 1981), pp. 41–58.

21. Likening motherhood to annihilation of the self, to a form of death for women, is a common pattern in women's writing. Alice Walker's *Meridian* (New York: Harcourt, 1976), is one of a host of possible examples, mentioned here again because of its many parallels to *Quicksand*. Walker's character, Meridian, haunted by the thought that she has "shatter[ed] her mother's emergent self," likens motherhood to being "buried alive, walled away from . . . life, brick by brick" (p. 51).

22. Robert Bone also makes this suggestion. He sees an "underlying moralism" in Larsen's tone. He adds, "Helga's tragedy in Larsen's eyes is that she allows herself to be declassed by her own sexuality. The tone of reproach is unmistakable," *The Negro Novel in America*, p. 105.

23. It has long been a stereotype that the church has provided black women a "safe" and controlled release of unexpressed sexual desires. In her essay "A Cultural Legacy Denied and Discovered: Black Lesbians in Fiction by Women," Jewelle Gomez describes "Black women who have hidden from their sexuality behind a church pew." The black church, she continues, has been "a place for Black women to redirect their energy from physical passions to pungent spirituality and socializing." See *Home Girls:*

A Black Feminist Anthology, ed. Barbara Smith (New York: Kitchen Table: Women of Color Press, 1983), pp. 120–21.

24. Larsen's use of the trope of descent in *Quicksand* departs significantly from its popular use in other Afro-American fiction. Used by such writers as James Weldon Johnson *(The Autobiography of an Ex-Colored Man),* Jean Toomer *(Cane),* Zora Neale Hurston *(Their Eyes Were Watching God),* Ralph Ellison *(Invisible Man),* Alice Walker *(Meridian),* among many others, the descent to the South is essential, whether psychically or spiritually, to their protagonists' health and survival. With Larsen, it is associated with a form of death.

25. See, for example, Hugh Gloster, *Negro Voices in American Fiction* (New York: Russell and Russell, 1948); J. Saunders Redding, *To Make a Poet Black* (Chapel Hill: University of North Carolina Press, 1945); Hiroko Sato, "Under the Harlem Shadows . . ."; and Robert Bone, *The Negro Novel in America.*

26. Beatrice Royster, "The Ironic Vision of Four Black Women Novelists: A Study of the Novels of Jessie Fauset, Nella Larsen, Zora Neale Hurston, and Ann Petry," Ph.D. diss., Emory University, 1975), p. 86.

27. Cheryl Wall, "Passing for What? Aspects of Identity in Nella Larsen's Novels," *Black American Literature Forum* 20 (spring/summer 1986): 97–111.

28. In her novel *Plum Bun,* published the same year as *Passing,* Jessie Fauset also used fairy tale conventions to deflect her critique of the romance and the role its underlying ideology plays in disempowering women.

29. Rachel Blau DuPlessis, *Writing beyond the Ending: Narrative Strategies of Twentieth-Century Women Writers* (Bloomington: Indiana University Press, 1985), p. 15.

30. Nancy Miller, "Emphasis Added: Plots and Plausibilities in Women's Fiction," in *Subject to Change: Reading Feminist Writing* (New York: Columbia University Press, 1988), p. 43.

6. Boundaries

1. This essay is a version of a keynote address on feminist criticism, presented at the University of Pennsylvania in April, 1987. A shorter version appeared under the title "The Self and the Other: Reading Toni Morrison's *Sula* and the Black Female Text," in Nellie McKay, ed., *Critical Essays on Toni Morrison* (Boston: G. K. Hall, 1988), and in Houston A. Baker, Jr., and Patricia Redmond, eds., *Afro-American Literary Study in the 1990s* (Chicago: University of Chicago Press, 1989).

2. Toni Morrison, *Sula* (New York: New American Library, 1973), p. 119. Subsequent references are to this edition and will be indicated parenthetically in the text.

3. W. E. B. Du Bois, "Negro Art," *The Crisis* (June 1921): 55–56.

4. Langston Hughes, "The Negro Artist and the Racial Mountain," in Donald Gibson, ed., *Five Black Writers,* pp. 227–28.

5. Addison Gayle, "Blueprint for Black Criticism," *First World* (January/February, 1977): 44.

6. See three essays by Henry Louis Gates, for example: "Preface to Blackness: Text and Pretext," in *Afro-American Literature: The Reconstruction of Instruction,* ed. Dexter Fischer and Robert Stepto (New York: MLA, 1979), pp. 44–69; "Criticism in the Jungle," in *Black Literature and Literary Theory,* ed. Henry Gates (New York: Methuen, 1984), pp. 1–24; and "Writing 'Race' and the Difference It Makes," *Critical*

Inquiry 12 (Autumn 1985):1–20. For critiques of the issue on "'Race,' Writing, and Difference," in which the last essay appears, see *Critical Inquiry* 13 (Autumn 1986).

7. I offer a more detailed accounting of the controversy in the next chapter.

8. Mel Watkins, "Sexism, Racism, and Black Women Writers," *The New York Times Book Review,* June, 1986, p. 36. For similar discussions, see Darryl Pinckney, "Black Victims, Black Villains," *The New York Review of Books* 34 (January 29, 1987): 17–20; and Richard Barksdale, "Castration Symbolism in Recent Black American Fiction," *College Language Association Journal* 29 (June 1986): 400–413.

9. "The Unglamorous but Worthwhile Duties of the Black Revolutionary Artist, or of the Black Writer Who Simply Works and Writes," in *In Search of Our Mother's Gardens* (New York: Harcourt Brace Jovanovich, 1983), p. 137.

10. Although a whole field of binary oppositions can be viewed as analogous to the male/female opposition, Cary Nelson rightly cautions against so rigid a reading. He argues persuasively that when such dualities are considered in cultural and historical context, the basic male/female opposition breaks down and the qualities associated with each side are often reversed. See "Envoys of Otherness: Difference and Continuity in Feminist Criticism," in *For Alma Mater: Theory and Practice in Feminist Scholarship,* ed. Paula Treichler and others (Urbana: University of Illinois Press, 1985), pp. 91–118.

11. Shoshana Felman, "Women and Madness: The Critical Phallacy," *Diacritics* 5 (Winter 1975): 3.

12. The historical equation of blackness with maleness in discourses on blackness is an issue urgently calling for extensive examination. For a discussion of how this equation has worked in discourses on slavery, see Deborah Gray White, *Ar'n't I a Woman: Female Slaves in the Plantation South* (New York: Norton, 1985). White examines slave women whose experiences are neglected, more often than not, from scholarship on slavery. According to White, the pattern began with the publication of Stanley Elkins's *Slavery, a Problem in American Institutional and Intellectual Life* (1959), in which he posited his controversial "Sambo" thesis of male infantilism and incompetence, which historians have since focused their energies on negating. That focus has effectively eclipsed black women from view. For a discussion of how these masculinist constructs have operated in the construction of Afro-American literary history, see Deborah E. McDowell, "In the First Place: Making Frederick Douglass and the Afro-American Narrative Tradition," in William L. Andrews, ed., *Critical Essays on Frederick Douglass* (Boston: G. K. Hall, 1991).

13. See Robert Stepto, *From behind the Veil: A Study of Afro-American Narrative* cited above. See also Henry Gates's preface to the special issue of *Critical Inquiry* "'Race,' Writing, and Difference," in which he describes the beginning of that tradition: the writings of John Gronniosaw, John Marrant, Olaudah Equiano, Ottabah Cugoano, and John Jea, all male. They, he argues, posited both "the individual 'I' of the black author as well as the collective 'I' of the race. Text created author; and black authors, it was hoped, would create or re-create the image of the race in European discourse" (p. 11).

14. Spillers, "A Hateful Passion, a Lost Love," *Feminist Studies* 9 (Summer 1983): 296.

15. Luce Irigaray, *This Sex Which Is Not One* (Ithaca: Cornell University Press, 1985), p. 217.

16. Thomas Docherty, *Reading (Absent) Character: Toward a Theory of Characterization in Fiction* (Oxford: Clarendon, 1983), p. 265.

17. I am adapting Docherty's distinction between "character as a 'becoming' rather than as an 'essence.'" See *Reading (Absent) Character,* p. 268.

18. Baruch Hoffman, *Character in Literature* (Ithaca: Cornell University Press, 1985), p. 79.

19. I borrow this point from Judith Kegan Gardiner, "The (US)es of (I)dentity: A Response to Abel on '(E)Merging Identities,'" *Signs* 6 (Spring 1981): p. 439.

20. Carole Gilligan, *In a Different Voice* (Cambridge: Harvard University Press, 1982), p. 147.

21. In *The Bluest Eye,* Morrison is similarly concerned with those women who view sex as a marital duty rather than a source of their own pleasure. Called the Mobile women, they try to rid themselves of the "dreadful funkiness of passion," give their "bod[ies] sparingly and partially," and hope that they will "remain dry between [their] legs" (pp. 68–69).

22. Toni Morrison, "Intimate Things in Place," *Massachusetts Review* (Autumn, 1977): 477.

23. See Bettye J. Parker, "Complexity: Toni Morrison's Women—An Interview Essay," in *Sturdy Black Bridges: Visions of Black Women in Literature,* ed. Roseann P. Bell, Bettye J. Parker, and Beverly Guy-Sheftall (New York: Anchor/Doubleday, 1979), p. 256.

24. For a discussion of this theme in other Morrison novels, see Renita Weems, "'Artists without Art Form': A Look at One Black Woman's World of Unrevered Black Women," *Conditions: Five* 2 (Autumn 1979): 48–58.

25. *Sula* is an intensely elegiac novel about loss, grieving, and the release of pain. The epigraph signals the concern. "It is sheer good fortune to miss somebody long before they leave you." It implies that leave-taking and loss are inevitable. At the end of the book Shadrack gives over to his grief for Sula, and when he does, he ceases to fill his life with compulsive activity. At Chicken Little's funeral, the women grieve for their own painful childhoods, the "most devastating pain there is" (p. 65). The narrator grieves for a community that has become increasingly atomistic with the passage of time. Barbara Christian also sees these qualities in the novel, reading the epilogue as "a eulogy to the Bottom." See "Community and Nature: The Novels of Toni Morrison," *The Journal of Ethnic Studies* 7 (Winter 1980): 64–78.

26. Wolfgang Iser, for example, discusses the two "selves" that interact in the reading process: one, the reader's own self or "disposition"; the other, that offered by the text. See *The Act of Reading* (Baltimore, Johns Hopkins University Press, 1978), p. 37. For a thorough overview and synthesis of theories of reading, see Susan R. Suleiman, "Introduction: Varieties of Audience-Oriented Criticism," in *The Reader in the Text,* ed. Susan R. Suleiman and Inge Crosman (Princeton: Princeton University Press, 1980), pp. 3–45.

27. "Toni Morrison," in *Dictionary of Literary Biography,* p. 191.

28. I borrow here from Jerome Beatty's afterword to *Sula* in *The Norton Introduction to the Short Novel,* second edition, p. 699.

29. Christopher Lehmann-Haupt, review of *Sula* in *The New York Times,* 123 (January 7, 1974): 29.

30. "Rootedness: The Ancestor as Foundation," in *Black Women Writers: A Critical Evaluation,* ed. Mari Evans (New York: Anchor/Doubleday, 1984), p. 341.

31. For a discussion of the absences in *Sula*, see Robert Grant, "Absence into Presence: The Thematics of Memory and 'Missing' Subjects in Toni Morrison's *Sula*," in Nellie McKay, ed., *Critical Essays on Toni Morrison*, pp. 90–103.

32. Norman Holland, "Unity, Identity, Text, Self," *PMLA* 90 (1975): 816. See also Jean Kennard, "Ourself behind Ourself: A Theory for Lesbian Readers," in Elizabeth Flynn and Patrocinio Schweikart, eds., *Gender and Reading* (Baltimore: Johns Hopkins University Press, 1986), pp. 63–80.

33. Holland, *Dynamics of Literary Response* (New York: Oxford University Press, 1968), p. 101.

34. Don Bialostosky, "Dialogics as an Art of Discourse in Literary Criticism," *PMLA* 10 (October 1986): 790.

35. Spillers, "Cross-Currents, Discontinuities: Black Women's Fiction," in Marjorie Pryse and Hortense Spillers, eds., *Conjuring: Black Women, Fiction, and Literary Tradition*, p. 250.

36. Frantz Fanon, "On National Culture," in *The Wretched of the Earth* (New York: Grove, 1968), p. 224.

37. Raymond Williams, *The Politics of Modernism: Against the New Conformists* (London: verso, 1989).

38. Arnold Adoff, ed., *Black on Black: Commentaries by Negro Americans* (New York: Macmillan, 1968), pp. 25, 26, 27.

39. Anthony Appiah, "Topologies of Nativism," *Yale Journal of Criticism* 2, no. 1 (Fall 1988): 169.

40. Barbara Johnson, "Response," in Houston A. Baker, Jr., and Patricia Redmond, eds., *Afro-American Literary Study in the 1990s* (Chicago: University of Chicago Press, 1989), p. 42.

7. Reading Family Matters

1. This is a longer version of a lecture given at Rutgers University in September 1987 at the symposium "Changing Our Own Words: Black Women, Criticism, and Theory." The essay was published in Cheryl Wall's volume of the same name by Rutgers University Press in 1990. I would like to thank Janice Knight, Cheryl Wall, and Richard Yarborough for their very helpful comments on an earlier draft of this chapter.

2. Mary Louise Pratt, "Interpretive Strategies/Strategic Interpretations," in Jonathan Arac, ed., *Postmodernism and Politics* (Minneapolis: University of Minnesota Press, 1986).

3. Mel Watkins, "Sexism, Racism, and Black Women Writers," *The New York Times Book Review*, pp. 1, 35.

4. A significant and controversial exception from a woman is Trudier Harris, "On *The Color Purple*, Stereotypes, and Silence," pp. 155–161. Though Harris focuses on *The Color Purple*, her assertions are echoed more broadly in readings of other novels by black women. She argues that *The Color Purple* satisfies white "spectator readers" by presenting stereotypical "black fathers and father-figures" who are "immoral [and] sexually unrestrained." See also Sondra O'Neale, "Inhibiting Midwives, Usurping Creators: The Struggling Emergence of Black Women in Fiction," in Teresa de Lauretis, ed., *Feminist Studies/Critical Studies* (Bloomington: Indiana University Press, 1986), pp. 139–156. Male exceptions include Calvin Hernton, *The Sexual Mountain and Black Women Writers* (New York: Anchor/Doubleday, 1987), 37–58; and Richard

Wesley "*The Color Purple* Debate: Reading between the Lines," *Ms.* (September 1986) 62: 90–92.

This tendency has been reflected especially in responses to and reviews of Alice Walker's *The Color Purple,* though most have centered disproportionately and inappropriately on Steven Spielberg's film adaptation of the novel. Jack Smith, chief of the Chicago bureau of *Time* magazine, compresses this oppositional tendency in his question: "Why were so many black women moved by *The Color Purple* and so many black activists/artists/militants [presumed to be male?] revulsed by the film—and the novel?" And not surprisingly, in his second question, Smith links these polar responses regressively to Shange's controversial choreopoem. He asks, "Why did so many black women walk out of *for colored girls* . . . shouting 'Amen,' while so many black men denounced the 'bitch' who wrote it?" "The Black Person in Art: How Should S/he Be Portrayed?" *Black American Literature Forum* 21 (Spring/Summer 1987): 22. Theologian Delores Williams's reading can be regarded as a response to Smith's questions. She sees *The Color Purple* as "feminist theology" affirming the belief that "women's liberation is the key to the redemption of our society. This social redemption depends upon . . . changing our consciousness about the maleness of God, about divine validation of heterosexuality and about authority as it relates to the masculine and feminine dimensions of culture." For these reasons, she adds, "we black feminists leave the cinema knowing we have seen something painfully significant about ourselves, men, God, and redemption." See "Examining Two Shades of 'Purple,'" *Los Angeles Times,* March 15, 1986. See also Williams's essay, "What Was Missed: *The Color Purple,*" *Christianity and Crisis* (July 14, 1986).

5. Richard Ohmann, "The Shaping of a Canon: U.S. Fiction, 1960–1975," in *Politics of Letters* (Middletown: Wesleyan University Press, 1987), pp. 71, 75.

6. Cathy Davidson, *Revolution and the Word* (New York: Oxford University Press), p. 111.

7. Paul Smith, *Discerning the Subject* (Minneapolis: University of Minnesota Press, 1988).

8. For discussions of gender and reading, see Elizabeth A. Flynn and Patrocinio P. Schweickart, eds., *Gender and Reading: Essays on Readers, Texts, and Contexts* (Baltimore: Johns Hopkins University Press, 1986).

9. Maureen Quilligan, *Milton's Spenser: The Politics of Reading* (Ithaca, N.Y.: Cornell University Press, 1983), p. 178.

10. Excerpts of Wallace's book were published in *Ms.* magazine in December 1979.

11. Among the most controversial critiques of this tendency are Henry Louis Gates, Jr., "Preface to Blackness: Text and Pretext," in Dexter Fisher and Robert Stepto, eds., *Afro-American Literature: The Reconstruction of Instruction* (New York: Modern Language Association of America, 1979), pp. 44–69; and "Criticism in the Jungle," in Henry Louis Gates, Jr., ed., *Black Literature and Literary Theory* (New York: Methuen, 1984), pp. 1–24.

12. Robert Staples, "The Myth of Black Macho: A Response to Angry Black Feminists," *Black Scholar* (March/April 1979): 26–27.

13. Janet Beizer, *Family Plots* (New Haven: Yale University Press, 1986), p. 7. I confine my comments to the essays in which the rhetoric is most insistently "profamily." To these could be added the following essays and newspaper and magazine features that protest the treatment of black men in the literature of black women. Some of them object specifically to the film version of *The Color Purple,* but make no

distinctions between film and novel: Gerald Early, "The Color Purple as Everybody's Protest Art," *Antioch Review* 44 (Summer 1986): 261–75; Richard Barksdale, "Castration Symbolism in Recent Black American Fiction," *College Language Association Journal* 29 (June 1986): 400–413; E. R. Shipp, "Blacks in Heated Debate over *The Color Purple*," *The New York Times,* January 27, 1986; "Seeing Red over Purple," *People Magazine,* March 10, 1986; Abdul Wali Muhammad, "Purple Poison Pulses," *Final Call,* January 27, 1986; Lynn Norment, *"The Color Purple," Ebony,* February 1986.

14. Christine Froula, "The Daughter's Seduction: Sexual Violence and Literary History," *Signs* 11 (Summer 1986): 621–44.

15. Despite abundant evidence that black women's "feminist" consciousness generally emerged organically from the material circumstances of their lives and can be documented well in advance of the second wave of the women's movement of the 1960s, this analysis continues to be perpetuated by black men. See bell hooks, *Feminist Theory: from margin to center* (Boston: South End, 1984); and Beverly Guy-Sheftall, "Remembering Sojourner Truth: On Black Feminism," in Pearl Cleage, ed., *Catalyst* (Atlanta, Georgia, n.d.), pp. 54–57.

16. David Bradley, "Telling the Black Woman's Story," *New York Times Magazine,* January 1984, p. 34.

17. Philip M. Royster, "In Search of Our Fathers' Arms: Alice Walker's Persona of the Alienated Darling," *Black American Literature Forum* 20 (Winter 1986): 357, 361. Royster keeps Walker's roles as daughter, wife, and mother clearly before the reader's eye, noting that she is a failed wife and an inadequate mother. See p. 353, especially.

18. Susan Willis, *Specifying: Black Women Writing the American Experience* (Madison: University of Wisconsin Press, 1987), p. 106.

19. Bradley, "Black Woman's Story," p. 30.

20. Royster, "Our Fathers' Arms," p. 363.

21. Watkins, "Sexism, Racism, and Black Women Writers," p. 36.

22. *Ibid.,* pp. 37, 36.

23. Richard Wright, *Native Son* (New York: Harper and Rowe, 1940), pp. 140, 224.

24. Marilyn Butler, "Against Tradition: The Case for a Particularized Historical Method," in Jerome J. McGann, ed., *Historical Studies and Literary Criticism* (Madison: University of Wisconsin Press, 1985), p. 37. See also J. P. Stern, "From Family Album to Literary History," *Critical Inquiry* 7 (Autumn 1975): 113–31. After Wittgenstein, Stern describes writing literary history as analogous to "pictures from a family album, not as scenes from a single story or drama" with sufficient continuity.

25. The novel was reviewed by Robert Towers in the August 12, 1982, issue under the heading "Good Men Are Hard to Find," though Towers admitted then that "the two books have about as much in common . . . as one of Roy Lichtenstein's comic-strip blowups and a WPA painting of cotton pickers in the field." Reed's public conflicts with black women writers are well known, which piques my curiosity about this pattern of "pairing" his work with Alice Walker's in literary reviews. See also Darwin Turner, "A Spectrum of Blackness," *Parnassus* 4 (1976): 202–218. For Reed's comments on this practice of pairing him with Alice Walker, see Mel Watkins, "An Interview with Ishmael Reed," *The Southern Review* 21 (July 1985): 603–614. There, Reed talks about his belief, captured in the title of a symposium that he sponsored, that "Third World Men [are] the Scapegoats of Feminist Writers."

26. Ishmael Reed, *Reckless Eyeballing* (New York: St. Martin's, 1986), 4.

27. See, as just one example, the courtroom scene near the end of Hurston's *Their Eyes Were Watching God,* in which Janie is acquitted of murdering Tea Cake. One of the group of black men outraged at the verdict says, "Well, you know whut dey say 'uh white man and uh nigger woman is de freest thing on earth.' Dey do as dey please," (Urbana: University of Illinois Press, 1937; rpt. 1978), p. 280.

28. Haki Madhubuti, "Lucile Clifton: Warm Water, Greased Legs, and Dangerous Poetry," in Mari Evans, ed., *Black Women Writers: A Critical Evaluation,* ed. Mari Evans (New York: Anchor/Doubleday, 1983), p. 159.

29. Haki Madhubuti, "Sonia Sanchez: The Bringer of Memories," in Evans, ed., *Black Women Writers,* pp. 419–20.

30. *Ibid.,* 432.

31. Madhubuti, "Lucile Clifton," pp. 150–51, 159, 156.

32. Judith Fetterley, "Reading about Reading: 'A Jury of Her Peers,' 'The Murders in the Rue Morgue,' and 'The Yellow Wallpaper,'" in Elizabeth Flynn and Patrocinio Schweickart, eds., *Gender and Reading,* pp. 150, 147.

33. Hernton, *The Sexual Mountain and Black Women Writers,* p. 38.

34. Peter Gay, *Education of the Senses* (New York: Oxford University Press, 1984), p. 436.

35. Houston Baker, *Modernism and the Harlem Renaissance* (Chicago: University of Chicago Press, 1987), p. 106.

36. Adolph Reed, "The Liberal Technocrat," *The Nation,* February 6, 1988, p. 168.

37. William Julius Wilson, *The Truly Disadvantaged: The Inner City, the Underclass, and Public Policy* (Chicago: University of Chicago Press, 1987), p. 7.

38. Reed, "The Liberal Technocrat," p. 168.

39. Alice Walker, *The Third Life of Grange Copeland* (New York: Harcourt Brace Jovanovich, 1970), pp. 9, 18.

40. All too little has been written about what black women experience within the family, a void partly created by the ideological discussions of the black family since the controversial Moynihan Report *(The Black Family: The Case for National Action).* Moynihan's "black matriarchy" thesis is well known and need not be replayed here. It is enough to say that the flood of liberal repudiations it elicited, however well-intentioned and sharply articulated, have done little to illuminate black women's subordination within the family. So strong have been the design and desire to refute Moynihan's description of black families as "tangles of pathology" with a mountain of "normalizing" data, that black women's experiences, thoughts, and feelings have been buried. In his monumental *The Black Family in Slavery and Freedom* (New York: Random House, 1981), Herbert Gutman acknowledged that his study was "stimulated by the bitter public and academic controversy surrounding" the Moynihan Report. He traces the development of the slave family and enlarged kin networks from 1750 to 1925, describing long-lasting slave marriages. But, as Angela Davis notes in *Women, Race, and Class* (New York: Random House, 1981), Gutman's "observations about slave women are generally confined to their wifely propensities." Similarly, in *Labor of Love, Labor of Sorrow: Black Women, Work, and the Family from Slavery to the Present* (New York: Basic, 1985), Jacquelyn Jones is at pains to prove that the "two-parent, nuclear family was the typical cohabitation" in slavery and freedom that protected the community at large from racial oppression. Only briefly does Jones, in an otherwise commendable study, indicate that, while racial oppression "could bind a

family tightly together," "it could also heighten tensions among people who had few outlets for their rage and frustration" (pp. 32, 34, 103).

41. Walker, *Grange Copeland*, p. 18.

42. Reed, *Reckless Eyeballing*, p. 77.

43. Pinckney, "Black Victims, Black Villains," p. 81.

44. Judith Fetterley, "Reading about Reading," and Annette Kolodny, "A Map for Misreading: Gender and the Interpretation of Literary Texts," in Elaine Showalter, ed., *The New Feminist Criticism* (New York: Pantheon, 1985), p. 57.

45. Fredric Jameson, *The Political Unconscious* (Ithaca, N.Y.: Cornell University Press, 1981), p. 9. For a discussion of the extent to which what happens during reading has been "already limited by decisions made before the book is ever begun," see Peter Rabinowitz, *Before Reading: Narrative Conventions and the Politics of Interpretation* (Ithaca, N.Y.: Cornell University Press, 1987), pp. 2 and following.

46. Alice Walker, "Source," in *You Can't Keep a Good Woman Down* (New York: Harcourt Brace Jovanovich, 1981). Subsequent page references are given in the text.

47. Shari Benstock, "At the Margin of Discourse: Footnotes in the Fictional Text," *PMLA*, 98 (March 1983): 205.

48. *Ibid.*, 221.

49. Margaret Homans, *Bearing the Word* (Chicago: University of Chicago Press, 1986), p. 160.

50. *Ibid*, p. 31.

51. Alice Walker, "In the Closet of the Soul," in *Living by the Word* (New York: Harcourt Brace Jovanovich, 1988), p. 82.

52. Shoshana Felman, *Writing and Madness* (Ithaca, N.Y.: Cornell University Press, 1985), p. 161.

53. Gloria Naylor and Toni Morrison, "A Conversation," *Southern Review* 21 (July 1985): 579.

54. *Massachusetts Review* 28 (Winter 1987): 688.

55. There are striking parallels between the reception of contemporary black women novelists and that of their counterparts, black feminist critics, in the academy. In a very insightful and refreshing discussion, Theodore Mason discusses the controversial issue of *New Literary History* featuring essays by Joyce Joyce, Houston Baker, and Henry Louis Gates. Mason invokes the battle royal scene from Ralph Ellison's *Invisible Man* to explain this controversy between two black men and a black woman, arranged by the white male editor of the journal, who watches his orchestrated combat with amusement. See "Between the Populist and the Scientist: Ideology and Power in Recent Afro-American Literary Criticism, or 'The Dozens' as Scholarship," *Callaloo* 36 (Summer 1988): 606–615.

56. Anthony Barthelemy, "Mother, Sister, Wife: A Dramatic Perspective," *Southern Review* 21 (July 1985): 787.

57. I borrow this phrasing from Alice Jardine, *Gynesis: Configurations of Woman and Modernity* (Ithaca, N.Y.: Cornell University Press, 1985), p. 37.

8. Witnessing Slavery after Freedom—*Dessa Rose*

1. A version of this chapter appeared as "Negotiating between Tenses: Witnessing Slavery After Freedom—*Dessa Rose*," in Deborah E. McDowell and Arnold Ramper-

sad, eds., *Slavery and the Literary Imagination* (Baltimore: Johns Hopkins University Press, 1989), pp. 144–63.

2. Ralph Ellison, William Styron, Robert Penn Warren, and C. Vann Woodward, "The Uses of History in Fiction," *Southern Literary Journal* 1 (Spring 1969): 60.

3. Bernard W. Bell, *The Afro-American Novel and Its Tradition* (Amherst: University of Massachusetts Press, 1987), p. 289; and Henry Louis Gates, Jr., "The Language of Slavery," in *The Slave's Narrative*, ed. Charles Davis and Henry L. Gates, Jr. (New York: Oxford University Press, 1985).

4. Of course, there were novels of slavery published before the 1960s, but, in terms of sheer numbers, it is a subject engaged by far more authors of this century. Nineteenth-century novels of slavery include the major antebellum novels—William Wells Brown's *Clotel; or the President's Daughter: A Narrative of Slave Life in the United States* (1853); Martin Delaney's *Blake; or the Huts of America* (1859); Harriet E. Wilson's *Our Nig* (1859); and James Howard's *Bond and Free* (1866)—and, though not focused exclusively on slavery, Frances E. W. Harper's *Iola Leroy* (1892). Twentieth-century examples include Arna Bontemps's historical romances: *Black Thunder* (1936) and *Drums at Dusk* (1939). See Hazel Carby, "Ideologies of Black Folk: The Historical Novel of Slavery," in Deborah E. McDowell and Arnold Rampersad, eds., *Slavery and the Literary Imagination* (Baltimore: Johns Hopkins University Press, 1989) for a discussion of what she describes as a paradox. She argues that, though it is "central to the Afro-American literary imagination . . . as a mode of production and as a particular social order, slavery is rarely the focus of the imaginative physical and geographical terrain of Afro-American novels."

5. Recent novels about slavery include Ernest Gaines's *The Autobiography of Miss Jane Pittman* (1971), Ishmael Reed's *Flight to Canada* (1976), Barbara Chase-Riboud's *Sally Hemings* (1979), Octavia Butler's *Kindred* (1979), Charles Johnson's *The Oxherding Tale* (1982), Sherley Anne Williams's *Dessa Rose* (1984), and Toni Morrison's *Beloved* (1987). Even when recent novels by black Americans do not focus exclusively on slavery or use it as a narrative point of departure, they nevertheless position their characters in a necessary confrontation with some story about slavery. Examples include Avey in Paul Marshall's *Praisesong for the Widow* (1983) and Ursa in Gayl Jones's *Corregidora* (1975).

6. Hortense Spillers, "Changing the Letter: The Yokes, the Jokes of Discourse, or, Mrs. Stowe, Mr. Reed," in Deborah E. McDowell and Arnold Rampersad, eds., *Slavery and the Literary Imagination* (Baltimore: Johns Hopkins University Press, 1989) pp. 37, 42.

7. John Blassingame, "Using the Testimony of Ex-Slaves: Approaches and Problems," in *The Slave's Narrative*, ed. Charles Davis and Henry L. Gates, Jr., p. 83.

8. For a general survey of the history of these warring interpretations, see William L. Van Deburg, *Slavery and Race in American Popular Culture* (Madison: University of Wisconsin Press, 1984).

9. See Charles Rowell, "Poetry, History and Humanism: Interview with Margaret Walker," *Black World* (December 1975): 10.

10. Sherley Anne Williams, author's note to *Dessa Rose* (New York: William Morrow, 1986), p. 5. All further references to the novel are to the first edition and are given in parentheses in the text.

11. The controversy that quickly erupted when *Confessions of Nat Turner* was published was widespread among black writers and intellectuals, most of whom main-

tained that Styron's imagined Nat Turner bore little resemblance to the actual historical figure. See John Henrik Clarke, ed., *William Styron's Nat Turner: Ten Black Writers Respond* (Boston: Beacon, 1968). And for a critique of Styron's critics, see Seymour L. Gross and Eileen Bender, "History, Politics, and Literature: The Myth of Nat Turner," *American Quarterly* 23 (October 1971): 487–518.

12. A version of the first section of *Dessa Rose* was titled "Meditations on History," no doubt an act of signifying on Styron, which appeared in Mary Helen Washington, ed., *Midnight Birds: Stories of Contemporary Black Women Writers* (New York: Anchor/Doubleday, 1980), pp. 200–248.

13. Frances Foster notes importantly that in the published slave narratives that black women contributed to the genre, their sexual abuse is noticeably deemphasized. She observes that they "never present rape or seduction as the most profound aspect of their existence." "'In Respect to Females . . .': Differences in the Portrayals of Women by Male and Female Narrators," *Black American Literature Forum* 15 (Summer 1981): 67.

14. Jenny Franchot, "The Punishment of Esther: Frederick Douglass and the Construction of the Feminine," in Eric Sundquist, ed., *New Essays on Frederick Douglass* (Cambridge University Press, 1990), p. 141.

15. In discussing *Beloved* with Charlayne Hunter-Gault, Morrison described "the eagerness with which publishers and people in the book industry were [long] interested in books by black people that said, 'Tell me how angry you are. . . . Tell us how horrible it is for you.' And so there was a sly encouragement to . . . expose the horrors of being the victim, which some people played into. But it was like feeding the vampire with one's own blood." "The MacNeil-Lehrer Report," September 29, 1987.

16. See Sherley Anne Williams, *Give Birth to Brightness: A Thematic Study in Neo-Black Literature* (New York: Dial, 1972); "Papa Dick and Sister-Woman: Reflections on Women in the Fiction of Richard Wright," in Fritz Fleishmann, *American Novelists Revisited: Essays in Feminist Criticism* (Boston: G. K. Hall), pp. 394–415; "The Blues of Contemporary Afro-American Poetry," *Massachusetts Review* 18 (Autumn 1977): 542–54; and "Some Implications of 'Womanist' Theory," *Callaloo* 9 (Spring 1986): 303–308.

17. "'I yam, what I am': the topos of un(naming) in Afro-American literature," in Henry Louis Gates, Jr., ed., *Black Literature and Literary Theory* (New York: Methuen, 1984), p. 157.

18. Williams also uses architectural space/place to ironize and mock Nehemiah's assumed superiority, for his "Big House" is Hughes's run-down farmhouse in which he has an "'attic half' that was little better than a loft" (p. 26), a far cry from the "Great Houses" of cavalier Virginia that had once opened their doors to him.

19. I borrow this phrase from Margaret A. Simons, "Racism and Feminism: A Schism in the Sisterhood," *Feminist Studies* 5 (Summer 1979): 384–401.

20. For a discussion of the feminist interrogation and critique of gender-linked vision, see Craig Owens, "The Discourse of Others: Feminists and Postmodernism," in Hal Foster, ed., *The Anti-Aesthetic: Essays on Post-Modern Culture* (Port Townsend, Wash.: Bay Press, 1983), pp. 57–77, especially 70–77.

21. Dessa describes to Harker, "White folks had taken everything in the world from me except my baby and my life and they had tried to take them. And to see him, who had helped to save me, had friended with me . . . laying up, wallowing in what had

hurt me so—I didn't feel that nothing I could say would tell him what that pain was like" (p. 173).

22. M. M. Bakhtin, *The Dialogic Imagination,* ed. Michael Holquist (Austin: University of Texas Press, 1981), p. 424.

23. See William L. Andrews, *To Tell a Free Story: The First Century of Afro-American Autobiography, 1760–1865* (Urbana: University of Illinois Press, 1986).

24. In an important and influential essay, "The Blues Roots of Contemporary Afro-American Poetry," Williams states that "the beginning of a new tradition" of Afro-American literature is "built on a synthesis of black oral traditions and Western literate forms," *Massachusetts Review* 17 (Autumn 1977): 554.

25. Henri Bergson, *Laughter* (New York: Doubleday, 1956), pp. 121–22.

26. Toni Morrison, interview with Charlayne Hunter-Gault, "The MacNeil-Lehrer Report," September 29, 1987.

27. This is precisely the predicament of Harriet Jacobs or Linda Brent at the end of *Incidents in the Life of a Slave Girl.* She is free of Mr. Flint, but not from the power of Mrs. Bruce, who has the financial means to purchase Linda's freedom.

28. Some would say that the "new order" *Dessa Rose* imagines is utopian and idealized. For example, in a recent review of Gloria Naylor's novel *Mama Day,* David Nicholson criticizes *Dessa Rose* for "retreating into an imaginary past." See "Gloria Naylor's Island of Magic and Romance," *Washington Post Book World* (February 28, 1988). I would suggest, rather, that Williams does not so much "retreat" to this imaginary past as she "confronts" it.

9. Transferences

1. This is a longer version of a talk presented at the Commonwealth Center for Literary and Cultural Change, University of Virginia, as part of a general symposium ("Is Knowledge Gendered?") and a specific panel on "Race and Gender in the Teaching of Historical Knowledge." I adapted the panel's focus in order to consider how "historical knowledge" gets constructed in the realm of literary studies. I thank Susan Fraiman and Rick Livingston for helpful comments and suggestions.

2. Audre Lorde, "Age, Race, Class, and Sex," in *Sister Outsider: Essays and Speeches by Audre Lorde* (Trumansburg, N.Y.: Crossing, 1984), p. 123.

3. Arthur C. Danto, *Narration and Knowledge* (New York: Columbia University Press, 1985), p. 343.

4. See Richard King, "Memory and Phantasy," *Modern Language Notes* 98 (December 1983): 1200. See also Pierra Nora, "Between History and Memory: Les Lieux de Memoire," *Representations* (Spring, 1989); Eric Hobsbaum and Terrence Ranger, eds., *The Invention of Tradition* (Cambridge, England, 1983).

5. While certainly not peculiar to this tradition, this philosophy of history has long been prevalent in the writings of African Americans, especially in the historical, or documentary, fiction produced so insistently for the past twenty years. Random examples would include John A. Williams's two metahistorical novels, *The Man Who Cried I Am* and *Captain Blackman* (1972), in both of which history is a suspicious text constructed by paramilitary, conspiratorial agents. Other examples include Ishmael Reed's *Flight to Canada* (1976) and Sherley Anne Williams's *Dessa Rose,* derived from her short story "Meditations on History." For a discussion of history and documentation in African American fiction, see Barbara Foley, "The Afro-American Documentary

Novel," in *Telling the Truth: The Theory and Practice of Documentary Fiction* (Ithaca, N.Y.: Cornell University Press, 1986). The now-familiar argument that the generic conventions of narrative are evident in the construction of history has been articulated in works such as Hayden White's *Tropics of Discourse, The Content of the Form: Narrative Discourse and Historical Representation* (Baltimore: Johns Hopkins University Press, 1987), and *Metahistory* (Baltimore: Johns Hopkins University Press, 1973).

6. Renato Rosaldo, "Others of Invention: Ethnicity and Its Discontents," *Voice Literary Supplement,* February, 1990, p. 27.

7. Hortense Spillers, "Interstices: A Small Drama of Words," in Carole Vance, ed., *Pleasure and Danger: Exploring Female Sexuality,* p. 74.

8. In *Orientalism,* Edward Said also talks about the "powerful series of political and ultimately ideological realities [that] inform scholarship today. No one can escape dealing with, if not the East/West division, then the North/South one, the have/have not one, the imperialist/anti-imperialist one, the white/colored one," (New York: Vintage/Random House, 1979).

9. Definitions are in order here, but they are difficult to pin down. Although the term "theory" operates much like a mantra in contemporary criticism, it is difficult to find anything but vague definitions of the term. Randomly chosen attempts at definition would include Jonathan Culler's, which defines theory as a "nickname" used "to designate works that succeed in challenging and reorienting thinking in fields other than those to which they ostensibly belong because their analyses of language, or mind, or history, or culture offer novel and persuasive accounts of signification." See *Framing the Sign: Criticism and Its Institutions* (Norman: University of Oklahoma Press, 1988), p. 15. In *Criticism in the University,* Graff and Gibbon define theory as "simply a name for the questions which necessarily arise when principles and concepts once taken for granted become matters of controversy." Bruce Robbins uses theory to "refer to all those otherwise diverse conceptual innovations in the last twenty-five years or so which have combined to produce the single result of reshaping literary criticism." He goes on to say, "Theory is the body of external examiners, foreign and domestic, who have been called in and asked to put the status quo to the test, each applying her or his own criteria. In historical terms, theory has been an invitation to the critical examination and displacement of established practice." See "The Politics of Theory," *Social Text* 18 (1987): 5. What all these definitions lack, perhaps inevitably, is specificity and an awareness that "theory" is a term freighted with contemporary understandings and fraught with ambiguity. (Before 1960, the annual bibliography of the MLA contained no category of scholarly work designated by the term "theory.") Biodun Jeyifo draws an interesting and useful distinction between "theory," wrongly identified as a singular and uniform formation, and "theoreticism," the "specialized jargon through which 'theory' supposedly achieves its purchase on the power of generalization." See "Literary Theory and Theories of Decolonization," unpublished manuscript.

10. For further discussion of this idea, see Pierre Bourdieu, *Distinction: A Social Critique of the Judgment of Taste* (Cambridge: Harvard University Press, 1984). In "The Self-Evaluations of Critical Theory," Evan Watkins notes similarly that "how we tell ourselves the history of recent theoretical developments . . . takes place in [that] shady zone between the boundaries of intellectual work and social situation." *Boundary 2* 12–13 (1984): 359–78.

11. Such a perception derives in large part from the nasty battle waged on the pages of *New Literary History* 18 (1987). See Joyce Ann Joyce, "The Black Canon:

Reconstructing Black American Literary Criticism"; Henry Louis Gates, Jr., "'What's Love Got to Do With It?': Critical Theory, Integrity, and the Black Idiom"; Houston A. Baker, Jr., "In Dubious Battle"; and Joyce Ann Joyce, "'Who the Cap Fit': Unconsciousness and Unconscionableness in the Criticism of Houston A. Baker, Jr., and Henry Louis Gates, Jr." Barbara Christian's "The Race for Theory" added significantly to that perception.

12. Valerie Smith, "Split Affinities: The Case of Interracial Rape," in Marianne Hirsh and Evelyn Fox Keller, eds., *Conflicts in Feminism* (New York: Routledge, 1990).

13. Hazel Carby, *Reconstructing Womanhood*, p. 15.

14. One could raise at least two serious objections here. The first is that a focus on what has been written *about* black feminist thinking eclipses a more constructive, perhaps a more empowering, focus on what has been written *by* black feminists.

In her review of Patricia Hill Collins's *Black Feminist Thought*, for example, Farah Griffin commended Collins for moving black feminism "to a new level" by spending "little time castigating white feminists or black men for their failures in regard to black women." She praises Collins for focusing instead "on an exploration and analysis of thought produced by black women themselves. In so doing, she reinforces their status as subjects and agents of history." See *Women's Review of Books* 8 (February 1991): 14. While I would dispute Griffin's perception that the work of black feminists has been, to this point, determinedly other-directed, I regard her implied call for a necessary shift of focus and address *within* the work of black feminism as absolutely essential. But such a shift alone is insufficient, for it ignores the often unequally positioned sites of knowledge production and their influence on how and if the work of black feminists is read, on how and if it is read in a way that restructures, not simply annexes, knowledge in conditioned reflex acts.

One could raise a second objection: that my focus is too strictly and narrowly academicist, and curiously so if we consider that although its main address is now the UNIVERSITY, black feminist thinking does not stake its origins or find its shelter there, and even when academia is its central site, it strives to extend its borders. While the focus is narrow, its implications and imperatives for the organization and construction of "historical knowledge" are much broader.

15. For a discussion of the use of what Martin Jay terms "charismatic names" to legitimate critical arguments, see "Name Dropping or Dropping Names? Modes of Legitimation in the Humanities," in M. Kreiswirth and M. Cheetham, eds., *Theory between the Disciplines*.

16. For a discussion of Sojourner Truth as "standard exhibit in modern liberal historiography," see Phyllis Marynick Palmer, "White Women/Black Women: The Dualism of Female Identity and Experience in the United States," *Feminist Studies* 9 (Spring 1983): 151–69.

17. Rather than attempt to provide an extensive inventory here, let me call attention to certain benchmark statements from women of color about the injunction to theorize. In her controversial essay "The Race for Theory," Barbara Christian discusses the pressures she feels to "produce a black feminist literary theory as if [she] were a mechanical man," *Gender and Theory*, ed. Linda Kauffman (London and New York: Basil Blackwell, 1989), p. 227. Gloria Anzaldua notes that "what passes for theory these days is forbidden territory" for women of color, which makes it "*vital* that we occupy theorizing space," even as we understand that "what is considered theory in the dominant academic community is not necessarily what counts as theory for women

of color," introduction, *Making Face, Making Soul/Haciendo Caras: Creative and Critical Perspectives by Women of Color* (San Francisco: Aunt Lute Foundation, 1990), p. xxv.

18. Denise Riley, *"Am I That Name?" Feminism and the Category of 'Women' in History* (Minneapolis: University of Minnesota, 1988), p. 1. By her admission, Riley's double move is a concession to pragmatism. She maintains that "it is compatible to suggest that 'women' don't exist—while maintaining a politics of 'as if they existed'— since the world behaves as if they unambiguously did" (p. 112).

19. Constance Penley, *The Future of an Illusion: Film, Feminism, and Psychoanalysis* (Minneapolis, 1989), p. 179.

20. Gayatri Spivack, "The Politics of Interpretation," in W. J. T. Mitchell, *The Politics of Interpretation* (Chicago: University of Chicago Press, 1982), p. 346.

21. Michelene Malson, Jean O'Barr, Sarah Westphal-Wihl, and Mary Wyer, eds., *Feminist Theory in Practice and Process* (Chicago: University of Chicago Press, 1989), p. 7.

22. Elizabeth Spelman, *Inessential Woman: Problems of Exclusion in Feminist Thought* (Boston: Beacon, 1988), p. 162.

23. In a very perceptive and persuasive chapter, Judith Roof argues that a "racial or lesbian commitment is defined as anachronistically political—'liberationist'—as activism instead of analysis." She asks, "Why for this moment are gender and class cerebral and race and sexual orientation experiential?" "All Analogies Are Faulty: The Fear of Intimacy in Feminist Criticism," in *A Lure of Knowledge: Lesbian Sexuality and Theory* (Columbia University Press, 1991).

24. Toril Moi, *Sexual/Textual Politics* (London and New York: Methuen, 1985), pp. 86, 87.

25. Jane Flax, *Thinking Fragments: Psychoanalysis, Feminism, and Postmodernism in the Contemporary West* (Berkeley: University of California Press, 1990), p. 140.

26. For a brilliant discussion of this scene and of the materiality in which black women were embedded more generally, see Haryette Mullen, "'Indelicate Subjects': African American Women's Subjectivity," *Subversions* (Winter 1991): pp. 1–7. See also Valerie Smith, "Black Feminist Theory and the Representation of the 'Other,'" in Cheryl Wall, ed., *Changing Our Own Words: Essays on Criticism, Theory, and Writing by Black Women* (New Brunswick: Rutgers University Press, 1989), pp. 38–57. There Smith discusses tendencies prevalent in the discourses of Anglo-American feminist and male Afro-Americanists to invoke the experiences of black women, who become fetishized Others. She also links this association of black women as embodied others to classic Western philosophy as well as to nineteenth-century cultural ideas and ideals of womanhood. Such ideas of womanhood excluded slave women who were pinned in the body and therefore associated with "animal passions and slave labor" (p. 45).

27. Nell Irvin Painter, "Sojourner Truth in Life and Memory: Writing the Biography of an American Exotic," *Gender and History* 2 (Spring 1990): 3–16. Painter traces the evolution of Sojourner Truth as historical legend and how the dominant representations of her, in both her time and ours, reflect various power asymmetries and hierarchies.

28. For example, it is seldom noted that during Reconstruction Truth assisted the resettlement of some blacks in the exodus to Kansas and worked on land reform.

29. Georg W. F. Hegel, "Geographical Basis of History," in *The Philosophy of History,* trans. J. Sibree (New York, 1991), p. 99.

30. Linda Kauffman, ed., *Gender and Theory* (New York, 1989), p. 2.

31. Michael Awkward, "Appropriative Gestures: Theory and Afro-American Literary Criticism," in Kauffman, *Gender and Theory*, p. 243.

32. Here I make an obvious allusion to Eve Sedgwick's influential study *Between Men: English Literature and Male Homosocial Desire* (New York: Columbia University Press, 1985), which examines the "bonds that link males to males," through and over the bodies of women.

33. Valerie Smith's observations about the trajectory of African American literary studies is well taken in this context. In "Gender and Afro-Americanist Literary Theory," in Elaine Showalter, ed., *Speaking of Gender* (New York: Routledge, 1989), she argues that the dynamics of the male acquisition of power actually inform the critical positions of each generation. She refers specifically to Houston Baker's essay "Discovering America: Generational Shifts, Afro-American Literary Criticism, and the Study of Expressive Culture." She does well to note that in his epigraph to this essay, Baker "casts the connection of black expressive culture to literary criticism and theory in terms of the perennial battle between fathers and sons."

34. Such questions have received considerable attention in recent years. See, to name only a few examples, Jane Tompkins, *Sensational Designs: The Cultural Work of American Fiction, 1790–1860* (New York: Oxford University Press, 1985); Paul Lauter, *Canons and Contexts* (New York: Oxford University Press, 1991); John Guillory, "Canon," in Frank Lentricchia and Thomas McLaughlin, eds., *Critical Terms of Literary Study* (University of Chicago Press, 1990); and Richard Ohmann, "The Shaping of a Canon: U.S. Fiction, 1960–1975," in *Politics of Letters* (Middletown, Conn.: Wesleyan University Press, 1987).

35. The special issue and its responses are collected in *'Race,' Writing, and Difference* (Chicago: University of Chicago Press, 1986).

36. In *Essentially Speaking* (New York: Routledge, 1989), Diana Fuss makes essentially the same point. In "'Race' Under Erasure? Poststructuralist Afro-American Literary Theory," while she praises Gates, who has "perhaps done the most to open the floodgates for poststructuralist African American theory," and Baker, who "pioneers a fourth generational movement" (p. 81), Fuss, a white woman, asks, "What accounts . . . for the apparent resistance on the part of many minority women critics to what Barbara Christian has labeled 'the race for theory'?" (p. 95). A simple binarism between poststructuralism and essentialism structures Fuss's argument in this chapter, the former represented by Henry Louis Gates, Houston Baker, and Anthony Appiah (and, presumably, herself); the latter, by black women. In Fuss's analysis, "essentialism" is a kind of shorthand, catchall term for all that is *not* poststructuralist theory, a negation projected and branded onto black women. Moreover, essentialism acts very much like the proverbial poststructuralist "floating signifier," coming in a variety of brands. It slides up and down the scale of value and meaning, depending on its proximity to the moves and vocabularies of poststructuralism. Interestingly, Fuss acknowledges that a form of essentialism inheres in the work of Gates and Baker, but she redeems their variety of essentialism, primarily because she views it as redemptive, having "saved" African American literary study from what she terms the "bedrock of essentialism." Implying the now familiar theory/practice (politics) opposition, Fuss asks, "Is it possible that there might be an order of political necessity to these more essentialist arguments advanced by black women?"

37. Jonathan Arac, Wlad Godzich, and Wallace Martin described the spread of

deconstruction in their preface to *The Yale Critics* (Minneapolis, 1987). In their estimation, "critics doing the new work most respected by a professionally authoritative
screening group have drawn heavily from the Yale critics. In 35 essays that recently
reached the editorial committee of PMLA, the American critics most cited were Miller
... de Man, Bloom, Hartman and Derrida." Yet another and related sign of their
powerful sway, Martin observed, was deconstruction's spread "from elite private institutions to public institutions," embracing "much more of the United States" and enroll-
ing much "broader student bodies." While some have denied deconstruction's imperial
status, arguing that it is only one of many discourses and, perhaps, one already displaced by competitors, a brief list of randomly chosen titles would suggest that even
these "competing" discourses are often articulated through the language and tendencies of deconstruction. And though not simply mimicking deconstruction, many attempt to establish grounds of compatibility with it. In "Feminism and Deconstruction"
(*Feminist Studies*, 14 [spring 1988]: 51–65), for example, Mary Poovey describes
deconstruction as a discourse with vast enabling possibilities for feminism. Michael
Ryan's *Marxism and Deconstruction* (Baltimore: Johns Hopkins University Press,
1982) is an effort at what he calls a "critical articulation," which is not only a comparative reading of the two discourses, but also an "attempt to develop a new form of
analysis which would be both marxism and deconstruction," an "alloy of the two"
(pp. xv, xiii). In the introduction to his *Black Literature and Literary Theory* (New
York: Methuen, 1984), Henry Louis Gates collects a group of essays that draw on
various critical methodologies and reading strategies, but believes the signal challenge
of black literary study is "to bring together, in a new fused form, the concepts of
critical theory and the idiom of the Afro-American and African literary traditions."
To undertake this complex process, he suggests that "Western critical theories [be used]
to read black texts" (p. 10). Gates's inclusion of essays that do not effect such a fusion
would seem to indicate no tendency on his part to prescribe; however, in the economy
of the volume, the Yale School and its varieties of deconstruction predominate. Even
though Gates's more recent essays call for black critics to "invent their own ... black,
text-specific theories," deriving from a "black formal cultural matrix," he also challenges them "not to shy away from white power—that is, literary theory," but to
"translate it into the black idiom." The hegemony of "theory" (or white power) in
this proposed hybridization is clear. The "New Historicism," one more recent con-
tender for the throne of theory, derives, as Elizabeth Fox-Genovese is right to note, "in
no small measure from its continuing affair with poststructuralist criticism—notably
deconstruction with which it is much less at war than one might think."

38. Barbara Smith, "Toward a Black Feminist Criticism."

39. One of the most pointed historical antecedents to the cases I have been tracing
in this chapter is Frederick Douglass's involvement with the abolitionist movement.
As Douglass gained knowledge and confidence in the movement, he desired to break
free of the confining role as "story-teller" handed him by the movement. He was
admonished by John Collins, general agent of the Massachusetts Anti-Slavery Society,
to "be yourself and tell your story.... Give us the facts, we will take care of the
philosophy." Quoted in Waldo E. Martin, Jr. *The Mind of Frederick Douglass* (Chapel
Hill: University of North Carolina Press, 1984), p. 22.

40. Terry Eagleton, *Literary Theory: An Introduction* (Minneapolis, University of
Minnesota Press, 1983), p. 203.

41. Biodun Jeyifo, "Literary Theory and Theories of Decolonization," unpublished

manuscript. Also see his "On Eurocentric Critical Theory: Some Paradigms from the Texts and Sub-Texts of Post-Colonial Writing," in Helen Tiffin and Stephen Slemon, eds., *After Europe: Critical Theory and Post-Colonial Writing* (Sydney, Dangaroo Press, 1989).

42. See her "feminist theory: a radical agenda" in *Talking Back: thinking feminist, thinking black* (Boston: South End Press, 1989), p. 36. See also Michele Wallace, who articulates a similar position in two essays from her collection *Invisibility Blues: From Pop to Theory* (London: Verso, 1990). In "Variations on Negation and the Heresy of Black Feminist Criticism," Wallace registers her concern that "black women writers and academics seem disproportionately under-represented in the sphere of knowledge production, in which literary criticism is included." While, in this essay, she concludes that "nobody in particular and everybody in general seems responsible for this situation" (pp. 215, 214), in "Negative Images: Toward a Black Feminist Cultural Criticism," she suggests that black women are largely responsible for this vacuum. She chastises them for producing "idealized and utopian black feminism, which remains almost entirely unarticulated and untheorized." Echoing Michael Awkward's point in "Appropriative Gestures: Theory and African American Literary Criticism," Wallace asserts, "I am firmly convinced that if black feminism, or the feminism of women of color, is going to thrive on any level as a cultural analysis, it cannot continue to ignore the way that Freud, Marx, Saussure, Nietzsche, Levi-Strauss, Lacan, Derrida and Foucault have forever altered the credibility of obvious truth, 'common sense' or any unitary conception of reality" (p. 248). The importance of the work in this heterogeneous list is more asserted than argued, and recalls again Martin Jay's point about the "charismatic names," the ritualized forms of citation used to legitimate critical arguments simply through the act of reference. See "Name Dropping or Dropping Names? Modes of Legitimation in the Humanities."

43. The familiar and assumed distinction between "literature" and "criticism" has been widely problematized in contemporary critical discussion, as literary critics have rejected the "secondary" roles of servants to the master and "primary" texts and claimed for themselves a status equal to that of creative writers. As Barbara Hernsstein Smith puts it, "theory cannot be seen as distinct from and opposed to literary 'creation' but as a central and inevitable aspect of it," "Value/Evaluation," in Frank Lentricchia and Thomas McLaughlin, eds., *Critical Terms for Literary Study,* p. 181. In "The Race for Theory," Barbara Christian wants Smith's refusal of the distinction between "theory" and "creative writing" to work in reverse. That is, she wants to blur the distinction between the two in order to argue that if "theory" can be "creative writing," creative writing can be theory. But in arguing that "people of color have always theorized . . . in narrative forms, in the stories [they] create, in riddles and proverbs," she falls into the same logic that traps bell hooks. In other words, to reverse the theory/creative binarism in order to claim for the literatures of "people of color" status as "theory" is still to give primacy to "theory."

44. Cornel West makes a similar argument in "The Dilemma of the Black Intellectual," *Cultural Critique* 1 (1985): "Charges of intellectual inferiority can never be met upon the opponent's terrain." Rather, "the terrain itself must be viewed as . . . unworthy of setting the terms of contemporary discourse" (p. 117). West goes on to discuss the "place" of black intellectuals in Marxist thought, noting, "the Marxist privileging of black intellectuals often reeks of condescension that confines" the roles of black

intellectuals to "spokespersons and organizers; only rarely are they allowed to function as creative thinkers who warrant serious critical attention" (p. 118).

45. Rey Chow, "'It's You, and Not Me': Domination and 'Othering' in Theorizing the 'Third World,'" in Elizabeth Weed, ed., Coming to Terms: Feminism, Theory, Politics (New York, 1989), p. 161.

46. Edward Said, The World, the Text, and the Critic (Cambridge: Harvard University Press, 1983), p. 143.

47. Valerie Smith, "Black Feminist Theory and the Representation of the 'Other,'" p. 46.

48. Jane Gallop, Marianne Hirsch, and Nancy K. Miller, "Criticizing Feminist Criticism," in Marianne Hirsch and Evelyn Fox Keller, eds., Conflicts in Feminism (New York: Routledge, 1990), pp. 364–65.

49. Ralph Ellison, "The World and the Jug," in Shadow and Act (New York: Vintage/Random House, 1972), p. 124.

50. Jane Gallop, Around 1981: Academic Feminist Literary Theory (New York: Routledge, 1992), p. 9.

INDEX

Abolitionist movement, 209n.39

Affective affiliations: black feminist criticism and, 19–20; sexual identity and, 180n.44

Afro-American literature: construction of history in, 204–205n.5; debate on portrayal of black male characters by black women writers, 102–104; novel of passing as genre of, 189n.12; "ordinary" and "poetic" discourse in, 45; poststructuralism and scholarship on, xvii. *See also* Black feminist criticism; Black women writers; Literary criticism; Literary history; Literary studies

Ain't I a Woman: Black Women and Feminism (hooks), 19

All the Women Are White, All the Blacks Are Men, But Some of Us Are Brave (Hull, Bell-Scott, and Smith), 18, 104

American Baptist Publication Society, 53

American Family Association, xvi

Am I That Name? Feminism and the Category of "Women" in History (Riley), 158–59

Ammons, Elizabeth, 55, 184n.24

Andrews, William, 29, 151

The Anxiety of Influence (Bloom), 48

Anzaldua, Gloria, 206–207n.17

Appiah, Anthony, 115, 116, 180–81n.44

Arac, Jonathan, 208–209n.37

Ar'n't I a Woman: Female Slaves in the Plantation South (White, 1985), 195n.12

Around 1981: Academic Feminist Literary Theory (Gallop), 174–75

Artist, black: debate on image of in *The Crisis*, 101–102; female as theme in novels of Morrison and Walker, 13; figure of in Fauset's *Plum Bun*, 74

Audience: politics and power of literary reviews, 120; for Walker's *The Color Purple*, 50–51. *See also* Readership; Reading

Authorship: Walker on process of in "The Source," 134. *See also* Writing

Awkward, Michael, 113–15, 116, 117, 163–65

Baker, Houston, 50, 127, 165–67, 208n.33

Bakhtin, Mikhail, 151, 186n.43

Baldwin, James, 15

Bambara, Toni Cade, 14

Baym, Nina, 29

Beacon Black Women Writers Series, xiii

Beizer, Janet, 121

Bell, Bernard, 141

Bell-Scott, Patricia, 104

Beloved (Morrison), 122, 203n.15

Benstock, Shari, 130

Benston, Kimberly, 145

Bergson, Henri, 152

Bernikow, Louise, 5

Betsey Brown (Shange, 1985), 135–36

Beyond the Gates (Phelps, 1883), 31

The Big Sea (Hughes), 72

Bildungsroman: character development in black women's novels, 36; and Fauset's *Plum Bun*, 65

Birthright (Stribling), 71

Black Aesthetic movement: literary image of black artist, 102; opening up of possibilities for black and women writers, 50–51

Black Bourgeoisie (Frazier), xvi

The Black Family in Slavery and Freedom (Gutman), 200n.40

Black feminist criticism: development and future directions of, 6–22; examination of works of black male writers, 14–15; gender and race in development of theory, 163–67; grounding strategies of, xviii; reevaluation of theory/practice di-

DEBORAH E. McDOWELL is Professor of English at the University of Virginia. She is coeditor, with Arnold Rampersad, of Slavery and the Literary Imagination and the author of essays on a range of African American texts.